CUTTING THROUGH APPEARANCES

The Practice and Theory of Tibetan Buddhism

CUTTING THROUGH APPEARANCES

The Practice and Theory of Tibetan Buddhism

Geshe Lhundup Sopa
Jeffrey Hopkins

Associate editor for Part Two: Anne C. Klein

With a Foreword by His Holiness The Dalai Lama

Snow Lion Publications
Ithaca, New York USA

Snow Lion Publications
P.O. Box 6483
Ithaca, New York 14851
USA

Printed in USA

ISBN 0-937938-81-5 Paper
ISBN 0-937938-82-3 Cloth

Library of Congress Cataloging-in-Publication Data

Cutting through appearances : the practice and theory of Tibetan Buddhism / [translated from the Tibetan with an introduction and notes by] Lhundup Sopa, Jeffrey Hopkins ; associate editor for part two: Anne C. Klein ; with a foreword by the Dalai Lama. — 2nd ed.
p. cm.
First ed. published under title: Practice and theory of Tibetan Buddhism.
Contains a translation of the Fourth Panchen Lama's Instructions on the three principal aspects of the path and an annotated translation of Kön-chok-jik-may-wang-po's Precious garland of tenets.
Includes bibliographical references and index.
ISBN 0-937938-82-3 (cloth) : $25.95. — ISBN 0-937938-81-5 (pbk.) : $15.95
1. Buddhism—Doctrines. 2. Spiritual life (Buddhism) 3. Buddhism—China-Tibet. III. Bstan-pa'i-ñi-ma, Panchen Lama IV, 1781-1854. Gsuṅ rab kun gyi sñiṅ po lam gyi gtso bo rnam pa gsum gyi khrid yig gźan phan sñiṅ po. English. 1989. IV. Dkon-mchog mtha'i rnam par bźag pa rin po che'i phreṅ ba. English. 1989. V. Title: Practice and theory of Tibetan Buddhism.
BQ7634.C88 1990
294.3'923—dc20 90-37764
CIP

Contents

Foreword

Buddhahood—the state of being a source of help and happiness for all sentient beings—is attained through method and wisdom. The chief method is the altruistic aspiration to highest enlightenment for the sake of all sentient beings, and the chief wisdom is the correct view of emptiness—the realization that phenomena do not exist in their own right.

An altruistic aspiration to highest enlightenment is induced by love and compassion which are in turn induced by applying knowledge of one's own plight in cyclic existence to others. It is first necessary to realize the manifold sufferings of cyclic existence, both the obvious, such as physical and mental pain resulting from war, and the non-obvious, such as the mere fact of having a mind and body which are so composed that the aggregation of secondary circumstances will create immense pain.

Realizing that one's own wish to avoid suffering and attain happiness is shared equally with all sentient beings, one can generate love—the wish that all sentient beings have happiness—and compassion—the wish that all sentient beings be free from suffering. It is possible, in turn, even to generate the motivation of a Bodhisattva wherein one assumes alone the burden of the welfare of all beings, from tiniest insects upwards. A Bodhisattva then seeks Buddhahood as a means toward the primary goal of helping others.

To achieve Buddhahood, the afflictions of desire, hatred, and ignorance as well as the predispositions they establish in the mind must be overcome. The means to do this are the realization of and subsequent prolonged meditation on emptiness—the absence of inherent existence of each and every phenomenon, from forms through to omniscient consciousness.

Within Buddhist schools, the view of emptiness or selflessness is presented in many ways, with the lower systems serving as means of penetrating the higher views. One gradually learns the compatibility of dependent-arising and emptiness and eventually can generate a wisdom consciousness capable not just of temporarily suppressing the afflictions but of removing forever the inborn misconception of the nature of phenomena which provides a false foundation for the afflictive emotions. By understanding that phenomena do not inherently exist but exist only nominally or imputedly, it becomes possible to develop the mind fully and thereby spontaneously effect the welfare of countless beings.

The two treatises in this volume—by the Fourth Paṇchen Lama and Gön-chok-jik-may-wang-bo—together with the supplementary commentaries should help to provide an understanding of the structure of this path.

Tenzin Gyatso
THE XIVTH DALAI LAMA

Preface

Homage to Mañjushrī.

This book offers an insight into the practical and theoretical aspects of Tibetan Buddhism. Part One epitomizes much of the daily practice of Tibetan monks and yogis. Though the text is taken from the Ge-luk-b̄a[1] order of Tibetan Buddhism, it typifies in many ways the practice of all Tibetan orders—N̄ying-ma, Ḡa-gyu, S̄a-ḡya,[2] and Ge-luk. The treatise was written by the Fourth Paṇ-chen Lama L̄o-sang-b̄el-den-d̄en-b̄ay-nyi-ma[3] (1781-1852/4) as a commentary to a short verse letter by D̄zong-ka-b̄a,[4] the founder of the Ge-luk-b̄a order, on the three principal aspects of the path to highest enlightenment.

Part Two presents a solid introduction both to the theory behind the practice and the theory being realized in practice. This treatise, which is also taken from Ge-luk-b̄a commentary, presents a map of the entire spectrum of the Buddhist schools of tenets, as seen from the viewpoint of a traditional mode of scholarship. Providing a student with a basis for continuing study of Buddhist philosophy, it details the presentations of

---

1 *dge lugs pa.*

2 *snying ma, bka' brgyud, sa skya.*

3 *blo bzang dpal ldan bstan pa'i nyi ma.*

4 *tsong kha pa blo bzang grags pa,* 1357-1419.

cyclic existence and selflessness in the four schools, Vaibāṣhika, Sautrāntika, Chittamātra, and Mādhyamika (which will be translated here as Great Exposition School, Sūtra School, Mind Only School, and Middle Way School). The text was written by Ḡön-chok-jik-may-w̄ang-b̄o[1] (1728-91), the reincarnation of Jam-ȳang-shay-b̄a,[2] author of the textbook literature for the Go-mang[3] College of Dre-b̄ung[4] Monastic University in Lhasa and D̄ra-s̄hi-kyil[5] Monastic University in the northeastern province of Tibet called Am-do.[6]

We wish to express a debt of gratitude to the late Professor Richard Robinson and to Professor Harvey Aronson for making many suggestions that improved the English of Part One. We particularly wish to express our thanks to Professor Anne Klein for providing the impetus for us to recast our translation of Part Two, the presentation of tenets, and to add commentary so that it might be more accessible. She helped not only to edit that part but also to compile the glossary and index.

About the second edition. In this second edition, we have expanded the over-all text by approximately one-third through adding an introduction and more explanatory material to Part Two as well as lengthening the glossary, bibliography, and notes. We also have added material on the authors of the Tibetan texts and, in retranslating Part Two, have compared seven editions of the text, noting significant variations and emendations.

Geshe Lhundup Sopa
Jeffrey Hopkins

---

1 *dkon mchog 'jigs med dbang po.*
2 *'jam dbyangs bzhad pa.*
3 *sgo mang.*
4 *'bras spungs.*
5 *bkra shis 'khyil.*
6 *a mdo.*

Technical Note

In Part One extensive portions of the six preparatory practices only mentioned in the text are given in full. Also, two stanzas of Ḏzong-ka-ḇa's basic text, omitted by the Paṇ-chen Lama, have been restored. Ḏzong-ka-ḇa's verse letter, which forms the basic text for the Fourth Paṇ-chen Lama's commentary, is set in italics.

In Part One, the material in square brackets has been added by the translators to facilitate understanding. In Part Two, short comments by the translators have been similarly set in brackets, with longer commentary indented.

The names of Tibetan authors and orders are given in 'essay phonetics' for the sake of easy pronunciation; for a discussion of the system used, see the Technical Note at the beginning of Jeffrey Hopkins, *Meditation on Emptiness* (London: Wisdom Publications, 1983), pp. 19-22. Transliteration of Tibetan in parentheses and in the glossary is done in accordance with a system devised by Turrell Wylie; see 'A Standard System of Tibetan Transcription', *Harvard Journal of Asiatic Studies*, Vol. 22, 1959, pp. 261-7. For the names of Indian scholars and systems used in the body of the text, *ch, sh,* and *ṣh* are used instead of the more usual *c, ś,* and *ṣ* for the sake of easy pronunciation by non-specialists.

Though the Tibetan has techniques for indicating greater and smaller meaning-breaks, it does not have paragraphs, and thus in the translation all paragraph-breaks have been added. Also, the Tibetan does not employ differences of print such as bold or italics for the sake of emphasis, etc.; thus, these have all been added in the translation.

Part One

PRACTICE: MEDITATION

Introduction

Part One is a meditation manual; it details how to prepare for and how to conduct a meditative session. It is highly practical with nothing said that does not fit directly into an actual meditation. It does not describe the levels of trance, the hindrances to meditation and their antidotes, or the powers of mind present at various levels of meditation. It elaborates only on those points that are directly applicable to the format of a session. The proofs for emptiness are not explained in detail, but how to meditate on emptiness is. The proofs for impermanence are not explained in detail, but meditation on renunciation of the impermanent and miserable is.

Because readers new to Buddhism need other works of instruction on doctrinal matters, in Part Two of this book we provide a translation and explanation of Ḡön-chok-jik-may-w̄ang-b̄o's *Precious Garland of Tenets*. It supplements the manual and in no way contradicts the explicit or implicit import of the instructions given. For, the practice of Tibetan Buddhism is founded on a thorough study of Buddhist theory, the practices being a means of internalizing theory to the point where it becomes spontaneously lived experience.

THE MEDITATION MANUAL

Due to beginningless conditioning to the three poisons of desire, hatred, and ignorance, the mind does not of its own course, unless it has been trained, abide in the right path. Therefore, practice is necessary. In the beginning practice is always artificial unless, through training in a previous lifetime, one's predispositions are awakened upon contacting the material again and the attitudes sought arise of their own force. However, for most, the beginning is a matter of hard conditioning to new ideas, and thus frequent repetition is necessary.

This manual gives in copious detail the instructions necessary for daily practice. A yogi would perform the whole meditation at least once and at most six times a day. However, beginning students often find that it takes considerable time to become acquainted with each phase of the meditation, and thus they concentrate on only a certain phase of the session until gaining a minimal familiarity. Beginners also tend to limit meditation to short periods of from ten to twenty minutes in order to avoid laxity or undue excitement.

Also, even though the aim is to perform the more complicated visualizations in all their detail, this is impossible for a beginner, who must use the technique of pretending to conduct the full visualization. This acts as a cause of actually being able to do so fully in the future.

Any persons outside the tradition who attempt such meditation are cautioned to beware of entering into difficult meditation without the proper preparation in terms of motivation and theory. One of the goals is to develop flexibility of mind, and if students begin to become rigid, they are advised to identify the mispractice and seek a means of alleviating the problem. Thus, any who newly seek to practice this text are to be cautioned that the advice of a skillful teacher is often necessary.

COMMENTS ON THE TEXT

This Tibetan meditation manual was written by the Fourth Paṇ-chen Lama, L̄o-sang-b̄el-den-d̄en-b̄ay-nyi-ma[1] (1781-1852/54) and is based on an epistolary verse essay by D̄zong-ka-b̄a[2] (1357-1419), the founder of an order that eventually came to be known as Ge-luk-b̄a. D̄zong-ka-b̄a was condensing the import of Buddha's sūtras in a short letter to his student, Tsa-ko-b̄ön-b̄o Ngak-w̄ang-drak-b̄a,[3] to whom he affectionately refers as 'child' in the last word of the poem. The Fourth Paṇ-chen Lama's text is not a commentary of notes nor a commentary on the difficult points of D̄zong-ka-b̄a's work. Rather, it is intended for practice. D̄zong-ka-b̄a's work is called *The Three Principal Aspects of the Path to Highest Enlightenment*,[4] and the main part of the commentary is concerned with the internalization of these three principal factors of the path: the intention definitely to leave cyclic existence, the aspiration to enlightenment for the sake of all sentient beings, and the correct view of emptiness. It is preceded by preliminary practices and followed by concluding ones. This is the basic structure of the book and of the meditation discussed.

These three principal aspects of the path are the essence of all the nearly countless scriptures of Buddha and their commentaries, and thus meditation based on them is not to be seen as merely partial or introductory. D̄zong-ka-b̄a's essay and the Fourth Paṇ-chen Lama's

---

[1] *blo bzang dpal ldan bstan pa'i nyi ma.*

[2] *tsong kha pa blo bzang grags pa.*

[3] *tsha kho dpon po ngag dbang grags pa.*

[4] *lam gtso rnam gsum*; P6087, Vol. 153. The text is found in volume *kha* of D̄zong-ka-b̄a's Collected Works.

commentary are both written from the point of view of the Great Vehicle[1] and, within that, what is considered to be the highest of the philosophical schools, the Middle Way Consequence School.[2] The book details the practices that are common requirements for both the sūtra and tantra paths. Though there are tantric practices that are considered to be 'higher' than those presented here, all of them require these three principal paths as prerequisites and none of them at any time forsakes these three. The intention definitely to leave cyclic existence is as essential to the practice of tantra as it is to that of sūtra; in tantra the discipline is even stricter than that of the sūtra systems. The aspiration to enlightenment for the sake of all sentient beings is the assumption of the burden of freeing all sentient beings from misery and joining them with happiness and one's consequent wish for Buddhahood, the state wherein one actually has the power to effect one's promise to free all beings through teaching the path. It forms the motivation for tantra practice as well as for sūtra practice. The correct view is the realization of emptiness, the realization that all phenomena do not exist inherently, are just imputations by thought, nominally existent and effective but not to be found under ultimate analysis. Emptiness itself is the life of sūtra and tantra.

What some tantras have that this text does not are certain difficult and dangerous practices for highly trained yogis to achieve in a very short time the aim of Buddhahood. Thus, undoubtedly the Paṇ-chen Lama chose Ḏzong-ka-ḇa's text for his basis because it provides the essentials of the path to Buddhahood and is not limited in scope to practices that aim at temporary beneficial results such as rebirths in higher realms.

Ḏzong-ka-ḇa is said to have received the precepts on

---

1 *theg pa chen po, mahāyāna.*

2 *dbu ma thal 'gyur pa, prāsaṅgika.*

the three principal aspects of the path from the deity who is the physical manifestation of the wisdom of all Buddhas, Mañjughoṣha, or Mañjushrī. Through devotion and meditation Dzong-ka-ba attained meetings with Mañjushrī, and this the Paṇ-chen Lama offers as recommendation for the book's reliability and great worth.

Preparations for Meditation

The manual begins with instructions on how to prepare for the actual meditation on the three principal aspects of the path to enlightenment. The preparations given are common throughout Tibetan Buddhism, not just for the particular meditation of this book, but for any meditation. They are called the six preparatory practices.

1 *Cleaning the place where one is meditating.* In order to receive a visit from Buddha, the meditator cleans the meditation room and arranges on an altar an image of Buddha, a scripture, and, for instance, a reliquary[1] to symbolize respectively the body, speech, and mind of a Buddha.

2 *Arranging offerings.* Offerings are set out in an appealing manner. They must be procured honestly: water, food, clothing, and so forth.

3 *Positioning one's body.* The posture recommended has seven features:

(a) Sitting on a soft and comfortable cushion in the lotus or half-lotus position.
(b) Keeping the eyes neither opened very wide nor closed tight, aimed at the point of the nose. One should avoid looking hard at the point of the nose, but should set the gaze there gently.
(c) Keeping the body straight with the backbone like a pile of coins.

---

[1] *mchod rten, stūpa.*

(d) Keeping the shoulders level.
(e) Keeping the head neither high nor low, unmovingly in a straight line from the nose to the navel.
(f) Setting the teeth and lips as usual with the tongue set against the back of the upper teeth.
(g) Breathing quietly and gently.

It is said that if one leans forward, ignorance is increased; if to the right, jealousy; if to the left, desire; if to the back, pride. Thus the proper posture is important.

After positioning the body, the field for the accumulation of meritorious power, including the Buddha, Bodhisattvas, one's own teachers, and so forth, is visualized in front of oneself. The motivation for taking refuge is reflected on. One is concerned with the sufferings of all ordinary beings in cyclic existence. One is concerned with their turning to a religion of utter solitary peace, perfecting neither their own nor others' aims. One is concerned with the afflictive emotions obstructing them from liberation from cyclic existence and with the obstructions preventing them from simultaneously cognizing all phenomena. Realizing that the Three Jewels have the power to protect all beings from these four ills, one then takes refuge, asking for help for all beings.

Refuge is taken in Buddha as the teacher of refuge, in the Doctrine as the actual refuge—principally in the sense of the true cessation of all afflictive emotions, or nirvana—and in the Spiritual Community as helpers toward refuge.

Rather than leaving the taking of refuge just as a petition, the manual instructs the meditator to simulate the actual aid of the Three Jewels for all sentient beings through visualizing ambrosia falling from the bodies of the Buddhas, Bodhisattvas, and so forth who are the sources of refuge and entering the minds and bodies of all beings, thereby purifying them of all obstructions. Also, with the statement of one's intention to attain

Buddhahood in order to help all sentient beings, the deities visualized in front of oneself are pleased and send a duplicate of themselves into the meditator. One suddenly turns into the lama and Buddha and thereupon performs the aiding of all beings through emanating from one's body a light that strikes and purifies all beings, establishing them in Buddhahood.

This type of practice is particularly tantric in that one is not just aspiring to Buddhahood but is mimicking while still on the path the condition of Buddhahood itself. Just as one does not consider the beings visualized in front of oneself to be mere visualizations or figments of imagination but the real refuges themselves, so one considers that one has actually for the moment become a Buddha. Because this technique is based on simulating the eventual effect of practice in terms of the physical forms and activities of a Buddha, the tantra system is called 'effect'. The sūtra system, since it does not involve meditation in which an aspect of the Form Bodies of a Buddha is cultivated while still on the path, is called 'cause'. This manual is a mixture of the two systems.

To establish the motivation for meditating on the three principal aspects of the path, the text calls for cultivation of the four immeasurables. These are: equanimity, love, compassion, and joy; they are 'immeasurable' because the field with respect to which one is meditating is the infinite field of all sentient beings throughout all space. Each of the four immeasurables passes through three stages of heightening force. The first is a statement of how nice it would be if all sentient beings had equanimity, happiness, freedom from suffering, and high status and the bliss of liberation. The second is the wish that they may come to have these. The third is to take upon oneself the burden of causing all sentient beings to have these. Only practitioners of the Great Vehicle have the third; however, Lesser Vehicle practitioners do have the other two, and thus it is said that they have limitless compassion or even great compassion. However, they do not have the great compassion that involves taking upon oneself the burden of freeing all sentient beings from suffering and joining all sentient beings with happiness.

The wish to free all without exception from suffering and the causes of suffering is mercy or compassion, and the wish to join all without exception with happiness and the causes of happiness is love. In contrast, worldly love and mercy are limited in the scope of the objects of attention; all persons are not valued similarly; some are considered to be close and some distant.

Having stated their intention to free all beings from suffering and establish them in happiness, meditators state their determination to attain Buddhahood in order to carry out this intention. The full development of this thought is *bodhicitta,* the aspiration to highest enlightenment for the sake of all sentient beings. With this motivation, one enters into cultivation of the three principal aspects of the path to highest enlightenment.

4 Visualization of the field of assembly. Visualization of the great teachers and masters of Buddhism is the fourth of the six preparatory practices. An important part of the meditation is an invitation to the actual deities to dissolve into the visualized beings. One drops all consideration of them as just visualizations, ceases any thought that they are actually somewhere else, and views these visualizations as the real beings themselves.

It is said that when Buddha was about to die, he was asked by his attendants on whom they should rely after his death. His answer was that he would enter any teacher whom they believed to be equal to Buddha. An aim of the practice of considering one's own guru, or lama, to be a Buddha, is to bring the highest value to the teaching which one receives though not imagining that Buddha and a better teaching are available elsewhere.

5 *Performance of the seven branches of practice together with offering maṇḍala.* This is done through recitation of verses from the *Prayers of Samantabhadra*. The seven parts are:

(a) Obeisance
(b) Offering
(c) Revealing one's own faulty deeds
(d) Admiring one's own and other's virtues
(e) Entreaty
(f) Supplication
(g) Dedication.[1]

The offering of maṇḍala involves giving the purified world system together with sun and moon and all imaginable marvels to the field of assembly.

6 *Supplication.* The last practice of preparation is supplication to the lineage of gurus of the three principal aspects of the path for aid in generating the proper attitudes and understanding.

The Three Principal Aspects of the Path

As mentioned above, the structure of the actual path is included within three principal aspects—the intention definitely to leave cyclic existence, the aspiration to enlightenment for the sake of all sentient beings, and the correct view of emptiness.

Intention to leave cyclic existence. Essential to developing an intention to leave the round of birth, aging, sickness, and death is an appreciation for the value of a life-situation in which it is possible to practice the teachings and then a realization of the precariousness of life.

It is said that in order to practice the teaching it is necessary to have several factors called 'leisure and for-

[1] In Tibetan, these seven are: *phyag 'tshal ba, mchod pa, bshags pa, rjes su yi rang, bskul ba, gsol ba, bsngo ba.*

tune'. Leisure[1] means to be free from the eight conditions of non-leisure:[2]

1 birth as a hell-being
2 birth as a hungry ghost
3 birth as an animal
4 birth in an uncultured area
5 possessing defective sense faculties
6 having wrong views
7 birth as a god of long life
8 birth in a world system where a Buddha did not come.

Fortune[3] means the five inner fortunes:

1 being a human
2 being born in a center of Buddhist teaching
3 having sound sense faculties

---

[1] *dal ba, kṣaṇa.* In Sarat Chandra Das, *A Tibetan-English Dictionary* (Calcutta, 1902), *dal ba* is translated as 'languor, ease, quietude, leisure; also the state of *dalwa*, and so the being at ease or in the state of leisurely comfort or repose.' In Vaman Shivaram Apte, *Sanskrit-English Dictionary* (Poona: Prasad Prakashan, 1957), the second meaning of *kṣaṇa* is 'leisure', the first being 'instant' which is obviously inappropriate here.

[2] *mi khom pa, akṣaṇa.* In Sarat Chandra Das, *A Tibetan-English Dictionary, mi khom pa* is translated as 'uninterrupted uneasiness, want of leisure'. Das refers to 'the eight states of perpetual uneasiness or the states where there are no opportunities for doing religious works'. In Vaman Shivaram Apte, *Sanskrit-English Dictionary, akṣaṇa* is translated as 'inopportune, unseasonable'; similarly, *kṣaṇa*, as cited in the previous note, is translated as 'leisure'. In Sir Monier Monier-Williams, *A Sanskṛit-English Dictionary* (London: Oxford, 1899; reprint, Delhi: Motilal, 1976), *akṣaṇa* is 'inopportune', and, again, the second meaning of *kṣaṇa* is 'a leisure moment, vacant time, leisure'. In Franklin Edgerton, *Buddhist Hybrid Sanskrit Grammar and Dictionary* (New Haven: Yale University Press, 1953; reprint, Delhi: Motilal, 1972), *akṣaṇa* is translated as 'inopportune birth, birth under such circumstances that one cannot learn from a Buddha'.

[3] *'byor pa, saṃpad.*

4 not having done the five actions of immediate retribution in a hell after death: killing one's father, killing one's mother, killing a Foe Destroyer,[1] with bad in-

---

[1] *dgra gcom pa, arhant*; one who has overcome ignorance, the principal foe. With respect to the translation of *arhant* (*dgra bcom pa*) as 'Foe Destroyer', we do this to accord with the usual Tibetan translation of the term and to assist in capturing the flavor of oral and written traditions that frequently refer to this etymology. Arhats have overcome the foe which is the afflictive emotions (*nyon mongs, kleśa*), the chief of which is ignorance, the conception (according to the Consequence School) that persons and phenomena are established by way of their own character.

The Indian and Tibetan translators were also aware of the etymology of *arhant* as 'worthy one', as they translated the name of the 'founder' of the Jaina system, Arhat, as *mchod 'os* 'Worthy of Worship' (see Jam-ȳang-shay-b̄a's *Great Exposition of Tenets*, ka 62a.3). Also, they were aware of Chandrakīrti's gloss of the term as 'Worthy One' in his *Clear Words*: *sadevamānuṣāsurāl lokāt pūnārhatvād arhannityuchyate* (Poussin, 486.5), *lha dang mi dang lha ma yin du bcas pa'i 'jig rten gyis mchod par 'os pas dgra bcom pa zhes brjod la* (409.20, Tibetan Cultural Printing Press edition; also, P5260, Vol.98 75.2.2), 'Because of being worthy of worship by the world of gods, humans, and demi-gods, they are called Arhats.' Also, they were aware of Haribhadra's twofold etymology in his *Illumination of the Eight Thousand Stanza Perfection of Wisdom Sūtra*. In the context of the list of epithets qualifying the retinue of Buddha at the beginning of the sūtra (see Unrai Wogihara, ed., *Abhisamayālaṃkārālokā Prajñā-pāramitā-vyākhyā, The Work of Haribhadra* [Tokyo: The Toyo Bunko, 1932-5; reprint ed., Tokyo: Sankibo Buddhist Book Store, 1973], 8.18), Haribhadra says:

> They are called *arhant* [=Worthy One, from root *arh* 'to be worthy'] since they are worthy of worship, religious donations, and being assembled together in a group, etc. (W9.8-9: *sarva evātra pūjā-dakṣiṇā-gaṇa-parikarṣādy-ārhatayarhantaḥ*; P5189, 67.5.7: *'dir thams cad kyang mchod pa dang // yon dang tshogs su 'dub la sogs par 'os pas na dgra bcom pa'o*).

Also:

> They are called *arhant* [= Foe Destroyer *arihan*] because they have destroyed (*hata*) the foe (*ari*).
> (W10.18: *hatāritvād arhantaḥ;* P5189, 69.3.6. *dgra rnams bcom*

tention causing blood to flow from the body of a Buddha, and causing dissension in the Spiritual Community
5 having faith in Buddha's scriptures.

Fortune also means the five outer fortunes:

1 a visitation from a Buddha
2 his teaching the excellent doctrine
3 his teaching remaining to the present
4 his followers still existing
5 the people of the area having mercy and love for others and thus teaching others.

Thus, a life of complete leisure and fortune precludes being anything other than a human. For, even the gods of the Desire Realm, though very happy, are lured by that happiness into complacency; therefore, one is exhorted to accumulate, while a human, the causes of happiness, the ten virtues which are the avoidance of the ten non-virtues:

1 killing
2 stealing
3 sexual misconduct
4 lying
5 divisive talk

---

pas na dgra bcom pa'o).

(Our thanks to Gareth Sparham for the references to Haribhadra.) Thus, we are not dealing with an ignorant misconception of a term, but a considered preference in the face of alternative etymologies—'Foe Destroyer' requiring a not unusual *i* infix to make *ari-han*, *ari* meaning enemy and *han* meaning to kill, and thus 'Foe Destroyer'. Unfortunately, one word in English cannot convey both this meaning and 'Worthy of Worship'; thus, we have gone with what clearly has become the predominant meaning in Tibet. (For an excellent discussion of the two etymologies of Arhat in Buddhism and Jainism, see L.M. Joshi's 'Facets of Jaina Religiousness in Comparative Light', L.D. Series 85, [Ahmedabad: L.D. Institute of Indology, May 1981], pp. 53-8.)

6 harsh speech
7 foolish talk
8 covetousness
9 harmfulness
10 wrong ideas.

The first three are physical; the middle four are verbal; and the last three are mental. One is exhorted to desist from these as much as possible because the effects of even tiny non-virtues can by very great. A moment of anger toward a Bodhisattva can destroy the virtue accumulated over a thousand aeons. Similarly, a moment of strong contrition can destroy the non-virtues of aeons. Cause and effect that are associated with the mind are said to be unlike cause and effect in the external world. Though a great oak tree grows out of an acorn, far greater effects in terms of intensity and duration are produced from deeds due to the importance of motivation.

Cyclic existence is a mass of suffering. Even the happiest beings in the Desire Realm are in a state of suffering. When the gods die, they face with a special 'clairvoyance' the horrors that are to come. They also perceive five signs of their approaching death:

1 dust gathering around the body
2 sweat coming from the armpits
3 fading of their garlands of flowers
4 body beginning to smell
5 discomfort with the environment.

The force of the actions that caused those beings to be born as gods ceases, and having exhausted great funds of good action, they are forced into lower rebirths. Humans, on the other hand, often have enough suffering to spur them into practice and sufficient leisure to be able to achieve results. Unlike animals, humans can begin new practices of virtue. Thus, human life is a rare and precious phenomenon that must be used meaningfully. The practice of virtues should at least be aimed at rebirth in a happy transmigration so that one can continue religious practice in order to be freed entirely from cyclic existence.

The development of an intention to leave cyclic existence entirely is accomplished in two phases. First, one learns to de-emphasize the appearances of the present lifetime, thereby establishing a more long-term perspective. Then, one de-emphasizes the appearances of future lifetimes. In the first phase, one passes from the narrow concern with the pleasures of the present lifetime; this is done by realizing (1) that the present situation endowed with pleasurable features is valuable, (2) that one will not stay long in this life, and (3) that lifetimes as animals, hungry ghosts, and hell-beings are bereft of such fortuitous circumstances. In the second phase, one expands one's perspective even more by developing an intention definitely to leave cyclic existence. This is done by reflecting on the effects of karma and the many varieties of suffering certain to be induced by one's own bad karma. One meditates on (1) suffering, whereby a wish to separate from cyclic existence is generated, (2) impermanence, whereby attachment to the mental and physical aggregates and this life is eliminated, and (3) selflessness, whereby attachment to the 'mine', one's sense powers and so forth, is overcome. Through this process, an attitude seeking liberation is developed in full form.

Altruistic aspiration to become enlightened. One's perspective is further expanded by meditatively cultivating a sense of closeness with all beings and by becoming aware of their suffering, as inferred from one's own situation which was realized earlier when generating the intention to leave cyclic existence.

The two wings of the bird flying to Buddhahood are wisdom and compassion. Without full development of compassion to the point where one takes upon oneself the burden of liberating all sentient beings from suffering and establishing them in happiness, a yogi can only attain the fruit of a Hearer[1] or Solitary Realizer.[2] Thus, after cultivating the wish to leave cyclic existence due to its misery, one extends through inference what one now knows about one's own condition to that of others and develops the wish to free all beings from suffering.

The yogi is directed to generate *bodhicitta*. *Bodhicitta* in general is of two types: ultimate and conventional. The ultimate *bodhicitta* is a Buddha's or Bodhisattva's wisdom of emptiness; it is the sign of a Bodhisattva's attainment of the path of seeing, the time of initially cognizing emptiness directly. Emptiness is realized earlier through inference, but this is the first direct cognition. From this point on, whenever Bodhisattvas directly cognize emptiness, their mental consciousness is an ultimate *bodhicitta*. The conventional *bodhicitta* is of two types: one is the aspiration to highest enlightenment for the sake of all sentient beings, and the other is that aspiration conjoined with the Bodhisattva deeds.

The *bodhicitta* being generated in the second part of the meditative session is the aspirational, conventional *bodhicitta*, and thus it has here been translated as 'the aspiration to enlightenment' often adding 'for the sake of all sentient beings'. For its generation, there are seven quintessential instructions of cause and effect:

1 recognition of all sentient beings as one's mothers
2 becoming mindful of their kindness
3 promising to repay their kindness
4 love
5 great compassion
6 the unusual altruistic attitude

---

1 *nyan thos, śrāvaka.*
2 *rang rgyal, pratyekabuddha.*

7 generation of the aspiration to Buddhahood for the sake of all beings.

The lineage of this system of practice is said to have extended from Shākyamuni Buddha to Maitreya to Asaṅga. The aim is to extend a sense of intimacy and closeness to all beings without exception. Non-partiality is what distinguishes pure love from worldly love. Worldly love is always partial.

The relationship with one's mother is used as the model because of the mother's extremely great kindness and care. Upon consideration, it was one's mother who taught one as a child to walk, talk, take sustenance, and so forth. Without this teaching, it is said that we would resemble bugs—helplessly incommunicative. In Buddhism, offspring are to feel thankful to their parents for their protection, sustenance, and teaching. It is said to be wrong to feel that parents somehow owe a good life to their offspring because they created him/her. Rather, the act of copulation of the parents provided a suitable home for one's consciousness which was in the intermediate state, after death and before rebirth. In comparison with many other modes and types of birth, one can only be thankful for what the parents have done. Any troubles that are encountered are created through the fructification of one's own former ill deeds. That fructification should be accepted without compounding the problem by creating new ill will.

Lamas often advise those who have difficulty reflecting on the kindness of the mother to set aside for the moment the tangle of bad thoughts and, instead, concentrate for the moment on her kindness and the marvellous protection and love which she afforded. If the relationship with one's mother is either not clear or too complicated, they advise that one use the relationship with one's closest friend as the model.

The final generation of the aspiration to enlightenment is the seventh stage of the seven cause and effect quintessential instructions. Yogis now are firm in their resolve to take upon themselves the burden of freeing all beings, and they reflect on whether they have the ability to do so. Realizing that they have difficulty even knowing with certainty what they are doing, they see that only a completely perfect Buddha has such ability. They ascertain that they must attain Buddhahood.

It is said that those of very sharp intellect first ascertain that Buddhahood would be the best means of helping others and then, before they pass on to the resolve to attain Buddhahood, reflect on whether the mind can be so purified that Buddhahood is actually possible. They realize that the mind is like a crystal which has become dirty and that the dirt can be cleaned away without destroying the crystal. In other words, they realize that the afflicted mind does not exist by way of its own character or from its own side but is produced from causes and conditions and thus is capable of being changed. They thereby ascertain that it is *possible* to attain Buddhahood; then they make a resolve to attain Buddhahood. When *bodhicitta* is produced in this manner, it is called a gold-like generation of the aspiration to highest enlightenment. For, just as gold is 'unchangeable', so Bodhisattvas from this point will never fall from their aspiration.

The generation of the conventional *bodhicitta* marks the beginning of the Bodhisattva path of accumulation. For three periods of countless aeons practitioners accumulate the stocks of merit and wisdom, especially practicing the six perfections. They also practice all six perfections in each perfection. For example, they perform the giving of giving, the ethics of giving, the patience of giving, the effort of giving, the concentration of giving, and the wisdom of giving; similarly, they perform the giving of ethics, the ethics of ethics, and so forth, totalling thirty-six. The wisdom of giving refers to the realization that giver, giving, gift, and receiver do not exist inherently or from their own side but are imputedly existent. This means that under analysis the giver and so forth cannot be found, but this does not mean that the giver is utterly non-existent or that giving need not be practiced. Rather, one practices giving within the context of realizing the merely nominal existence of agent, action, and object.

Correct view of emptiness. In order to cut out the root of cyclic existence, it is necessary to realize emptiness, first conceptually through inference and then in a totally non-dualistic direct cognition. Emptiness in the Consequence School, which is generally considered in Tibet to be the highest Buddhist philosophical system, is the lack of inherent existence, true existence, existence by way of the object's own character, existence in its own right, or existence as its own reality. This means that objects are only imputed in dependence upon bases of imputation. For instance, a chair is imputed in dependence upon a collection of four legs, a back, and a seat, but a chair is not any one of those parts individually, nor is it separate from those parts, nor is it the collection of those parts. If a chair were the collection of its parts, it would mean that each part was a chair or that the collection had no parts. Therefore, a chair exists only imputedly or by designation.

It is undeniable that phenomena appear to be their basis of imputation, that a chair appears to be the collection of its parts; however, this appearance, even to a sense consciousness, is wrong. Adherence to this false appearance must be challenged first with respect to the person (i.e., oneself) and then with respect to other phenomena through searching analytically in meditation to find the person or chair and discovering that they cannot be found among their bases of imputation.

Initially, it is necessary to see clearly what is being negated in the view of selflessness. Selflessness does not negate something that is existent; rather, it shows that something which is misconceived to exist does not exist. Thus, although true existence or inherent existence does not exist, a concept or image of true existence, its conception, and its conceiver do exist. The first step in meditation on the personal selflessness is to see this truly existent or self-sufficient self as it appears to our ordinary non-analytical intellect. One technique is to calm the mind, sit very quietly, and then think, 'I,' observing what happens. Another is to remember being falsely accused and watch the sense of a self-sufficient I that is generated and forms the center of one's response.

The inborn, habitual, or innate misconception of inherent existence is distinguished from the imputed or learned misconception of inherent existence. The latter is a misconception acquired through false teachings, scriptures, and proofs. The innate misconception, however, requires no teaching; it is the result of beginningless conditioning. The way that the inborn misconception of inherent existence apprehends the person is difficult to express concisely. The person is not perceived as if it were entirely separate from the mental and physical aggregates; for instance, when some part of the body, such as the stomach, is ill, we think, 'I am sick,' almost identifying the self with the stomach. However, the I is also not perceived as if it were completely the same as the aggregates. For example, if we see a particularly attractive person, we are apt to think, 'Might I become like that!' feeling even to exchange bodies with the person, whereas if we were utterly the same as our body, we could not even imagine such a thing. The I—as perceived by an inborn consciousness conceiving an inherently existent person—is, to our own sight, neither completely the same as nor completely different from the mental and physical aggregates. Still, an appearance of a seemingly self-sufficient I can and must be seen in order to identify the conception that must be destroyed. It will be replaced with the unadulterated conception of the person as imputed dependent on mind and body but not findable either among or separate from mind and body.

Similarly, the appearance of a self-sufficient body is described as a 'whole, looming body' with 'looming' having the sense of a big thing seen in the dark which turns out to be nothing. The body of flesh and bone also is described as 'bubbly', meaning that just as bubbles appear to be substantial phenomena but are seen to be destroyed quickly, so are flesh and bone. Also, just as bubbles come up and grow out from water, flesh and bone grow out into lumps. What is being investigated is whether something with parts is itself the collection of its parts or whether it is designated in dependence upon such a collection. Further, since each part is itself a whole, it is to be seen that parts are only imputedly existent. The theory is that all ordinary perceptions are misinformed about the nature of the object; things appear to exist inherently but do not exist this way. Through conditioning to emptiness, these misconceptions and false perceptions can be utterly eliminated.

Eventually yogis become so skilled that perception of appearance aids in understanding emptiness, for they understand that objects exist only imputedly and not inherently. This absence of inherent existence is emptiness. Also, reflection on emptiness aids in understanding appearances, for emptiness is the negative of inherent existence and not of nominal existence. Thus, appearances keep them away from the extreme of existence, and emptiness keeps them away from the extreme of non-existence. This indicates the high degree of skill required in delimiting just what is refuted in the view of emptiness—just inherent existence and not nominal existence.

Emptinesses are ultimate truths or highest object truths[1] because they are the objects of the highest wisdom and because they appear in direct cognition exactly the way they are. All other phenomena,[2] permanent and impermanent, are truths-for-a-concealer[3] because an ignorant consciousness, the concealer of the reality of emptiness through conceiving things to exist inherently, assumes they exist the way they appear. In other words, in direct perception all objects except emptinesses falsely appear to exist inherently and not just to exist imputedly, unfindable among their bases of imputation. Ignorance, here specifically the misapprehender of the nature of things, takes these appearances to be correct. Therefore, conventional objects are said to be truths—things that exist the way they appear—only with respect to ignorance.

This means that ignorance falsely establishes the *inherent* existence of objects; it does not mean that ignorance establishes the existence of objects. For, all phenomena conventionally exist validly.[4] It is their mode of existence that has been misinterpreted, and this is one reason why the phenomena of the universe are divided into the two truths: to show that for non-Buddhas conventional objects—all things except emptinesses—are truths only for ignorance. They do not exist the way they appear. By the very terminology itself, one is called to search for emptiness, the object of the highest wisdom.

Conclusion of the session. The meditation concludes with a dedication of the value of having performed the

---

1 *don dam bden pa, paramārthasatya.*

2 *chos, dharma.*

3 *kun rdzob bden pa, saṃvṛtisatya.*

4 *tshad mas grub pa, pramāṇasiddha.*

session. One is seeking through the dedication never to become separated from the two stages of tantra and the four wheels of the Great Vehicle. The two stages of tantra are:

1 the stage of generating the ripening of the mental continuum from ordinary to exalted perceptions through imagining oneself as a deity (an ideal person whose very appearance is one of wisdom and compassion) and one's environment as the habitat of a deity
2 the stage of completing the wisdom of the non-differentiation of emptiness and bliss, and one's actually becoming a deity.

The four wheels of the Great Vehicle are:

1 living in a place where the necessities for practicing the Great Vehicle are easily found
2 relying on a holy being who practices and teaches the Great Vehicle
3 having great aspirations for the practice of the Great Vehicle
4 having produced great merit in the past.

The purpose of seeking to remain with the Great Vehicle is that through practice of it Buddhahood can be achieved, and having the powers of a Buddha, one will be able to help others. Therefore, the dedication at the conclusion of the session is aimed toward one's own enlightenment for the sake of all sentient beings.

ABOUT THE AUTHOR OF THE MEDITATION MANUAL

The reincarnate line of Paṇ-chen Lamas was begun when the Fifth Dalai Lama, Ngak-w̄ang-l̄o-sang-gya-tso[1] (1617-1682), announced that one of his teachers, L̄o-

---

[1] *ngag dbang blo bzang rgya mtsho.*

sang-chö-ḡyi-gyel-tsen[1] (1567?-1662), would reappear after his death as a recognizable child-successor.[2] L̄o-sang-chö-ḡyi-gyel-tsen thereby came to be regarded as the First Paṇ-chen Lama; he was abbot of D̄ra-s̄hi-hlün-b̄o,[3] a large monastic university west of Lhasa at Shi-ḡa-d̄zay,[4] which from the time of the Third Dalai Lama, S̄ö-nam-gya-tso[5] (1543-88), had been 'entrusted to a series of adult lamas (viz. not yet reincarnating) who came to be regarded later as the spiritual predecessors of the Paṇ-chen Lamas.'[6]

In 1727-28, during the time of the Second Paṇ-chen Lama, L̄o-sang-ye-s̄hay,[7] there was a civil war in Tibet, and since the Seventh Dalai Lama was suspected of trouble-making by backing the losing side, the Yung-cheng Emperor (reigning from 1722 to 1735) banished him to Gar-tar[8] in eastern Tibet, for seven years. Before the Tibetans themselves, led by Po-hla-s̄ö-nam-d̄op-gyay,[9] gained control over the situation of the civil war, the Emperor made the Paṇ-chen Lama sovereign of D̄zang[10] Province and Western Tibet in order to counterbalance the power of the Dalai Lamas. As Snellgrove and Richardson say:[11]

---

[1] *blo bzang chos kyi rgyal mtshan.*
[2] This information is drawn from Snellgrove and Richardson, *Cultural History of Tibet,* (New York: Praeger, 1968), p. 220.
[3] *bkra shis lhun po.*
[4] *gzhis ka rtse.*
[5] *bsod nams rgya mtsho.*
[6] Snellgrove and Richardson, *Cultural History of Tibet,* p. 183.
[7] *blo bzang ye shes,* born 1663.
[8] *mgar thar.*
[9] *pho lha bsod nams stobs rgyas,* 1689-1747. For an account of his life, see K. Dondup, *The Water-Horse and Other Years: a history of 17th and 18th Century Tibet,* (Dharamsala: Library of Tibetan Works and Archives, 1984), pp. 73-100.
[10] *gtsang.*
[11] *Cultural History of Tibet,* p. 220.

> The Lama prudently accepted only a part of the donation, and the Dalai Lama and his successors never regarded it as conveying anything more than the subordinate position similar to that of a local hereditary ruler.

The Paṇ-chen Lamas became important personages in Tibet, such that, for instance, when the Eighth Dalai Lama was being chosen and an impasse had been reached due to the five great oracles' not agreeing on which from among three strong candidates was the reincarnation of the Dalai Lama, the Third Paṇ-chen Lama, Ḇel-den-ye-s̄hay,[1] made the choice. (He chose the one from his own province.)

Thus, by the time of the Fourth Paṇ-chen Lama, the author of our text, this line of lamas had assumed considerable importance in the central region of Tibet. In the colophon of our text, his name is given as L̄o-sang-ḇel-den-ḏen-ḇay-nyi-ma-chok-lay-ñam-gyel.[2] He is also called L̄o-sang-ḏen-ḇay-nyi-ma-chok-lay-ṇam-gyel and Paṇ-chen Ḏen-ḇay-nyi-ma. Living from 1781 to 1852/4, he wrote over five hundred eighty-one texts[3] (many of which are very short), contained in his Collected Works of nine volumes.

ABOUT THE TEXT

The text translated in Part One is the Fourth Paṇ-chen Lama's *Instructions on (Ḏzong-ka-ḇa's) 'Three Principal Aspects of the Path': Essence of All the Scriptures,*

---

[1] *dpal ldan ye shes*, born 1737.

[2] *blo bzang dpal ldan bstan pa'i nyi ma phyogs las rnam rgyal.*

[3] See Lokesh Chandra, ed., *Materials for a History of Tibetan Literature* (New Delhi: International Academy of Indian Culture, 1963), Part One, pp. 72-94, items 1462-2043; this count does not include the contents of volume *ka*, which was unavailable to Dr. Lokesh Chandra.

Quintessence of Helping Others.[1] It is found in volume *ca* of his Collected Works and is twenty-two folios.[2] Because many of the liturgical parts of the text are not given in full, being mentioned only by citing a line at the beginning and sometimes a line at the end, we have added these to the translation. We also had the text copied with these portions added and have made the text with a glossary of terms available for beginning Tibetan students on a private basis.[3] Two stanzas of Dzong-ka-ba's *The Three Principal Aspects of the Path to Highest Enlightenment,* omitted by the Paṇ-chen Lama in his commentary, have been restored; in all cases, our emendations are signalled in the footnotes. A collation of the topics presented in this section with those in Dzong-ka-ba's *Great Exposition of the Stages of the Path* is given in an Appendix.

---

[1] *gsung rab kun gyi snying po lam gyi gtso bo rnam gsum gyi khrid yig gzhan phan snying po.* Another translation of this text can be found in Geshe Wangyal, *Door of Liberation* (New York: Lotsawa, 1978), pp. 126-60. For the present Dalai Lama's oral commentary on Dzong-ka-ba's *Three Principal Aspects of the Path,* see Tenzin Gyatso, *Kindness, Clarity, and Insight* (Ithaca: Snow Lion, 1984) pp. 118-56, in which our translation of the root text was used.

[2] MHTL 1831. The edition which was used for this translation is a photographic copy of an edition in the library of the late Geshe Wangyal; the photographic copy was made by Richard B. Munn.

[3] All references to the text are to this edition.

Annotated translation of the Fourth Paṇ-chen Lama's

Instructions on (D̄zong-ka-b̄a's) 'Three Principal Aspects of the Path': Essence of All the Scriptures, Quintessence of Helping Others

The text has three overriding divisions: preparation for a session (Chapter 1), the actual session (Chapters 2 to 5), and the conclusion of a session (Chapter 6).

Guide to the Text

1 *Preparation for a Session of Meditation*

Oṃ svasti. I bow down and go for refuge to the feet of the excellent holy lamas who have great compassion. I pray to be taken care of by them at all times with great mercy.

This is a book of practices concerning the instructions on the three principal aspects of the path, extraordinary precepts actually bestowed by the protector Mañjughoṣha on the great Dzong-ka-ba, the King of Doctrine of the three realms.[1] It contains the essential meanings of all the scriptures of the Conqueror Buddha with commentary, collected in stages of practice for individuals. It details the two systems: how to act in the actual session of meditation and how to act between sessions.

---

[1] The Desire Realm, Form Realm, and Formless Realm.

PREPARATION

Perform, for instance, the six practices of preparation.[1] First, clean well the room where you are practicing. Second, beautifully arrange offerings [procured] without deceit. Third, on a comfortable cushion assume a posture having the seven features of Vairochana['s way of sitting]. Then, with respect to generating an attitude of refuge and so forth from within a special, virtuous attitude, the objects of refuge should first be set clearly [in front of you in visualization]:

> Directly in front of you there is a high and broad throne of jewels raised up by eight great lions. On that, on cushions of the spheres of variegated lotus and sun and moon, is your kind, fundamental lama in actuality but in the form of the Conqueror Shākyamuni with pure gold body, his head having the crown protrusion. His right hand presses the earth [in the gesture of calling the goddess of the earth to witness his achievement]. His left hand, in the pose of meditative equipoise, carries a bowl filled with ambrosia. He is wearing the saffron religious robes. A mass of light is generated from his body, which is adorned with the major and minor marks and has a nature of pure, clear light. In the middle of the mass of light he sits with his two legs in the adamantine posture. Surrounding him, collections of your actual and indirect lamas, deities, Buddhas, Bodhisattvas, Heroes, Sky-Goers, and Protectors of Doctrine are seated. On marvellous tables in front of each of them are the verbal doctrines taught by each in the form of books having the nature of light.

---

[1] The text gives only the beginning and end of these practices. We have provided the full reference. In the Tibetan text, see 2.4-2.7.

The members of the field of assembly are pleased with you. Abiding in the greatest faith, mindful of the virtues and kindness of the field of assembly, think:

> I and all sentient beings, my mothers, from beginningless time until now have undergone various sufferings of cyclic existence in general and of the three bad transmigrations[1] in particular. However, it is still difficult to comprehend the depth and limits of suffering.
>
> Now I have attained the special body of a human that has leisure and fortune, is difficult to find, and, if found, is extremely meaningful. If at this time of meeting with Buddha's precious teaching I do not attain the state of completely perfect Buddhahood, the supreme liberation that eradicates all suffering, I must again undergo the suffering at least of cyclic existence in general and perhaps also of the three bad transmigrations in particular.
>
> The power of protection from these sufferings exists in the lamas and the Three Jewels, who are sitting in front of me. I will attain the state of perfect Buddhahood for the sake of all sentient beings, my mothers. In order to do so, I will go for refuge to the lamas and the Three Jewels.
>
> I go for refuge to the Lamas. I go for refuge to the Buddhas. I go for refuge to the Doctrine. I go for refuge to the Spiritual Community.

Recite the abridged refuge:

> I go for refuge until perfect enlightenment to Buddha, the Doctrine, and the Supreme Community.

---

[1] Lives as animals, hungry ghosts, and hell-beings.

Think:

> From the bodies of all the objects of refuge, a stream of the five kinds of ambrosia [white, red, blue, yellow, and green] together with rays of light is falling and entering the bodies and minds of all sentient beings, myself and others. It is purifying all sickness, possession [i.e. madness], ill deeds,[1] and obstructions with their latencies beginninglessly accumulated. It is developing and furthering merit, life-span, and all the qualities of verbal and cognitive understanding. In particular, it also is purifying the ill deeds, obstructions, and discordant conditions together with their latencies which are in relation to lamas and the Three Jewels. May all sentient beings, myself and others, enter under the refuge of the lamas and the Three Jewels.

Believe that all have entered under the refuge of the Three Jewels.

Then, to [generate] an aspiration to enlightenment for all sentient beings, say:

> By whatever merit I have done, my gifts and so forth, may I accomplish Buddhahood for the sake of all beings.

Think at this time:

> By the roots of virtue arising from giving, ethics, and meditation, which I perform, or I ask others to perform, or which are done by others with my sympathy, may I attain the state of

[1] *sdig pa, pāpa*. This word is often translated as 'sins', but since this word often conveys the sense of a transgression against a creator deity, we have opted for 'ill deeds'. Nevertheless, these include transgressions against the natural order of things, as in the case of the ten non-virtues.

> completely perfect Buddhahood for the sake of all sentient beings. I *will* attain the state of completely perfect Buddhahood for the sake of all sentient beings. For the sake of achieving Buddhahood I will learn according to Buddha's way the [compassionate] deeds of the Children of the Conqueror Buddha.[1] I pray for transformative blessings[2] from the lamas and gods to enable me to do this.

Make the prayer with strong force. Thereby the gatherings of lamas and gods [visualized in space in front of you] are pleased; a duplicate separates from each of their bodies and dissolves into you. Thus, your body momentarily changes into the body of lama and Buddha. Rays of light emanate from your body transformed into lama and Buddha. By striking all the sentient beings living around you, the rays of light purify their ill deeds and obstructions. Think that they have been established in the state of lama and Buddha. This is said to be the extraordinary precept of the oral lineage of En-sa,[3] meditation in which one actualizes while on the path the result of the generation of the altruistic aspiration to enlightenment.

Then think:

> What causes the wandering of all sentient beings, my old mothers, in cyclic existence without independence?
>
> By the power of the two, desire and hatred [which are apprehensions of other beings as] in

---

[1] I.e., Bodhisattvas.

[2] These are blessings that transform the practitioner's body, speech, and mind into a more magnificent and capable state. Practitioners imagine that such transformative heightening of body, speech, and mind takes place as the prayer is recited.

[3] *dben sa/ dben sa pa blo bzang don grub.*

timate or alien, they wander in cyclic existence and thereby undergo suffering.

Therefore, if all sentient beings were to abide in the immeasurable equanimity that is free of desire and hatred, intimacy and alienness, how nice it would be! May they come to have these. I will cause them to have these. I pray for transformative blessings from the lamas and gods to enable me to do this.

If all sentient beings had happiness and the causes of happiness, how nice it would be! May they come to have these. I will cause them to have these. I pray for transformative blessings from the lamas and gods to enable me to do this.

If all sentient beings were free from suffering and the causes of suffering, how nice it would be! May they come to be free from these. I will cause them to be free from these. I pray for transformative blessings from the lamas and gods to enable me to do this.

If all sentient beings did not lack high status [as humans and gods] and the excellent bliss of liberation, how nice it would be! May they come not to lack these. I will cause them not to lack these. I pray for transformative blessings from the lamas and gods to enable me to do this.

Make the supplication with strong force and imagine the purification of all sentient beings through the falling ambrosia.

[The generation of the aspiration to enlightenment in general is the development of the thought:] 'I must attain, regardless of anything, the precious state of a completely perfect Buddha, quickly, quickly for the sake of all sentient beings, my mothers.' The generation of the attitude of altruistic enlightenment in particular [in this book is the development of the thought]: 'For the sake of attaining Buddhahood I will begin meditation on the instructions of the three principal aspects of the path.' Mentally promise firm adherence to this, and also say it many times.

Then, the objects of refuge [which are visualized in space in front of you] melt into light by stages from the outside [to the inside of the group] and dissolve into the Foremost Lama[1] in the center, [D̄zong-ka-b̄a]. The Foremost Lama also melts into light and dissolves into your forehead between the eyebrows. Consider this as transformative blessing for your mental continuum.

[The fourth of the six practices of preparation is] the clear setting of the field of accumulation [of merit] in visualization in front of you:

> There is the broad and extensive trunk of a wish-granting tree in the space directly in front of you. The top has leaves, flowers, and fruit. On its top of one hundred thousand petals, eight great lions are supporting a high and broad throne of jewels. On that, on cushions of variegated lotus and sun and moon is your kind fundamental lama in actuality but in the form of the great D̄zong-ka-b̄a, King of Doctrine, with clear white body and mouth smiling with pleasure. He is wearing the three religious robes and the golden paṇḍita's hat. His two hands are performing the gesture of the wheel of doctrine at his heart and hold stems of lotuses which extend over his shoulders.
>
> On the blossoming lotus above his right shoulder, the wisdom of all the Buddhas shines forth in the form of a sword. The light fills all worlds. All the collections of the darkness of ignorance

---

[1] *rje bla ma. rje* has the sense of 'foremost' as in *rdo rje,* literally, the foremost of stones, a diamond. 'Foremost Lama' is a general term, but here in this Ge-luk-b̄a meditation it refers to D̄zong-ka-b̄a, the founder of the order.

[particularly the apprehension of inherently existing entities] are consumed by the fire burning forth from its point.

On the blossoming lotus above his left shoulder is a volume of the *Perfection of Wisdom of One Hundred Thousand Stanzas*, the sole mother of all the Buddhas of the three times [past, present, and future].[1] Letters of melted gold shine from the sapphire pages; the emanation of rays of light from the letters clears away the darkness of sentient beings' ignorance. Also, the letters are not just shapes; they clearly proclaim the initial process of generating the aspiration to enlightenment through to finally bringing about the welfare of transmigrators in cyclic existence through the twenty-seven activities of a Buddha—together with the grounds, paths, and fruits. Think that potentialities predisposing you to the Great Vehicle path can be established just by the sound's coming to the mind.

The Conqueror Shākyamuni Buddha is sitting in the heart of the Foremost Lama. The Conqueror Vajradhara is sitting in the heart of Sākyamuni Buddha. In each of the hair pores of the Foremost Lama's body there are numberless Buddha fields. Rays of light emanate from all parts of his body in the ten directions. At the points of these rays inconceivable magical creations, equal in number to sentient beings, emanate and perform actions for the sake of those transmigrators.

The Foremost Lama sits encircled by a five-colored rainbow, his legs crossed in the adamantine posture. On a ray of light that has emanated up-

---

[1] The perfection of wisdom is the 'mother' of all Buddhas in the sense that their attainment of Buddhahood is a result mainly of it.

ward from his heart, the beings—from the Conqueror Vajradhara through to the fundamental lama who actually bestowed this teaching on you—sit one above the other. Not including the Conqueror Vajradhara, all from Mañjushrī through to your own fundamental lama are each in actuality the lama himself in the form of an orange Mañjushrī. His right hand holds aloft a sword; his left hand holds a volume at his heart. Meditate on these as having completely a nature of light.

On the point of a ray of light emanating to the right from the heart of the Foremost Lama, the lamas of the lineage of the extensive [compassionate] deeds sit on cushions of lotus and moon. On the point of a ray of light emanating to the left from the heart of the Foremost Lama, the lamas of the lineage of the deep view [that phenomena do not exist by way of their own being] sit on cushions of lotus and moon. On the point of a ray of light emanating to the front from the heart of the Foremost Lama, the lamas who have actual doctrinal relationship to you sit on cushions of lotus and moon.

Surrounding the Foremost Lama, collections of deities, Buddhas, Bodhisattvas, Heroes, Sky-Goers, and Protectors of Doctrine sit on lion thrones. On marvellous tables in front of each of the members of the field of assembly are the verbal doctrines taught by each of them in the form of books having a nature of light. At the crown of the head of each of the members of the field of assembly appears a white *oṃ*; at the throat a red *āḥ*; at the heart a blue *hūṃ*. Rays of light emanate in the ten directions from the *hūṃ* at the heart.

[You have been imagining beings of wisdom in the sky

in front of you]. Now invite the actual wisdom-beings, who are like those imagined, from their usual places [such as Amitābha from Sukhāvatī]. All come and dissolve into each of the imagined beings. Thus, firmly consider each as an entity which includes all three refuges [Buddha, Doctrine, and Spiritual Community].

Then, generate [visualize, feel, and so forth] yourself as a deity, and offer ritual ablution, clothing, and so forth [to the beings of wisdom]. If these are done, it makes a great difference with respect to clarifying the mind for cultivating the path and for pacifying uncleanliness, defilements, and so forth. Yet, even if the ablution is not done, it is said there is no fault which would nullify [the practice].

Produce a bath-house:[1]

> In a bath-house of very pleasant fragrance,
> With a base of crystal, clear and sparkling clean,
> With attractive, flaming pillars of precious stone,
> And covered with a canopy of shining pearls.

Offer ablution:

> Just as the gods offered ablution
> [To Buddha] just after his birth,
> So with pure divine water
> I also offer ablution.
> *Oṃ sarva-tathāgata-abhiṣekata-samaye śrīye aḥ hūṃ.*

> I offer ablution to the Vajradhara, King of Conquerors,
> Whose body is formed from tens of millions of perfect, good virtues,
> Whose speech fulfils the hopes of limitless transmigrators,

[1] The text only refers to the practice of ablution and so forth, which we have provided in full. In the Tibetan text, see 19.4-23.6.

Whose mind sees all to be known just as it is.
Oṃ sarva-tathāgata-abhiṣekata-samaye śrīye aḥ hūṃ.

I offer ablution to the lineage of extensive deeds.
I offer ablution to the lineage of the profound view.
I offer ablution to the lineage empowering practice.
I offer ablution to the lineaged lamas.
Oṃ sarva-tathāgata-abhiṣekata-samaye śrīye aḥ hūṃ.

I offer ablution to the teachers, the Buddhas.
I offer ablution to the protection, the Doctrine.
I offer ablution to the leaders, the Spiritual Community.
I offer ablution to the sources of refuge, the Three Jewels.
Oṃ sarva-tathāgata-abhiṣekata-samaye śrīye aḥ hūṃ.

Wipe their bodies:

I wipe their bodies with a clean cloth, infused with fragrance, unequalled.
Oṃ hūṃ traṃ hrīḥ aḥ kāya-viśodhanaye svāhā.

Anoint their bodies:

Just as a goldsmith polishes pure gold,
So I anoint the shining bodies of these Kings
Of Conquerors with the best of fragrances, strong perfumes
Suffusing all the billion [worlds of this world system].

Offer clothing:

With indestructible faith I offer
Fine, soft, light, divine clothing to those
Who have attained an indestructible adamantine body.
Thereby, may I too attain an adamantine body.

Offer ornaments:

> Because the Conquerors possess the natural ornaments of [a Buddha's] major and minor marks,
> They cannot be decorated with other ornaments.
> Still, through my offering the best of precious ornaments
> May all transmigrators attain a body adorned with the major and minor marks.

Petition them to remain:

> O Conquerors, because you love me and all transmigrators,
> I petition you to remain here
> Through your magical emanations
> As long as I make offerings.

In order to pacify ill deeds and infractions, which are conditions opposed to cultivating the path, and in order to increase merits, which are conditions concordant with cultivating the path, perform the seven branches of practice together with offering maṇḍalas [the fifth practice of preparation]. These seven include the essentials for the accumulation of merit and purification of obstructions.

Doing it in the long way, bow down and say whatever names of Buddhas, Bodhisattvas, and lineaged lamas you know. In the short form, say:[1]

> I bow down respectfully to the spiritual guides,
> The eyes that see all the countless scriptures,
> The best fords for the fortunate progressing to liberation.

---

[1] The text only refers to the remainder of the obeisance and offering which we have provided in full. In the Tibetan text, see 24.3-26.2.

They clearly act through skill in means aroused
by love.

1. Obeisance

I bow down with pure body, speech, and mind
To all without exception of all
The lions of humans, the Tathāgatas[1] of the three
times
In the worlds of the ten directions.

By the power of my aspirations for good deeds
I bow down to all the Conquerors with extreme
respect,
Myself adopting forms as numerous as the particles of the worlds,
And with all the Conquerors vivid before my
mind.

I consider that in one particle are Buddhas as nu-
merous
As the particles of the worlds, sitting in the midst
Of Bodhisattvas, and that the Conquerors fill all
Without exception of the entities of phenomena.

I praise all the Sugatas[2] and express
The qualities of all the Conquerors with all
The oceans of sounds of the melodious intoner
[the tongue],
Inexhaustible oceans of praise.

2. Offering

I offer to all the Conquerors
Excellent flowers, excellent garlands,
Pleasant sounds, fragrant oils,

---

1 Literally, 'Ones Gone Thus'. Buddhas are called 'Ones Gone Thus' because all Buddhas of the past, present, and future travel the same path to omniscience.

2 Literally, 'Those Gone To Bliss', i.e., Buddhas.

Superior umbrellas, superior lamps, and excellent
incense.

I offer to all the Conquerors
Excellent clothing, superior fragrances,
Fragrant powders, and mounds of incense equal
to Mount Meru,[1]
And all specially arrayed marvels.

I also consider all extensive, unequalled acts
Of offering to be for all the Conquerors.
By the powers of faith in good deeds
I bow down and revere all the Conquerors.

Say that softly with visualization of the field of assembly and bow down.

At this interval, confess each of the three vows [the vow of individual liberation, the Bodhisattva vow, and the tantric vow], and in particular recite the *Confession of Infractions* and bow down as much as possible.

Say softly, with visualization of the field of assembly and of the falling ambrosia, the following prayer.[2]

3. Confession

I confess individually all ill deeds
Done by me with body, speech,
Or mind through the power
Of desire, hatred, and ignorance.

4. Admiration

I admire and will emulate the meritorious actions
Of all the Conqueror Buddhas of the ten directions,

---

[1] The mountain at the center of our world-system, according to Buddhist cosmology.

[2] The text only refers to the remainder of the seven-branched service, which we have provided in full. In the Tibetan text, see 26.8-27.11.

The Buddha Children, the Solitary Realizers, those still learning,
Those with no more learning, and all transmigrators.

5. Entreaty

I entreat all the protectors, who have found nonattachment
And progressively awakened into enlightenment
And are the lights of the world systems of the ten directions,
To turn the unsurpassed wheel [of doctrine].

6. Supplication

With pressed palms I supplicate those planning
To show nirvana to the world to dwell here
Even as many aeons as the particles in the realms
To help and bring happiness to all transmigrators.

7. Dedication

I dedicate toward perfect enlightenment
All the little virtue I have accumulated
Through obeisance, offering, confession,
Admiration, entreaty, and supplication.

Then, offer maṇḍala [the purified world system] extensively:

Oṃ vajra-bhūmi āḥ hūṃ. Ground of most powerful gold. *Oṃ vajra-rekhe āḥ hūṃ*. In the center surrounded by an outer rim of iron mountains, the king of mountains, Meru. To the east, Videha with Deha and Videha. To the south, Jambudvīpa with Chāmara and Aparachāmara. To the west, Godānīya with Sāthā and Uttaramantriṇa. to the north, Kuru with Kurava and Kaurava. Mountains of jewels, wish-granting trees, wish-granting cows, naturally grown maize, precious chariots, precious jewels, precious consorts, precious ministers, precious elephants, precious horses, precious generals, vessels of great treasure, goddess of beauty, goddess of garlands, goddess of song, goddess of dance, goddess of flowers, goddess of incense, goddess of light, goddess of perfume, suns, moons, precious umbrellas, banners of victory, and in the center all the marvellous wealth of gods and humans. I offer these to the glorious excellent lamas—the kind fundamental lamas and their lineages—and to the divine company of Ḏzong-ka-ḇa, the King of Subduers Shākyamuni Buddha, and Vajradhara together with their retinues. Please accept these through your compassion for the sake of transmigrators. Having taken them, please empower me with transformative blessings.

I offer this ground anointed with incense,
Strewn with flowers, adorned with Meru, the
four continents,
Sun, and moon and visualized as a Buddha Land.
May all transmigrators enjoy this Pure Land.

To the lamas, deities, and Three Jewels I offer in
visualization
The body, speech, mind, and resources of myself
and others,
Our collections of virtue in the past, present, and
future,
And the wonderful precious maṇḍala with the
masses of Samantabhadra's offerings.
Accepting them through your compassion,
please empower me with blessings.
Idaṃ guru-ratna-maṇḍalakaṃ niryātayāmi.

Making a petition, recite three times this prayer, *The Three Great Aims*, which was composed by the Foremost Lama [D̄zong-ka-b̄a] himself:

> I pray for transformative blessings in order to stop all the various wrong thoughts, beginning from not respecting the spiritual guide through to conceiving persons and phenomena to exist inherently. I pray for transformative blessings in order to generate easily all the various correct attitudes, from respecting the spiritual guide through to realizing the reality of selflessness. I pray for transformative blessings in order to pacify immediately all internal and external obstacles.

[The sixth preparatory practice is a supplication.] Make a supplication to the lineage of lamas who teach the principal aspects of the path, saying:[1]

> I supplicate the Conqueror Vajradhara, protector of mundane existence and solitary peace,
> Who does not abide in the extremes of mundane existence and solitary peace,
> Who through wisdom has ended the bonds of mundane existence,
> And who through compassion has put far away the liking for a solitary peace.
>
> I supplicate the protector Mañjushrī, body of wisdom
> Unifying all the treasures of wisdom
> Of countless Buddhas exceeding even
> A number equal to the particles of the realms.
>
> I supplicate to the feet of B̄a-wo-dor-jay[2]
> All of whose webs of doubt were manifestly cleared away

---

[1] The text only refers to the supplication, which we have provided in full. In the Tibetan text, see 29.2-32.9.
[2] *dpa' po rdo rje.*

By the holy Mañjushrī through the power of his
  prayers
Like a great wave set rolling long ago.

I supplicate to the feet of the glorious lama
  D̄zong-ka-b̄a
Who manifested the Three Buddha Bodies
  through his well-reasoned realization
Of the way the two truths actually are and
  through
His practice of the union of method and wisdom.

I supplicate to the feet of the world's scholar,
  Gen-dün-drup,[1]
Lion expounding the good path, glittering with
  the mane
Of the hundred thousand books
In the forest of the Sugata's scriptures.

May I be empowered to generate effortlessly
Faith and respect at all times through only remembering
The kind masters, who are the foundations of all
  qualities
Of auspicious virtue, mundane and supramundane.

May I be empowered to produce contentment of
  mind,
Few desires, abiding in discipline, heartily seeking liberation,
Speaking honestly, forever being conscientious,
  acquaintance with superior friends,
Perceiving everything as pure, and lack of bias.

May I be empowered to produce in my mental
  continuum

---

[1] *dge 'dun grub*, the First Dalai Lama.

Untainted realization of the shortness of time and a profound aversion
For goods and respect through remembering not just the words
That death is definite and the time of death unsure.

May I be empowered effortlessly to generate
Compassion and a disinclination toward achieving only my own happiness
Through identifying all embodied beings as kind mothers
And thus becoming aware of the suffering of stricken beings.

May I be empowered to understand in accordance
With the thoughts of the Superior, the father Nāgārjuna, and his spiritual son [Āryadeva],
The deep meaning of dependent-arising free from extremes,
The sole medicine curing all the sickness of extreme conceptions.

Taking as an example the virtue of this prayer,
May all the roots of virtue of myself and others
In the past, present, and future not ripen for even a moment
As anything unfavorable to superior enlightenment:

Desire for profit, fame, companions,
Enjoyments, goods, and others' respect.
May all my roots of virtue become in birth after birth
Causes only of supreme enlightenment.

May the forms of these pure wishes be accomplished

Through the Conqueror's and his Children's
marvellous transformative blessings,
Through the universal truth of dependent-arising,
And through my pure extraordinary thoughts.

Make these supplications with strong force in order to generate quickly in your mental continuum realization of the three principal aspects of the path to highest enlightenment.

2 *Understanding the Path and Promising to Cultivate It*

Meditate continuously on the gatherings of lamas and gods visualized in space in front of you, and think:

> In general, the foundation of all good qualities is faith. In particular, the foundation of all accumulations of goodness in this life and the future, the fundamental support of all achievements—supreme and common[1]—the excellent cause of producing, keeping, increasing, and completing all stages and paths is proper reliance on an excellent spiritual guide. Therefore, at the beginning I must experience reliance upon a spiritual guide. Such reliance is the basis of the path.

---

[1] The supreme achievement or feat (*dngos grub, siddhi*) is Buddhahood; common achievements include such feats as flying in the sky, cleansing an area of contagion, understanding treatises immediately upon reading them, and so forth.

The ways of relying on a spiritual guide are two: reliance in thought and reliance in deed. With respect to the first, how to rely on a spiritual guide in thought, clearly set [i.e., visualize] in the space in front of you the virtuous spiritual guides who teach you doctrine, and firmly think:

> These spiritual guides of mine are actually Buddhas. In the precious tantras the completely perfect Buddha says that in the degenerate era the Conqueror Vajradhara shows himself in the physical form of virtuous spiritual guides and performs deeds for the sake of transmigrators in cyclic existence. Just so, these virtuous spiritual guides of mine are only showing a form of body different [from Vajradhara's customary body]. Except for that, they are the Conqueror Vajradhara who in the degenerate era displays the physical form of virtuous spiritual guides in order to take care of those who did not have the fortune actually to see the Buddha.
>
> These kind fundamental lamas of mine are not only in fact real Buddhas; their kindness is even greater than all the Buddhas'. If all the former Conquerors and the Bodhisattvas forsook me, unable to tame me, these kind fundamental lamas, not able to bear it because of their compassion, perform the deeds of the Conqueror. Even if Buddha actually came, the deep doctrines he would teach would not be better expressed.
>
> In the past, our teacher, Buddha, the King of Conquerors, for the sake of only one stanza of doctrine, even put a thousand iron nails into his body and used his body to burn a thousand lamps. Without regret he gave up his son, his wife, his own body, and all usable things, whatever he had. He had to do unthinkably difficult

> deeds. Without my having to do any such difficult deeds, these kind fundamental lamas, like a father teaching his child, liberally teach me deep precepts, the Great Vehicle doctrines, complete and without mistake. If I can meditate on their teaching, it can easily give me the states of high status[1] and even of liberation from cyclic existence as well as omniscience. There is no way at all to return such kindness.

Meditate thus until the hairs of the body rise and tears well from the eyes.

The ways of relying on spiritual guides through deeds are to please them with the three delights. These three delights are to offer things to them, to venerate them with body and speech, and to achieve what they teach. Of these, the main one is to achieve what they teach. Therefore, think:

> According to the lamas' teaching, I must practice the meaning of all the scriptures, together with their commentaries, included in the three principal aspects of the path.

Mentally promise firm adherence to this.

How are all the meanings of the scriptures with their commentaries included in the three principal aspects of the path? The chief content of all the scriptures and their commentaries is only the means for freeing trainees from bad transmigrations in particular and cyclic existence in general and establishing them in the state of Buddhahood. In order to attain Buddhahood, it is necessary to learn its two causes, method and wisdom. Further, the chief method is the altruistic aspiration to highest enlightenment, and the chief wisdom is the correct

---

[1] High status (*mngon mtho, abhyudaya*) here refers elevated states of existence within cyclic existence, these being lives as gods, demigods, and humans.

view that no phenomenon exists by way of its own being.

In order to generate these two paths in your mental continuum, it is necessary at the beginning to generate all the features of the thought that you will definitely leave cyclic existence. This thought is a wish for liberation from cyclic existence. If you do not want liberation from cyclic existence, you cannot generate the altruistic aspiration to enlightenment and love and compassion, which are wishes to free other sentient beings from cyclic existence.

The main means of attaining a Buddha's Form Body is the collection of merit. The heart, root, and excellent essential of all the collections of merit is just the precious altruistic aspiration to highest enlightenment. The main cause of attaining a Buddha's Wisdom Body, which is the mind of the Conqueror, is the collection of wisdom. The heart, root, and excellent essential of all the accumulations of wisdom is just the correct view that no phenomenon exists by way of its own being.

Therefore, all the essentials of the path are included in the three: the intention definitely to leave cyclic existence, the altruistic aspiration to highest enlightenment, and the correct view. The practice of these is the excellent pith of all quintessential instructions. In just this way the protector Mañjushrī earnestly exhorted the great D̄zong-ka-b̄a, a King of Doctrine.

Thus, first of all, the root of all accumulations of goodness derives from reliance on a spiritual guide. Hence, at the beginning it is necessary to have practical experience in relying on a spiritual guide. The basic text, D̄zong-ka-b̄a's *Three Principal Aspects of the Path to Highest Enlightenment*, says:

> I bow down to the holy lamas.

This also [implicitly] indicates all the other surrounding practices of preparation just explained.

When first cultivating the path, you must gain a rough idea of the entire body of the path. Aim in thought, 'I must cultivate such a number and series of paths.' It is necessary to make a promise of firm adherence to a particular meditation and not to pass from it to other subjects. D̄zong-ka-b̄a's basic text says:

> I will explain as well as I can
> The essential meaning of all the Conqueror's scriptures,
> The path praised by the excellent Conqueror Children,
> The port for the fortunate wishing liberation.
>
> Whoever are not attached to the pleasures of transient existence,
> Whoever strive to make leisure and fortune worthwhile,
> Whoever are inclined to the path pleasing the Conqueror Buddha,
> Those fortunate ones should listen with a clear mind.

3 *The First Principal Aspect: Developing an Intention to Leave Cyclic Existence*

Dzong-ka-ba's *Three Principal Aspects of the Path* says:[1]

> Without a complete intention definitely to leave cyclic existence
> There is no way to stop seeking pleasurable effects in the ocean of existence.
> Also, craving cyclic existence thoroughly binds the embodied.
> Therefore, in the beginning, an intention to leave cyclic existence should be sought.

This section has two parts: how to meditate on the means to overcome excessive emphasis on the appearances of this life and how to meditate on the means to overcome excessive emphasis on the appearances of future lives.

---

[1] The text (42.1) omits this transitional stanza from Dzong-ka-ba's work, which we have added.

MEANS TO OVERCOME EXCESSIVE EMPHASIS ON THE APPEARANCES OF THIS LIFE

Dzong-ka-ba's *Three Principal Aspects of the Path* says:

> Leisure and fortune are difficult to find
> And life has no duration.
> Through familiarity with this,
> Emphasis on the appearances of this life is reversed.

This section has two parts: thought on the meaningfulness of leisure and fortune and thought on the difficulty of finding leisure and fortune.[1]

MEANINGFULNESS OF LEISURE AND FORTUNE

Continuously meditate on the lamas and gods in front of you, and think:

> Leisure[2] means having the time to accomplish the excellent doctrine of Buddha. Fortune means having all the inner and outer conditions conducive to realizing the doctrine.
>
> Therefore, this life of complete leisure and fortune which we have obtained is extremely worthwhile. Using such a life, we can accomplish giving, ethics, patience, effort, and so forth, which are the causes of the wonderful body and resources of high status. In particular, in a life of leisure and fortune we can generate the three

---

[1] The text (43.8), before editing, wrongly read: 'There are three [parts]: thought on the difficulty of finding precious leisure and fortune, thought that the time of death is indefinite, and thought of the sufferings in bad transmigrations.' The Paṇ-chen Lama's own headings on the individual sections confirm the editorial emendation.

[2] For a short discussion of the attributes of leisure and fortune, see pp. 24-26.

> vows and can easily accomplish the state of perfect Buddhahood in one short lifetime during the degenerate era. This life of worthwhile leisure and fortune is difficult to find, and if it is found, its essence should be used without wasting it pointlessly. I pray for transformative blessings from the lamas and gods to enable me to do this.

DIFFICULTY OF FINDING LEISURE AND FORTUNE

Clearly visualize the gatherings of lamas and gods in front of you, and think:

> This life of complete leisure and fortune is not only meaningful but also extremely difficult to find. Most beings, including humans, for the most part engage in the ten non-virtuous actions,[1] which are obstacles to obtaining leisure and fortune. In particular, in order to obtain all aspects of a life-support of complete leisure and fortune one needs a basis [of a complete action] of ethics [which establishes the main potency in the mind that, when empowered, produces a human life]. One needs helping causes, giving and so forth [which establish potencies that supplement the main potency]. One also needs conjunction of one life to another by means of a stainless vow [to gain enlightenment for the sake of others].
>
> Those who muster such causes are extremely few. Those in bad transmigrations—animals, hungry ghosts, and hell-beings—seem to be beyond hope of obtaining even a happy transmigration [as a human, demi-god, or god]. Also, as

[1] The ten non-virtues are killing, stealing, sexual misconduct, lying, divisive talk, harsh speech, foolish talk, covetousness, harmfulness, and wrong ideas.

> rare as a star at noon is the obtaining of a life-support of complete leisure and fortune by those already in happy transmigrations. Therefore, the essence of this life of complete leisure and fortune, difficult to find and meaningful when found, must be used without wasting it pointlessly.

This is how to use the essence of this life of leisure and fortune:

> I will continuously rely on the lamas who are inseparable from Buddha, and I will practice the essentials of the Great Vehicle precepts taught by them. Thereby, I will attain perfect Buddhahood in only one lifetime. I pray for transformative blessings from the lamas and gods to enable me to do this.

MEANS TO OVERCOME EXCESSIVE EMPHASIS ON THE APPEARANCES OF FUTURE LIVES

D̄zong-ka-b̄a's *Three Principal Aspects of the Path* says:

> If you think again and again
> About actions and their inevitable effects
> And the sufferings of cyclic existence,
> Emphasis on the appearances
> Of future lives will be reversed.

This section has two parts: thought about deeds and their inevitable effects and thought on the sufferings of cyclic existence.

ACTIONS AND THEIR EFFECTS

Clearly visualize the collection of lamas and gods in front of you, and think:

It is said in the scriptures of the Conqueror Buddha, 'From causes that are virtuous actions, only effects of happiness arise; suffering does not arise. From causes that are non-virtuous actions, only effects of suffering arise. Though one creates even tiny causes—virtues and ill deeds—extremely great effects—happiness and suffering—arise. If virtuous and non-virtuous actions are not done, one does not experience effects of happiness and suffering. If interference with virtuous and sinful causes already made is not encountered, the actions done will not be fruitless; effects—happiness and suffering—will certainly come forth.'

I will generate firm faith trusting what was taught with regard to the greater power of actions from the point of view of the field of activity, the thought, the object, and the agent. Then I will learn the right way to adopt virtues and discard non-virtues. Among the ten virtues I will, as much as possible, achieve even tiny virtues, and among the ten non-virtues, I will not pollute the three doors of body, speech, and mind with even tiny non-virtues. I pray for transformative blessings from the lamas and gods to enable me to do this.

SUFFERINGS OF CYCLIC EXISTENCE

This section has two parts: thought on the sufferings of cyclic existence in general and thought on the sufferings of individual cyclic existences.

Sufferings of cyclic existence in general

Clearly visualize the gatherings of lamas and gods in front of you, and think:

> Once one has taken birth in cyclic existence due to [former polluted] actions and the afflictive emotions [of desire, hatred, and ignorance], one does not pass beyond suffering. Because enemies become friends and friends become enemies, there is no certainty about someone's helping or harming. However much the happiness of cyclic existence is enjoyed, not only is there no final satisfaction, but also attachments are extended, bringing about many unbearable sufferings. However good a body one obtains, as it must be given up again and again, there is no certainty with regard to obtaining a certain type of body. Because the gap between lives is closed again and again beginninglessly, the limits of birth are not to be seen. No matter what prosperity of cyclic existence is obtained, because finally it must definitely be forsaken, there is no certainty with regard to obtaining prosperity. Because one must go alone to the next life, there is no certainty with regard to friends.
>
> Thus, at this time of obtaining a life of complete leisure and fortune which is difficult to find and is, if found, extremely worthwhile, I will do whatever I can to attain the state of lama and Buddha who have abandoned all the sufferings of cyclic existence. I pray for transformative blessings from the lamas and gods to enable me to do this.

Sufferings of individual cyclic existences

Clearly visualize the gatherings of lamas and gods in front of you, and think:

Once one has the contaminated aggregates of body and mind,[1] one does not pass beyond suffering. Thus, what need is there to consider whether the three bad transmigrations—animals, hungry ghosts, and hell-beings—involve suffering!

Based on the contaminated aggregates of a human, one experiences hunger, thirst, hot, cold, and so forth. One also experiences separation from attractive friends, meeting unattractive enemies, searching for but not finding the desired, the undesired falling upon oneself, birth, aging, sickness, death, and so on.

Based on the contaminated aggregates of demi-gods, one experiences mental suffering from an unbearable jealousy of the glorious fortune of gods, and one experiences physical suffering [from consequently engaging in war].

Based on the contaminated aggregates of gods of the Desire Realm, when there is fighting with the demi-gods, one experiences the cutting off of limbs, the loss of the body, murder, and so forth. There is also the undesirable foreknowledge from the arising of the signs of death that one must separate from the glorious fortune of gods and experience the terrible suffering of a bad transmigration.

Based even on the contaminated aggregates of beings in the Form and Formless Realms, one experiences the measureless suffering of falling to a bad transmigration upon the exhaustion of the impetus of the former good actions [that caused

---

[1] Ordinary mind and body are contaminated in the sense that they are products of actions (*las, karma*) that are involved with afflictive emotions.

> the birth in the upper realm]. For, freedom to remain in those realms was not attained.
>
> In short, once these contaminated aggregates exist, they act as a base for birth, aging, sickness, death, and so forth in this life. The suffering of pain and the suffering of change are attracted to both this and future lives. In short, just the existence of the contaminated aggregates means that they are entities compounded from a force other than their own—former [polluted] actions and afflictive emotions.
>
> Therefore, I will do whatever I can to attain the state of lama and Buddha that frees one from the suffering of cyclic existence having the nature of contaminated aggregates. I pray for transformative blessings from the lamas and gods to enable me to do this.

Dwell thus on thoughts about cyclic existence in general and about particular cyclic existences without desirous attachment for any of the prosperity of cyclic existence—like the nausea of a prisoner for the prison. A strong intention to seek liberation all day and night will be generated. When this happens, it is an indication that the intention definitely to leave cyclic existence has been generated.

It is as D̄zong-ka-b̄a's *Three Principal Aspects of the Path* says:

> If, having meditated thus, you do not generate admiration
> Even for an instant for the prosperity of cyclic existence
> And if an attitude seeking liberation arises day and night,
> Then the intention definitely to leave cyclic existence has been generated.

Then, it says:

> Also, if this intention definitely to leave cyclic existence
> Is not conjoined with generation of a complete aspiration to highest enlightenment,
> It does not become a cause of the marvellous bliss of unsurpassed enlightenment.
> Thus, the intelligent should generate the supreme altruistic aspiration to become enlightened.

4 *The Second Principal Aspect: Cultivating an Altruistic Aspiration to Enlightenment*

The cultivation of an aspiration to highest enlightenment begins with recognition of all sentient beings as mothers. This is done having first attained even-mindedness towards all sentient beings.

HOW TO ACHIEVE EVEN-MINDEDNESS

First, clearly imagine in front of you a neutral sentient being who has neither helped nor harmed you. Then think:

> All persons want happiness and do not want suffering; thus, I must not help some apprehending them as intimate and must not harm others apprehending them as alien. I must create an even-mindedness that is free of desire and hatred, intimacy and alienness, with regard to all sentient

> beings. I pray for transformative blessings from the lamas and gods to enable me to do this.

When you become even-minded toward a neutral being, clearly imagine in front of you a sentient being who is definitely pleasant to your mind. Then cultivate an even-mindedness [which is devoid of desire and hatred]. Not becoming even-minded is due to the power of desire. Think that you have been born in beginningless cyclic existence by desiring the pleasant in the past and thereby stop attachment and meditate.

When you become even-minded toward a pleasant being, clearly imagine in front of you a sentient being whom you definitely find unpleasant. Then, cultivate even-mindedness [free of desire and hatred]. Not becoming even-minded is due to the generation of anger through single-mindedly apprehending the person to be disagreeable. If you do not become even-minded with regard to him/her, think that this is not a situation for generating an altruistic aspiration to enlightenment and thus stop anger and meditate.

When you become even-minded toward an unattractive being, clearly imagine in front of you both a sentient being who is very pleasant, such as your mother, and one who is very unpleasant, such as an enemy. Then think:

> These two are the same because from their point of view they want happiness and do not want suffering. From my point of view, this one who is now apprehended as a friend has been my chief enemy countless times through beginningless cyclic existences. This one who is now apprehended as an enemy has been my mother limitless times through beginningless cyclic existences. Thus who should be desired? Who should be hated? I will create an even-mindedness free from desire and hatred, intimacy and alienness. I

> pray for transformative blessings from the lamas and gods to enable me to do this.

When you have become even-minded toward an attractive being and an unattractive being together, cultivate an even-mindedness toward all sentient beings. The way to do this is to think:

> All sentient beings are the same. From their point of view they want happiness and do not want suffering. Also, from my point of view all sentient beings are friends. Therefore, I will create an even-mindedness free of desire and hatred, intimacy and alienness, toward all of them. I will not help some because of apprehending them as intimate and will not harm others because of apprehending them as alien. I pray for transformative blessings from the lamas and gods to enable me to do this.

HOW TO CULTIVATE RECOGNITION OF ALL SENTIENT BEINGS AS MOTHERS

After that, there is the meditation that starts from recognition of all sentient beings as mothers and goes through to the altruistic aspiration to highest enlightenment. Continuously meditate on the lamas and gods in front of you, and think:

> Why are all beings my friends? Cyclic existence is beginningless; therefore, my births are also beginningless. In the continuum from one birth to another there is not even one country or place where I have not been born. My births there are countless. There is not even one type of body of a sentient being that I did not formerly have. The times I had such bodies are countless. There is not even one sentient being who has not been my mother. The times each was my mother are

> countless. There is not even one sentient being who has not been my mother in a human body. The times each has been my mother are countless, and each will be my mother again in the future. Therefore, of course, they are my mothers who protected me with kindness.

HOW TO CULTIVATE THOUGHT OF THE KINDNESS OF MOTHERS

If experience arises with regard to recognizing all sentient beings as mothers, think of their kindness. Continuously meditate on the lamas and gods in front of you, and visualize the clear form of your own mother of this life, not in her youth but in her old age. Then think:

> This mother of mine was my mother not only in this life but also countless times again and again in the beginningless continuum of lives. In particular, in this life she initially protected me with love in the womb. Then when I was born, she placed me on a soft cushion; she rocked me to and fro on the tips of her ten fingers. She held me to the warmth of her flesh; she pleased me with her loving smile; she looked at me with happy eyes. She cleaned away mucus from my nose with her mouth;[1] she wiped away my filth with her hand.
>
> My mother suffered more from my being slightly sick than she would have, for instance, if she herself were dying. She lovingly gave me food and riches which she obtained with strained muscles, without looking to her own life and without caring about ill deeds, sufferings, and all the bad talk of others that she might incur. My

---

[1] In the days before tissue paper, Tibetan mothers licked the mucus from a child's runny nose and spit it out.

> mother provided measureless help and happiness for me in accordance with her capacity. She protected me from measureless harm and suffering; therefore, her kindness is extremely great.

When experience arises with respect to your mother's kindness, meditate also on the kindness of other relatives and friends, such as your father. Clearly imagine the form of your father and so forth and think:

> In the beginningless continuum of lives he was my mother innumerable times. He protected me with kindness when he was my mother just as my mother of this lifetime protected me with kindness. Therefore, his kindness is extremely great.

When experience arises with respect to the kindness of all relatives, meditate on all neutral sentient beings. Clearly imagine them in front of you. Think:

> It indeed appears that now these have no connection with me, but they have been my mother innumerable times in the beginningless continuum of lives. When they were my mother, they protected me with kindness just as my mother of this life protected me. Thus, their kindness is extremely great.

When experience arises with respect to the kindness of all neutral beings, meditate on sentient beings who are enemies and the like. Clearly imagine in front of you the forms of enemies, and think:

> What is accomplished by apprehending these as enemies? They have been my mother countless times in the beginningless continuum of lives. When they were my mother, they provided measureless help and happiness for me. They protected me from measureless harm and suf-

> fering. In particular, I could not stay even a little while without them [because I loved them so much]. They also could not stay even a little while without me [because they loved me so much]. Thus, they had such an intimate sentiment toward me numberless times. That they have become enemies at the present occasion is due to bad actions (*karma*); otherwise, they are only my mothers who protected me with kindness.

When experience arises with respect to the kindness of enemies, contemplate the kindness of all sentient beings.

HOW TO MEDITATE ON REPAYING THEIR KINDNESS

After thinking of their kindness as before, meditate on repaying their kindness. Continuously meditate on the lamas and gods in front of you, and think:

> The mothers who have beginninglessly protected me with kindness are mentally agitated through being possessed by the afflictive emotions of desire, hatred, and ignorance. Due to not having attained independence of mind, they are crazed. They lack the eye that sees the paths of high status[1] and definite goodness.[2] They have no virtuous spiritual guide, no leader of the blind. They stumble each moment by the punishment of bad deeds, passing along the edge of the abyss of frightful cyclic existences in general and bad transmigrations in particular. If I forsook them, I

---

[1] High status refers to preferable states within cyclic existence—those of humans, demi-gods, and gods.

[2] There are two levels of definite goodness, liberation from cyclic existence and Buddhahood.

> would be extremely shameless. Therefore, to repay their kindness, I will free them from the sufferings of cyclic existence and will establish them in the bliss of liberation. I pray for transformative blessings from the lamas and gods to enable me to do this.

HOW TO CULTIVATE LOVE

Imagine an intimate such as your mother, and think:

> How can she have bliss non-polluted [with thoughts of an inherently existing self]? She does not even have happiness polluted [with thoughts of an inherently existing self]. She goes along with what is now claimed to be happiness, which turns into suffering. Through wishing for happiness she strives, strives, yearns, yearns; however, she is making the causes of bad transmigrations and sufferings in the future. In this life, also, except for making suffering, fatigued and tired, she does not in the least have real bliss. Therefore, if she had happiness and all the causes of happiness, how nice it would be! May she come to have these. I will cause her to have these. I pray for transformative blessings from the lamas and gods to enable me to do this.

When experience arises with respect to the thoughts of love, imagine other relatives and friends such as your father. Then imagine neutral sentient beings, then enemies, and finally all sentient beings. Meditate as before.

HOW TO CULTIVATE GREAT COMPASSION AND THE UNUSUAL ALTRUISTIC ATTITUDE

Think:

> My kind fathers and mothers, throughout all of

space, are bound without independence by polluted actions (*karma*) and afflictive emotions. They are swept along powerlessly in the river of continuous cyclic existence by the currents of desire, existence [desire in the form and formless realms], ignorance, and wrong views. They are battered by the turbulent waves of birth, aging, sickness, and death.

Their modes of action through body, speech, and mind are completely and tightly bound by the tight bonds of various actions difficult to oppose. They have entered beginninglessly into the iron cage of apprehending an inherently existent self and its belongings, which stays in the center of the heart and is difficult for anyone to open. Thus, what is there to say about their being on the path going to liberation and omniscience? Without seeking even the path going to temporary happy transmigrations, the huge, thick, black cloud of ignorance that obscures the adopting of the good and the discarding of the bad has beclouded them. If I do not liberate these stricken beings tortured ceaselessly by the three sufferings—the suffering of pain, the suffering of change, and the pervasive suffering of being conditioned [by a process of uncontrolled actions and afflictive emotions]—who will liberate them? If I were to abandon such stricken beings, my kind mothers, seeing them drowning in the ocean of cyclic existence, I would be shamelessly vulgar. I would be ashamed before the eyes of all the Buddhas and Bodhisattvas, and my wish to learn the Great Vehicle would also be only words. Therefore, now I will do whatever I can to generate an ability to free these stricken beings, my kind mothers, from cyclic existence and establish them in the state of Buddhahood.

In this way, a complete form of a compassionate attitude that is unusual [in that you have taken upon yourself the burden of liberating all beings] should be generated with strong force.

HOW TO CULTIVATE AN ALTRUISTIC ASPIRATION TO HIGHEST ENLIGHTENMENT

Think:

> Do I have the ability to establish all sentient beings in the state of Buddhahood?
>
> If now I am unsure of where I am going, I have no ability to establish even one sentient being, myself, in the state of perfect Buddhahood. Also, even if I attain the state of a [Hearer or Solitary Realizer] Foe Destroyer, aside from furthering a tiny bit the aims of sentient beings, I will have no ability to establish all sentient beings in the state of Buddhahood. Who has such power? A completely perfect Buddha has. Therefore, I will do whatever I can to attain the state of a completely perfect, unsurpassed Buddha for the sake of all sentient beings, my mothers. I pray for transformative blessings from the lamas and gods to enable me to do this.

After generating an altruistic aspiration to highest enlightenment you should learn the activities of Bodhisattvas. Though the Bodhisattva activities involve limitless forms of practice, in brief, they mean that within the context of being motivated by a precious aspiration to enlightenment for the sake of all sentient beings, you generate deep, penetrating ascertainment of the nature of the two truths in reliance on correct reasoning.

If experience arises through the turning of the mind to each of the six perfections and if the power of intellect proceeds to increase, perform all six perfections—giving, ethics, patience, effort, concentration, and wisdom—in each perfection. All the meanings of the Great Vehicle scriptures and the commentaries are included in the six perfections. Learn that all the activities of the Bodhisattvas do not pass beyond the six perfections.

Also, the four ways of gathering students are included in the six perfections. 'The gathering of students by giving gifts' is easy to understand [as being included in the perfection of giving]. 'Speaking pleasantly' is included in the giving of doctrine, which is a part of giving. From among the three types of ethics—the ethics of restraining ill deeds, the ethics that are the composite of virtuous practices, and the ethics of aiding the aims of sentient beings—'teaching others to fulfil their aims' and 'one's acting according to this teaching' are included in the ethics of aiding the aims of sentient beings. [The main aims of sentient beings are the attainment of high status as humans and gods and the attainment of definite goodness—liberation from cyclic existence and Buddhahood.]

On the other hand, the four ways of gathering students can be presented separately from the perfections, for Bodhisattvas first learn to control their own mental continuums, and, once having ripened their own continuums, they aid the aims of others. Therefore, in order to teach that it is necessary [to perform the perfections first and gather students later] the four ways of gathering students are often taught separately from the six perfections.

In short, say:

> I will do whatever I can to attain the precious state of a completely perfect Buddha quickly, quickly for the sake of all sentient beings. In order to do that, I will generate an aspirational intention to attain highest enlightenment and will

> train properly in the points of training [concerning the altruistic aspiration]. Then I will generate a practical intention to gain highest enlightenment in conjunction with the Bodhisattva deeds and will learn properly all the Bodhisattva deeds that are included in the six perfections and the four ways of gathering students. I pray for transformative blessings from the lamas and gods to enable me to learn these.

Make the petition with strong force.

You should experience as much as you can in the actual session a turning of the mind toward the altruistic aspiration to highest enlightenment and its exhortations. Between sessions also, you should learn to conjoin all activities of the three modes [of action—physical, verbal, and mental—] with an aspiration to highest enlightenment for the sake of all sentient beings. Again and again you should clearly establish love, mercy, and the aspiration to highest enlightenment as the basis of all ways of behavior. Even though only a fabricated aspiration to enlightenment is produced [rather than a spontaneous and effortless one], if whatever deeds you do are conjoined with this aspiration they will become a means of finishing the collection of merit.

In the past King Prasenajit asked Buddha, the Supramundane Victor:

> With too many activities, I am unable to remain single-mindedly in the practice of virtues. I wish to be able to practice the Great Vehicle without the degeneration of my activities as king. How can I do this?

Buddha answered:

> Kings who are unable to remain at all times single-minded with regard to the practice of virtues

> because they have many activities should cultivate this aspiration to enlightenment for the sake of all beings in relation to all ways of behavior. They should be motivated in whatever they do by this aspiration. If they do this, everything they do will become a means of attaining Buddhahood without neglecting the royal duties.

Because this is extremely important, that Bodhisattvas should learn to accompany everything they do with the aspiration to enlightenment was urgently taught also in Shāntideva's *Compendium of Instructions*[1] quoting as the source this passage from the *Advice to King Prasenajit Sūtra.*

Moreover, when physical pain and mental suffering arise, meditate on giving pleasure to others and taking pain to yourself. Think:

> May the physical sickness and the mental suffering of all sentient beings throughout all of space leave them and be added to my physical sickness and mental suffering.

If happiness and the wonderful particulars of prosperity come to your body and mind, meditate on giving and taking. Think:

> I will give this happiness and fortune to all sentient beings [and take their unhappiness and misfortune].

When eating food, think:

> I will eat this food to nourish my body for the sake of all sentient beings. In addition, it is said that there are eighty-four thousand germs in my body, and by giving this food to them I attract

---

[1] *bslabs pa kun las bsdus pa, śikṣāsamuccaya.* For an English translation of this text, see C. Bendall and W.H.D. Rouse, *Sikṣā Samuccaya* (Delhi: Motilal, 1971).

> them now with things; in the future I will attract them by giving them doctrine.

Generate such thought, and without wasting activities pointlessly, conjoin whatever you eat, drink, or do with generation of an altruistic aspiration to highest enlightenment. Even when lying down, you should go to sleep within an aspiration to enlightenment. Think:

> I will nourish my body with sleep for the sake of all sentient beings. I will nourish and further with sleep the various creatures in my body which sleep replenishes.

When cleaning the house, generate the thought:

> I will clean away the mess of actions and afflictive emotions of all sentient beings.

At the time of bathing, cleaning your hands and so forth, generate the thought:

> I will wash away the defilement of afflictive emotions in all sentient beings.

When opening a door, generate the thought:

> I will open the door of liberation to lead all sentient beings out of bad transmigrations and to lead them to the state of Buddhahood.

When offering lamps to an image, generate the thought:

> I will clear away the darkness of ignorance of all sentient beings throughout all of space.

Learn from these examples to conjoin all actions of the three modes [physical, verbal, and mental] with an aspiration to enlightenment. Learn from the mouths of excellent lineaged lamas and read in detail the Great Vehicle scriptures because the exhortations on the altruistic aspiration to enlightenment are as extensive and limitless as space.

About the ways of cultivating the generation of an altruistic aspiration to highest enlightenment, Ḏzong-ka-ḇa's *Three Principal Aspects of the Path* says:

> Also, if this thought definitely to leave cyclic existence
> Is not conjoined with generation of a complete aspiration to highest enlightenment,
> It does not become a cause of the marvellous bliss of unsurpassed enlightenment.
> Thus, the intelligent should generate the supreme altruistic aspiration to become enlightened.
>
> [All ordinary beings] are carried by the continuum of the four powerful currents,
> Are tied with the tight bonds of actions difficult to oppose,
> Have entered into the iron cage of apprehending self [inherent existence],
> Are completely beclouded with the thick darkness of ignorance,
>
> Are born into cyclic existence limitlessly,
> And in their births are tortured ceaselessly by the three sufferings.[1]
> Thinking thus of the condition of mothers who have come to such a state,
> Generate the supreme altruistic intention to become enlightened.

This is the system of practice as it appears in the quintessential instructions of the oral transmission.

---

[1] The suffering of mental and physical pain, the suffering of change, and the suffering of pervasive conditioning.

5 *The Third Principal Aspect: Cultivating the Correct View*

This section has two parts: meditation ascertaining the selflessness of persons and meditation ascertaining the selflessness of other phenomena.

HOW TO MEDITATE SO AS TO ASCERTAIN THE SELFLESSNESS OF PERSONS

Endless forms of reasoning for the ascertainment of selflessness were taught in the scriptures of the Conqueror Buddha. However, if it is ascertained through the four essentials for beginners, it easily becomes clear.

FIRST ESSENTIAL: ASCERTAINING THE MODE OF APPEARANCE OF WHAT IS NEGATED IN THE VIEW OF SELFLESSNESS

Even in deep sleep we hold tightly, tightly, in the center of the heart, the thought 'I, I.' This is a consciousness innately misconceiving [an inherently existent] self. For example, without your having done a bad deed another accuses you, 'You did such and such a bad deed', and thinking 'I, I' tightly, tightly in the center of the heart, you reflect, 'Without my doing such a bad deed he/she accuses me like this.' At that time, the way the I is apprehended by a consciousness innately misconceiving inherent existence is clearly manifest.

Therefore, at that time how and as what the mind apprehends the self should be analyzed with a subtle part of the mind. If the later analytical attention is too strong, the former consciousness that conceives 'I, I' will be abandoned and will not appear at all [and thus cannot be watched]. Hence, allow the general mind to generate firmly and continuously the entity of the consciousness thinking 'I', and analyze it with another subtle portion of consciousness.

When you analyze in this way, the first essential is to understand how the I is conceived by a consciousness innately misconceiving an inherently existent self:

> This I is not other than my own five aggregates, or body and mind. The I is not any of the five aggregates taken singly nor is it either of the two, body and mind, taken singly. Also, the I is not just conceptually imputed to only the glittering collection of the five aggregates or a collection of the two, body and mind. Hence, there is an I that from the beginning is self-sufficient.

This deluded conception of an I that from the start is self-sufficient is the innate apprehension of an inherently existent I. The [inherently existent] I that is its object is what is negated [in the view of selflessness].

This way of identifying what is negated should be realized nakedly in your mental continuum without its being just an idea explained by others or a general image evoked by words. This is the first essential, ascertaining the mode of appearance of what is negated.

SECOND ESSENTIAL: ASCERTAINING ENTAILMENT

Since this I, which is conceived by a mind thinking 'I' tightly, tightly in the center of the heart, exists in relation with your five mental and physical aggregates, it is entailed that this I is necessarily either one with or different from the five aggregates. Other than these two, there is not at all a third way of their existing. Phenomena must invariably exist in the form of one of these. Think and decide that other than these two ways of existing, there is no third category of the existence of phenomena.

THIRD ESSENTIAL: ASCERTAINING THE ABSENCE OF TRUE SAMENESS

If it is thought that the I is the same as the five mental and physical aggregates, then just as one person has five aggregates, the I would also be five continuums. Or, in another way, just as the I is one, the five mental and physical aggregates would become a partless one. There are many such fallacies. Therefore, think that such an I [a self-sufficient I] is not one with the five aggregates.

FOURTH ESSENTIAL: ASCERTAINING THE ABSENCE OF TRUE DIFFERENCE

Such an I is not one with the five mental and physical aggregates; however, you might think that it is different from the five aggregates.

After eliminating each of the aggregates, forms and so forth, the aggregate of consciousness can be identified separately, 'This is the aggregate of consciousness.' Just so, after eliminating each of the mental and physical aggregates, the I should be identified separately, 'This is the I.' However, it is not so. Therefore, think that such an I does not exist separately from the five aggregates.

Dwell thus on the analysis of the four essentials and determine that the I as conceived by the innate sense of an inherently existent self is non-existent. The continuum of this conviction should be sustained single-mindedly, without laxity and without excitement. Moreover, if this conviction becomes weaker in strength, beginners—relying on having done the analysis of the four essentials as above—should develop again a conviction of the unreality [of an I which exists by way of its own character and is not just imputed by thought]. Those of higher intelligence [have nakedly ascertained the way the self-sufficient I actually does appear]. Relying on having analyzed whether the I as it is perceived by an innate consciousness apprehending I exists or not, they should develop a conviction of the unreality [of such a solidly existent I] similar to the analysis of the four essentials.

At that time you should sustain single-mindedly the following two facets of understanding emptiness. From the point of view of ascertainment, firm definite knowledge determines that the I does not inherently exist. Second, from the point of view of appearance there is an utter, clear vacuity which is only the absence of what is negated, that is, the true existence of I. Sustaining these two single-mindedly is how to sustain the space-like meditative equipoise.

Subsequent to meditative equipoise, all phenomena, the I and so forth, should be meditated on as the sport [of emptiness] like a magician's illusions. In other words, rely on developing a strong conviction of truthlessness [the knowledge that phenomena do not inherently exist] during meditative equipoise, and also afterwards learn to view all that appears, even though appearing [to exist inherently], as the sport [of emptiness], like a magician's illusions, truthless and false.

HOW TO MEDITATE SO AS TO ASCERTAIN THE SELFLESSNESS OF OTHER PHENOMENA

This section has two parts: meditation ascertaining that compounded phenomena[1] do not inherently exist and meditation ascertaining that uncompounded phenomena[2] do not inherently exist.

HOW TO ASCERTAIN THE ABSENCE OF INHERENT EXISTENCE OF COMPOUNDED PHENOMENA

Take the body as an example of a compounded phenomenon. It undeniably appears to us [who do not know that phenomena do not inherently exist] that the body is a whole, looming body, self-sufficient, and is not just imputed by thought in relation to this body which is only a collection of five limbs of bubbly flesh and bone. This is the mode of appearance of what is negated [in the view of selflessness].

If such a whole body exists in relation with this body which is only a collection of five limbs of bubbly flesh and bone, it is one with or different from this body which is only a collection of five limbs of bubbly flesh and bone.

If they are one, then because this body which is only a collection of five limbs of bubbly flesh and bone is produced from the semen and blood of the father and mother, the drop of semen and blood that is the foundation of the entrance of consciousness would [absurdly] become the body which is only a collection of five limbs of bubbly flesh and bone. Also, just as there are five limbs, the body would become five bodies that are collections of five limbs.

---

1 *'dus byas, saṃskṛta.*

2 *'dus ma byas, asaṃskṛta.*

[Then you might think that such a whole body] is different [from this body which is only a collection of five limbs of bubbly flesh and bone. In that case] after eliminating each of the limbs, head and so forth, [the identification] 'This is it,' should be shown with respect to the body, but it is not possible. Therefore, develop conviction knowing that such an inherently existent body is totally non-existent, and sustain the realization single-mindedly.

HOW TO ASCERTAIN THE ABSENCE OF INHERENT EXISTENCE OF UNCOMPOUNDED PHENOMENA

Take space as an example. There are many parts to space—directions and intermediate directions; analyze whether space exists as one with or different from these. Meditate as before and develop definite conviction in the unreality [of inherently existent space].

In short, sustain well the two yogas. The first is the yoga of space-like meditative equipoise. In it one sustains single-mindedly the conviction that there is not even a particle of any of the phenomena of cyclic existence and nirvana, such as I, aggregate, mountain, fence, and house, that exists in its own right and is not just imputed by thought. The second is the yoga of illusion, the subsequent realization which [after the yoga of meditative equipoise] knows all objects of perception to be false entities that have the unreality of having arisen dependent upon a collection of major and minor causes. This meditative equipoise, which depends on sustaining the two yogas, is conjoined with a bliss of mental and physical pliancy that is induced by the power of analysis. It is assigned as actual special insight.[1]

About cultivating a correct view, Dzong-ka-ba's *Three Principal Aspects of the Path* says:[2]

---

[1] *lhag mthong, vipaśyanā.*

[2] The text (96.3) is missing the first stanza, which is transitional be-

If you do not have the wisdom realizing the way things are,
Even though you have developed the thought definitely to leave cyclic existence
As well as the altruistic intention, the root of cyclic existence cannot be cut.
Therefore work at the means of realizing dependent-arising.

Whoever, seeing the cause and effect of all phenomena
Of cyclic existence and nirvana as infallible,
Thoroughly destroys the mode of misapprehension of these objects [as inherently existent]
Has entered on a path pleasing to Buddha.

As long as the two, realization of appearances—the infallibility of dependent-arising—
And realization of emptiness—the non-assertion [of inherent existence],
Seem to be separate, there is still no realization
Of the thought of Shākyamuni Buddha.

When [the two realizations exist] simultaneously without alternation
And when, from only seeing dependent-arising as infallible,
Definite knowledge destroys the mode of apprehension [of the conception of inherent existence],
Then the analysis of the view [of emptiness] is complete.

Further, the extreme of [inherent] existence is excluded [by knowledge of the nature] of appearances [existing only as nominal designations],

---

tween the second and third aspects. It has been added for the sake of completeness.

And the extreme of [total] non-existence is excluded [by knowledge of the nature] of emptiness [as the absence of inherent existence and not the absence of nominal existence].
If within emptiness the way of the appearance of cause and effect is known,
You will not be captivated by extreme views.

The meaning of Dzong-ka-ba's words conveys the mode of practice as it appears in the precepts of the oral lineage.

6 *Finishing the Session*

In the actual session you have developed as much as possible experience in transforming the mind through analytical and stabilizing meditation. To conclude the session say many times:

> I bow down, worship, and go for refuge to the feet of the lama undifferentiable from Mañjushrī.

Think that by strongly making the prayer to the gatherings of lamas and gods, all the members of the field of the accumulation of merit gradually melt into light from the outside to the center and dissolve into Mañjushrī and the Foremost Lama [D̄zong-ka-b̄a who is one with Mañjushrī]. Mañjushrī together with the Foremost Lama dissolves into you. Thereby, all physical impurities—sickness and so forth—and all mental ill deeds and obstructions are purified, and you suddenly appear in the body of Mañjushrī.

Your own body has been radiantly transformed into the body of Mañjushrī, and the emanation of rays of light from it, by striking all the sentient beings throughout all of space, establishes all sentient beings in the state of Mañjushrī. Also, consider that the impurities of all inanimate objects are purified and that all inanimate things become as inestimable mansions [having the nature of light]. Contemplate as much as possible the billions of purified inanimate things and animate beings. Then establish a series of mantra in the heart of yourself and all sentient beings radiantly transformed into Mañjushrī, reciting as much as you can, *oṃ a ra pa tsa na dhīḥ* [three, seven, twenty-one, etc., times; the last time repeat *dhīḥ dhīḥ dhīḥ dhīḥ dhīḥ dhīḥ* ... as many times as possible].

At the end say:

After I have quickly attained
Through the virtue of this session
The state of Mañjushrī, may I establish
All transmigrators in his state.

I dedicate and consider the very wholesome virtue
Done in this session as a cause of accomplishing
All the prayers of all the Ones Gone To Bliss
And their children of the past, present, and future,
And as a cause of [the world's] maintaining
The excellent doctrine, verbal and realized.

Through the power of this virtue
May I finish travelling the path
Of the intention definitely to leave cyclic existence,
The altruistic aspiration to highest enlightenment,
The correct view, and the two stages of tantra[1]
In all my continuum of lives, never losing the four wheels of the Great Vehicle.[2]

---

[1] The stages of generation and completion in Highest Yoga Tantra.

[2] The four wheels of the Great Vehicle are (1) to live in a place

I will follow like children after their father, making sincere effort to achieve the three principal aspects of the path which include the essentials of all the scriptures.

The basic text, Ḏzong-ka-ḇa's *Three Principal Aspects of the Path* says:

> When you have realized thus just as they are
> The essentials of the three principal aspects of the path,
> Resort to solitude and generate the power of effort.
> Accomplish quickly your final aim, my child.[1]

In this way the lama Mañjunātha [Ḏzong-ka-ḇa] advised us followers with compassion.

If your mind becomes well practiced with respect to the path of the common vehicle, you should enter the immutable vehicle, the Vajra Vehicle, the unsurpassed quick path of purification in one short lifetime of the degenerate era without taking three countless aeons. Also, you should please with the three delights a tantric lama who has all the qualifications, and your mental continuum will be ripened through the pure powers of initiation.

Maintain dearer than your life the protection of pledges and vows accepted at the time of initiation. Based on that, search well for the essentials of the two stages of the profound path, the essential meaning of the ocean of tantras. If unmistaken ascertainment of the meaning is found, apply yourself to yoga in four sessions [each day]. There is no greater practice than learn-

---

where the necessities for practicing the Great Vehicle are easily found, (2) to rely on a holy being who practices and teaches the Great Vehicle, (3) to have great aspirations for the practice of the Great Vehicle, and (4) to have produced great merit in the past.

[1] Ḏzong-ka-ḇa is addressing Tsa-ko-ḇön-ḇo, the person to whom he wrote this epistolary poem.

ing thus the entire body of the paths of both sūtra and tantra. This is the ultimate pith of quintessential instructions extracting the essence of lama Mañjunātha's mind.

Lama Mañjunātha himself said [in his *Condensed Exposition of the Stages of the Path*]:

> Generate properly thus the common path
> Necessary for the two superior Great Vehicle paths,
> The Perfection Vehicle—the cause—and the Mantra Vehicle—the effect.
> Then, enter the great ocean of tantra
> Relying on a protector, a skilful captain,
> And obtain the complete instructions,
> Thereby making meaningful the attainment of leisure and fortune.
> I, a yogi, practiced such.
> You, wishing liberation, please do so as well.

You should turn about in your mental continuum these practices, from respecting an excellent spiritual guide properly in both thought and deeds through to learning the two stages of the profound path. Practice each day in four sessions or at least in one session. If so, the excellent essence will be extracted from this life of leisure. The precious teaching of the Conqueror Buddha can further the mental continuums of yourself and others.

Author's Dedication: I dedicate whatever very wholesome virtues, like a conch and jasmine, are obtained from making effort in this way in order that the teaching of the Conqueror Buddha, the sole basis of the livelihood of all beings, may remain for a long time. May this lamp of teaching perfected well with countless difficulties by Mañjunātha [Ḏzong-ka-ḇa] remain as long as this earth remains, and may it clear away the darkness of mind of all transmigrators. May the excellent King of Doctrine, Dam-j̄en,[1] with his retinue—who promised never to cease protecting and sustaining the teaching of Mañjunātha—be a friend always to the accomplishment of this doctrine.

Printer's Dedication: Thus, this *Instructions on (D̄zong-ka-b̄a's) 'Three Principal Aspects of the Path': Essence of All the Scriptures, Quintessence of Helping Others* was written by the glorious and good Conqueror over all factions, the Shākya monk L̄o-sang-b̄el-den-d̄en-b̄ay-nyi-ma in a room of the Ḡa-dam[2] mansion. By this printing may the precious teaching of Shākyamuni Buddha increase and extend in all directions.

Donor's Dedication: Oṃ svasti. In order that all beings might use this broad tree—a composite of the teaching of the Conqueror Buddha, a source of help and happiness—for the good fruit of superior liberation, I established this endless river of doctrinal giving at the great doctrinal college of D̄ra-s̄hi-hlün-drup.[3]

Sarvajagataṃ.

---

[1] *dam can*; a protector deity.
[2] *bka' gdams.*
[3] *bkra shis lhun grub.*

Part Two

THEORY: SYSTEMS OF TENETS

Introduction

Part Two is an annotated translation of an eighteenth century Tibetan text from a genre called 'presentations of tenets',[1] which in Tibet mainly refers to delineations of the systematic schools of Buddhist and non-Buddhist Indian philosophy. In this context, 'philosophy' is, for the most part, related with liberative concerns—the attempt to extricate oneself (and others) from a round of painful existence and to attain freedom. Focal topics and issues of these schools are presented in order to stimulate the metaphysical imagination—to encourage development of an inner faculty that is capable of investigating appearances so as to penetrate their reality.

The basic perspective is that the afflictive emotions, such as desire, hatred, enmity, jealousy, and belligerence, that bind beings in a round of uncontrolled birth, aging, sickness, and death, are founded on misperception of the nature of persons and other phenomena. Thus, when the reality of these is penetrated and this in-

---

[1] *grub mtha'i rnam bzhag, siddhāntavyavasthāpana.*

sight is teamed with a powerful consciousness of concentrated meditation, the underpinnings of the process of cyclic existence can be removed, resulting in liberation. Also, when wisdom is further empowered through the development of love, compassion, and altruism—as well as by deeds motivated by these—the wisdom consciousness is capable of achieving an all-knowing state in which one can effectively help a vast number of beings.

Because of this basic perspective on the situation of beings trapped by false ideation in a round of suffering, *reasoned* investigation into the nature of persons and other phenomena is central to the process of spiritual development, though, as we have seen in Part One, it is not the only concern. Systems of tenets, therefore, are primarily studied not to refute other systems but to develop an internal force that can counteract one's own *innate* adherence to misapprehensions that are part and parcel of ordinary life and are not just learned from other systems and do not just arise from faulty analysis. Thus, the aim of studying schools of philosophy is to gain insight into the fact that many perspectives that are basic to ordinary life are devoid of a valid foundation and thereupon to replace these with well-founded perspectives. The process is achieved through (1) first engaging in *hearing* great texts on such topics and getting straight the verbal presentation, (2) then *thinking* on their meaning to the point where the topics are ascertained with valid cognition, and (3) finally *meditating* on the same to the point where these realizations become enhanced by the power of concentration so that they can counteract innate tendencies to assent to false appearances.

Since it is no easy matter to penetrate the thick veil of false facades and misconceptions, it became popular in the more scholastic circles of India to investigate not just what the current tradition considered to the best and final system but also the supposedly 'lower' systems. This provided a gradual way to approach extremely subtle topics without confusing them with less subtle ones. Within such an outlook, a tradition of comparative study of the views of the different schools of thought developed in India and became even more systematized in Tibet. That the primary concern was indeed with developing the *capacity* to appreciate a profound view of a high system of philosophy is evidenced by the amount of time actually spent by students probing the workings of the so-called lower schools. Since the philosophies of those schools were appreciated, they were studied in considerable detail.

Because of the need to get a handle on the plethora of Buddhist systems, the genre of 'presentations of tenets' assumed considerable importance in Tibet. The main Indian precursors were texts such as the *Blaze of Reasoning* by Bhāvaviveka[1] (500-570 ?)[2]—and the *Compendium of Principles* by the eighth century scholar Shāntarakṣhita[3] with a commentary by his student Kamalashīla. Both Shāntarakṣhita and Kamalashīla visited Tibet in the eighth century and strongly influenced the direction that Buddhism took there.

In Tibet, the genre came to be more highly systematized, the presentations assuming a more developed

---

[1] *rtog ge 'bar ba, tarkajvālā.* This is Bhāvaviveka's commentary on his *Heart of the Middle* (*dbu ma snying po, madhyamakahṛdaya*). For a partial English translation of the latter (chap. III. 1-136), see Shotaro Iida. *Reason and Emptiness* (Tokyo: Hokuseido, 1980). For an excellent history of Indo-Tibetan Buddhism, see David L. Snellgrove, *Indo-Tibetan Buddhism: Indian Buddhists and Their Tibetan Successors* (Boston: Shambhala, 1987).

[2] See David Seyfort Ruegg, *The Literature of the Madhyamaka School of Philosophy in India* (Wiesbaden: Otto Harrassowitz, 1981), p. 61.

[3] *de kho na nyid bsdud pa'i tshig le'ur byas pa, tattvasaṃgrahakārikā.* A translation into English is available in: G. Jha, *The Tattvasaṃgraha of Śāntirakṣita with the commentary of Kamalaśīla*, Gaekwad's Oriental Series Vol. lxxx and lxxxiii (Baroda: Oriental Institute, 1937-9).

structure.[1] Some of these texts are long; for instance, a lengthy text entitled *Treasury of Tenets, Illuminating the Meaning of All Vehicles*[2] was written by the great fourteenth century scholar L̄ong-chen-rap-jam[3] of the N̄ying-ma order of Tibetan Buddhism. Another, the *Explanation of 'Freedom From Extremes Through Understanding All Tenets': Ocean of Good Explanations*[4] was authored by the great fifteenth century scholar D̄ak-tsang S̄hay-rap-rin-chen[5] of the S̄a-ḡya order. The latter criticized many of the views of the founder of the Ge-luk-b̄a order, D̄zong-ka-b̄a (author of the root text in Part One), for being self-contradictory and thus gave rise to the most extensive text of this genre in Tibet, written in large part as a refutation of D̄ak-tsang S̄hay-rap-rin-chen, the *Explanation of 'Tenets', Sun of the Land of Samantabhadra Brilliantly Illuminating All of Our Own and Others' Tenets and the Meaning of the Profound [Emptiness], Ocean of Scripture and Reasoning Fulfilling All Hopes of All Beings*, also known as the *Great Exposition of Tenets*,[6] by Jam-ȳang-shay-b̄ay-dor-jay Ngak-w̄ang-d̄zön-drü.[7] Jam-ȳang-shay-b̄a's text is replete with citations of Indian sources but is written, despite its length, in a laconic style (unusual for him) that can leave one

---

[1] For more discussion on this genre of Tibetan literature, see Katsumi Mimaki, *Blo gsal grub mtha'* (Kyoto: Université de Kyoto, 1982), pp. 1-12, and the David Seyfort Ruegg's foreword to Geshé Ngawang Nyima, *Introduction to the Doctrines of the Four Schools of Buddhist Philosophy* (Leiden, 1970).

[2] *theg pa mtha' dag gi don gsal bar byed pa grub pa'i mtha' rin po che'i mdzod.*

[3] *klong chen rab 'byams/ klong chen dri med 'od zer*, 1308-1363.

[4] *grub mtha' kun shes nas mtha' bral grub pa zhes bya ba'i bstan bcos rnam par bshad pa legs bshad kyi rgya mtsho.*

[5] *stag tshang lo tsā ba shes rab rin chen*, born 1405.

[6] *grub mtha'i rnam bshad rang gzhan grub mtha' kun dang zab don mchog tu gsal ba kun bzang zhing gi nyi ma lung rigs rgya mtsho skye dgu'i re ba kun skong/ grub mtha' chen mo.*

[7] *'jam dbyangs bzhad pa'i rdo rje ngag dbang brtson grus*, 1648-1721.

wondering why certain citations are made. Perhaps this was part of the reason why the eighteenth century Mongolian scholar J̄ang-ḡya Röl-b̄ay-dor-jay[1]—whom Jam-ȳang-shay-b̄a, then an old man, helped to find as a child as the reincarnation of the last J̄ang-ḡya—composed a more issue-oriented text of the same genre entitled *Clear Exposition of the Presentations of Tenets, Beautiful Ornament for the Meru of the Subduer's Teaching*.[2] After Jam-ȳang-shay-b̄a passed away, his reincarnation, Ḡön-chok-jik-may-w̄ang-b̄o,[3] became J̄ang-ḡya's main pupil. In 1733 Ḡön-chok-jik-may-w̄ang-b̄o wrote an abbreviated version of these texts, entitled *Presentation of Tenets, A Precious Garland*,[4] which is translated here.

In this sub-genre of brief Presentations of Tenets are earlier texts such as Jay-d̄zun Chö-ḡyi-gyel-tsen's[5] *Presentation of Tenets*,[6] the Second Dalai Lama Ge-dün-gya-tso's[7] *Ship for Entering the Ocean of Tenets*,[8] Paṇ-chen S̄ö-nam-drak-b̄a's[9] *Presentation of Tenets, Sublime Tree Inspiring Those of Clear Mind, Hammer Destroying the Stone Mountains of Opponents*,[10] and Drak-b̄a-s̄hay-drup's[11] *Condensed Essence of All Tenets*.[12] A medium length Pre-

---

1 *lcang skya rol pa'i rdo rje*, 1717-86.

2 *grub pa'i mtha'i rnam par bzhag pa gsal bar bshad pa thub bstan lhun po'i mdzes rgyan*.

3 *dkon mchog 'jigs med dbang po*, 1728-91.

4 *grub pa'i mtha'i rnam par bzhag pa rin po che'i phreng ba*.

5 *rje btsun chos kyi rgyal mtshan*, 1469-1546.

6 *grub mtha'i rnam gzhag*.

7 *dge 'dun rgya mtsho*, 1476-1542.

8 *grub mtha' rgya mtshor 'jug pa'i gru rdzings*.

9 *paṇ chen bsod nams grags pa*, 1478-1554.

10 *grub mtha'i rnam bzhag blo gsal spro ba bskyed pa'i ljon pa phas rgol brag ri 'joms pa'i tho ba*.

11 *grags pa bshad sgrub, co ne ba*, 1675-1748.

12 *grub mtha' thams cad kyi snying po bsdus pa*. For a list of other such brief texts, see the Bibliography in Katsumi Mimaki, *Blo gsal grub mtha'*, (Kyoto: Université de Kyoto, 1982), p. XLVI, etc., as well as the Introduction, pp. 5-12.

sentation of Tenets that also treats the other schools of Tibetan Buddhism in a somewhat biased fashion was written by Jang-ḡya's biographer and student, who was also a student of Ḡön-chok-jik-may-w̄ang-b̄o, Tu-ḡen-lo-sang-chö-ḡyi-nyi-ma.[1] His text is called *Mirror of the Good Explanations Showing the Sources and Assertions of All Systems of Tenets*.[2]

Most likely, Ḡön-chok-jik-may-w̄ang-b̄o chose to write such a concise text so that the general outlines and basic postures of the systems of tenets could be taught and memorized without the encumbrance of a great deal of elaboration. For similar reasons, we chose to translate and annotate Ḡön-chok-jik-may-w̄ang-b̄o's text in Part Two of this book in order to flesh out the theoretical topics, especially on emptiness, raised in Part One. At many places its brevity makes the issues being discussed inaccessible, and, therefore, we have added commentary both in brackets within sentences and in indented material to make the text more approachable. Our additional commentary has nearly doubled the size of the text, but we have nevertheless maintained Ḡön-chok-jik-may-w̄ang-b̄o's basic commitment to conciseness and have not sought to elaborate in detail the controversies that exist among the Tibetan monastic colleges on almost every one of these topics. We have sought to preserve the author's aim of providing an easy avenue to grasping the issues that revolve around the nature of persons and phenomena according to this system of traditional education.

FORMAT OF THE TEXT

Ḡön-chok-jik-may-w̄ang-b̄o's text presents the principal

---

[1] *thu'u bkvan blo bzang chos kyi nyi ma,* 1737-1802.

[2] *grub mtha' thams cad kyi khungs dang 'dod tshul ston pa legs bshad shel gyi me long.*

tenets of Indian schools, both Buddhist and non-Buddhist. He treats six renowned non-Buddhist schools very briefly and gives more detail on the four Buddhist schools and their main sub-schools. In the order of their presentation (the list of Buddhist schools represent an ascent in order of estimation) these are:

Non-Buddhist Schools

Vaisheṣhika and Naiyāyika (Particularists and Logicians)
Sāṃkhya (Enumerators)
Mīmāṃsa (Analyzers or Ritualists)
Nirgrantha (The Unclothed, better known as Jaina)
Chārvāka (Hedonists)

Buddhist Schools

Lesser Vehicle
- Great Exposition School[1]
  - 18 sub-schools
- Sūtra School[2]
  - Following Scripture
  - Following Reasoning

Great Vehicle
- Mind Only School[3]
  - Following Scripture
  - Following Reasoning
- Middle Way School[4]
  - Autonomy School[5]
  - Consequence School[6]

The structure of four schools is itself largely an artificial creation. For instance, the so-called Great Exposition School is, in fact, a collection of at least eighteen schools

---

1 *bye brag smra ba, vaibhāṣika.*
2 *mdo sde pa, sautrāntika.*
3 *sems tsam pa, cittamātra.*
4 *dbu ma pa, mādhyamika.*
5 *rang rgyud pa, svātantrika.*
6 *thal 'gyur pa, prāsaṅgika.*

that never recognized themselves as belonging to a single, over-arching school. Also, their tenets are so various (some prefiguring Great Vehicle schools) that it is extremely difficult to posit tenets common to all eighteen; thus, rather than attempting such, the Tibetan scholars who engaged in classifying systems presented representative tenets as explained in the root text of Vasubandhu's *Treasury of Manifest Knowledge*[1] as if these constitute the general tenet structure of such an over-arching system, even though they are merely *typical* of assertions found in these eighteen sects. The pretended amalgamation into a single school is a technique used to avoid becoming bogged down in too much proliferation so that the main purpose of this genre of exegesis—the presentation of an ascent to the views of systems considered to be higher—can be effected. With respect to the Great Exposition School, therefore, it should not be thought that there is not a wide variety of opinion differing greatly from this general presentation. Strictly speaking, even the name 'Great Exposition School' should be limited to followers of the *Mahāvibhāṣhā*, a text of Manifest Knowledge that was never translated into Tibetan.

Also, the division of the Sūtra School into those following scripture and those following reasoning is highly controversial. The former are said to be followers of Vasubandhu's own commentary on his *Treasury of Manifest Knowledge*, in which he indicates disagreement with many assertions of the Great Exposition School presented in his own root text. The latter—the Proponents of Sūtra Following Reasoning—are said to be followers of Dignāga and Dharmakīrti who (despite Dignāga's and Dharmakīrti's not having asserted external objects) assert external objects—objects that are different entities from the

---

[1] *chos mngon pa'i mdzod, abhidharmakośa.*

consciousnesses perceiving them. Again, neither of these groups saw themselves as sub-divisions of a larger school called the Sūtra School.

Similarly, the two sub-divisions of the Mind Only School are those following scripture—who depend on the writings primarily of Asaṅga and his half-brother Vasubandhu (after the latter converted to Asaṅga's system)—and those following reasoning—who depend on what is accepted to be the main system of Dignāga's and Dharmakīrti's writings. Again, it is unlikely that these two groups perceived themselves as being sub-schools of a larger school. Rather, the groupings are made by way of similarities between their systems and within a wish to keep to an accepted dictum that there are only four schools of tenets.

Also, the names of the two sub-divisions of the Middle Way School—the Autonomy School and the Consequence School—were, as is clearly admitted by D̄zong-ka-b̄a and his followers, never used in India. Rather, these names were coined in Tibet in accordance with terms used by Chandrakīrti in his writings. Thus, the very format of the four schools and their sub-divisions does not represent an historical account of self-asserted identities but is the result of centuries of classification of systems in India and Tibet in order to get a handle on the vast scope of positions found in Indian Buddhism.[1]

Given this situation, the format of four schools should be used as a horizon that opens a way to appreciate the plethora of opinions, not as one that closes and rigidifies investigation. In Tibet, students are taught this four-fold classification first, without mention of the diversity of opinion that it does not include, but then over decades of study the structure of such presentations of schools

---

[1] For discussion of the divisions of the Middle Way School, see Peter della Santina, *Madhyamaka Schools in India* (Delhi: Motilal Banarsidass, 1986).

of thought is gradually recognized by many students as a technique for gaining access to a vast store of opinion, a way to focus on topics crucial to authors within Indian Buddhism. The task of then distinguishing between what is clearly said in the Indian texts and what is interpretation and interpolation over centuries of Tibetan commentary becomes a fascinating enterprise for the more hardy among Tibetan scholars. The devotion to debate as the primary mode of education provides an ever-present avenue for students to challenge home-grown interpretations and affords a richness of critical commentary within the tradition that a short presentation of tenets does not convey.

TOPICS

In Ḡön-chok-jik-may-w̄ang-b̄o's text, each Buddhist school is treated under four major topics, the last having numerous subdivisions:

1 Definition
2 Subschools
3 Etymology
4 Assertions of tenets
 Assertions on the basis
  Objects: the two truths, etc.
  Object-possessors (i.e., subjects)
   Persons
   Consciousnesses
   Terms
 Assertions on the paths
   Objects of observation of the paths
   Objects abandoned by the paths
   Nature of the paths
 Assertions on the fruits of the paths

First, a reader is given, for general orientation, a definition of the school, its sub-schools, and an etymology of its name. Then, the tenets of the school are introduced. The topics considered under the heading of 'assertions of tenets' reveal the liberative orientation of the inquiry. The assertions are divided into three categories—presentations of the basis, the paths, and the fruits of the path. The presentation of the basis refers to assertions on classes of phenomena, which provide the *basis* for practicing the spiritual *paths*, which, in turn, produce attainments, the *fruits of the path*. It is clear from this order that the reason for learning philosophical positions on phenomena is to be able to practice a path in order to transform the mind from being mired in a condition of suffering to being enlightened into a state of freedom from suffering.

The general structure of basis, paths, and fruits probably takes its lead from the emphasis in texts of the Middle Way School on three coordinated sets of twos:

- the two truths—conventional and ultimate—which are the basis
- the two practices—method and wisdom—which are the paths
- the Two Buddha Bodies—Form Bodies and Truth Body—which are the final fruits of the path.

According to the Great Vehicle, taking as one's *basis* conventional truths, one practices the *paths* of method—love, compassion, and the altruistic intention to become enlightened as well the compassionate deeds that these induce—in dependence upon which one achieves the *fruit* of the Form Bodies of a Buddha. Also, taking as one's *basis* ultimate truths, one practices the *paths* of wisdom—especially the realization of the final status of persons and phenomena, their emptiness of inherent existence—in dependence upon which one achieves the *fruit* of a Truth Body of a Buddha. This threefold format of basis, path, and fruit that finds its main expression in the Great Vehicle seems to have supplied the structure for the genre of presentations of tenets for both the Lesser Vehicle[1] and the Great Vehicle.

Also, within the section on the basis, the emphasis on the two truths in all four schools derives from the fact that the two truths are a prime subject in the tenets of the highest school, the Middle Way School. As the great scholar Gung-tang Ḡön-chok-ḏen-ḇay-drön-may,[2] who was the chief student of Ḡön-chok-jik-may-w̄ang-ḇo, the author of our text, says,[3] the prime way that the Great Exposition School and the Sūtra School delineate the meaning of the scriptures is by way of the four noble truths, whereas such is done by way of the three natures in the Mind Only School and by way of the two truths in the Middle Way School. Thus, the emphasis given in this presentation of tenets to the four schools'

---

[1] The term 'Lesser Vehicle' (*theg dman, hīnayāna*) has its origin in the writings of Great Vehicle (*theg chen, mahāyāna*) authors and was, of course, not used by those to whom it was ascribed. Substitutes such as 'non-Mahāyāna', 'Nikāya Buddhism', and 'Theravādayāna' have been suggested in order to avoid the pejorative sense of 'Lesser'. However, 'Lesser Vehicle' is a convenient term in this particular context for a type of tenet system or practice that is seen, in the tradition which provides the perspective of this book, to be surpassed—but not negated—by a higher system. The 'Lesser Vehicle' is not despised, most of it being incorporated into the 'Great Vehicle'. The monks' and nuns' vows are Lesser Vehicle as is much of the course of study in Ge-luk-ḇa monastic universities—years of study are put into the topics of Epistemology (*tshad ma, pramāṇa*), Manifest Knowledge (*chos mngon pa, abhidharma*), and Discipline (*'dul ba, vinaya*), all of which are mostly Lesser Vehicle in perspective. ('Lesser Vehicle' and 'Low Vehicle' are used interchangeably in this book.)

[2] *gung thang dkon mchog bstan pa'i sgron me*, 1762-1823. He wrote two biographies of Ḡön-chok-jik-may-w̄ang-ḇo that are included in the latter's Collected Works (see the first volume).

[3] *Beginnings of a Commentary on the Difficult Points of (Ḏzong-ka-ḇa's) 'Differentiation of the Interpretable and the Definitive', the Quintessence of the 'Essence of the Good Explanations'* (*drang nges rnam 'byed kyi dga' 'grel rtsom 'phro legs bshad snying po'i yang snying*), (Sarnath: Guru Deva, 1965), 80.6-80.12 and 235.9ff.

delineations of the two truths derives from the system that the author and his tradition have determined to be the highest, the Middle Way School. This is not to say that the two truths are not important topics in all four schools, for they are; rather, the two truths are not *the* central topic in the other schools in the way that they are in the Middle Way School.

Object-Possessors. Having presented a school's assertions on objects, the text considers object-possessors, or subjects. Simply because, in general, subjects are themselves also objects, they are a sub-class of objects, but they are treated as a distinct category within a division of objects into objects and object-possessors. Object-possessors are treated as being of three types—persons (since they possess objects), consciousnesses (since they are aware of objects), and terms (since they refer to objects).

One might wonder why there is a presentation of assertions on persons if Buddhist schools advocate a view of selflessness. In this Tibetan delineation of Indian schools of Buddhism, the term 'self' in 'selflessness' refers not to persons but to an over-reified status of phenomena, be these persons or other phenomena. Consequently, even though it is said that *in general* 'self',[1] 'person',[2] and 'I'[3] are co-extensive, in the particular context of the selflessness of persons, 'self' and 'person' are not at all co-extensive and do not at all have the same meaning. In the term 'selflessness of persons', 'self' refers to a falsely imagined status that needs to be refuted, and 'persons' refers to existent beings who are the basis with respect to which that refutation is made. All of these schools, therefore, are said to posit persons as existent phenomena, not just creations of ignorance.

1 *bdag, ātman.*
2 *gang zag, pudgala.*
3 *nga, ahaṃ.*

A question between the schools is just what a person is. According to Ḡön-chok-jik-may-w̄ang-b̄o and his Ge-luk-b̄a predecessors, all schools except the Middle Way Consequence School posit something from within the bases of designation of a person as being the person. In contrast, the Consequence School holds that even though a person is designated in dependence upon mind and body, the person *is* neither mind nor body, being just the I that is *designated* in dependence upon mind and body. Following the lead of Chandrakīrti, recognized by most as the founder of the Consequence School, Ḡön-chok-jik-may-w̄ang-b̄o identifies, within all of the other schools, assertions that some factor among the five aggregates of forms, feelings, discriminations, compositional factors, and consciousnesses is the person when sought analytically. The Proponents of the Great Exposition, in general, are said to hold that the mere *collection* of the mental and physical aggregates is the person, whereas some of the five Saṃmitīya subschools are said to maintain that all five aggregates are the person—Ḡön-chok-jik-may-w̄ang-b̄o's suggestion being that, for them, *each* of the five aggregates is the person (although the absurdity of one person being five persons would seem difficult not to notice). Another subschool, the Avantaka, is said to assert that the mind alone is the person.

Similarly, in the Sūtra School, the Followers of Scripture are said to assert that the continuum of the aggregates is the person, whereas the Followers of Reasoning are said to maintain that the mental consciousness is the person. In the Mind Only School, the Followers of Scripture hold that the mind-basis-of-all[1] is the person, whereas the Followers of Reasoning assert that the mental consciousness is. Again, in the Autonomy School, both Yogic Autonomists and Sūtra Autonomists

---

[1] *kun gzhi rnam par shes pa, ālayavijñāna.*

are said to assert that a subtle, neutral mental consciousness is the person that is found upon searching for it among its bases of designation.

For the most part, Ḡön-chok-jik-may-w̄ang-b̄o's delineation of what from among the person's bases of designation these schools assert to be the person is a matter of conjecture and not a reporting of forthright statements of such in these schools' own texts. Though it is clear that most of these schools (if not all) accept that persons exist, it is by no means clear in their own literature that they assert that something from within the five aggregates that are the bases of designation of a person is the person. Rather, it would seem that, as presented in the ninth chapter of Vasubandhu's *Treasury of Manifest Knowledge*, persons are merely asserted to be non-associated compositional factors[1] and thus an instance of the fourth aggregate, compositional factors, without a specific identification of any of the five aggregates that are a person's bases of designation as being the person. For instance, one could quite safely say that there is not a single line in the whole of Indian Mind Only literature that explicitly presents an assertion that the mind-basis-of-all is the person that is found when sought analytically. Rather, such an assertion is deduced from the fact that the Mind Only School Following Scripture (that is to say, the followers of Asaṅga) asserts that the mind-basis-of-all travels from lifetime to lifetime carrying with it the karmic predispositions established by earlier actions. Bhāvaviveka, on the other hand, seems openly to assert that the mental consciousness is the person, when, in response to a challenge, he says that if the opponent is attempting to establish for him that consciousness is the person, he is proving what is already established for him.[2] In any case, the empha-

[1] *ldan min 'du byed, viprayuktasaṃskāra.*
[2] See Jeffrey Hopkins, *Meditation on Emptiness*, pp. 695-696.

sis put in Ge-luk-b̄a treatises on identifying for each of these schools what, from among the five aggregates that are the basis of the designation of a person, is the person comes from their acceptance of Chandrakīrti's claim to a *unique* assertion that nothing from among them is the person.

Thus, it can be seen that the very structure (basis, paths, and fruits) and the choice of topics (such as the two truths and assertions on the person) do not altogether arise from prime concerns within a particular school but are brought over from focal issues in other schools, particularly those considered to be higher. That topics of prime concern in the 'higher' schools dominate to some extent the presentation of the tenets of all four schools is natural, given that the main aim is to draw readers into realizing the impact of the views of the 'higher' systems and is not to give isolated presentations of these schools' views or a predominantly historical account.

Consciousnesses. The main focus of the tenets concerning consciousness is to identify the range of types of minds in terms of misapprehension and correct apprehension. The purpose is to provide a psychological structure for the therapeutic paths that cause a person to proceed gradually from misconceived notions about the nature of persons and other phenomena to states of mind that can counteract innate misconceptions. The liberative directionality of the over-all enterprise informs the course of the discussion, the main interest being to separate correctly perceiving from improperly perceiving consciousnesses and to identify the difference between conceptual and non-conceptual consciousnesses, the latter, when they realize selflessness, being more powerful for overcoming obstructions to liberation and to full enlightenment.

The topics of consciousness are presented in their richest detail in the chapter on the Sūtra School, specifically the Sūtra School Following Reasoning; correspondingly, the topic of terms is discussed most fully in the chapter on the Great Exposition School. Thus, in many respects the book is to be read cumulatively, bringing over to another system those assertions that, although they come from a different system, are concordant with its outlook. The book does not always make clear what is to be carried over and what is not; such information is, however, supplied by the oral tradition through a competent teacher.

Paths. Having presented a general outline of phenomena, the basis, Ḡön-chok-jik-may-w̄ang-b̄o presents the various schools' tenets on the spiritual paths founded on their respective assertions on the basis. The paths are described in terms of (1) the main objects of meditation, (2) the main misconceptions that are abandoned through such meditation, and (3) the lay-out of the paths.

In all four schools, paths are presented for Hearers, Solitary Realizers, and Bodhisattvas. It might seem, at first reading, to be surprising that even the Lesser Vehicle schools—the Great Exposition and Sūtra Schools—have presentations of paths for Bodhisattvas, since Bodhisattvas are associated primarily with the Great Vehicle; however, a distinction is made between *philosophical schools* which are divided into Lesser Vehicle and Great Vehicle and *practitioners of paths* which also are divided into Lesser Vehicle and Great Vehicle. The philosophical schools are divided in this way in accordance with whether they present a selflessness of phenomena (Great Vehicle) or whether they do not (Lesser Vehicle). Since the Great Vehicle tenets systems—the Mind Only and Middle Way Schools—present a selflessness of phenomena in addition to a selflessness of persons, they also speak of 'obstructions to omniscience', these being what prevent simultaneous and direct cognition of all phenomena as well as their final nature. The Lesser Vehicle schools, on the other hand, do not make such a presentation even though they present Buddhahood as having an all-knowingness through which a Buddha can *serially* know anything, but not simultaneously.[1]

Even though the Lesser Vehicle schools—the Great Exposition and Sūtra Schools—do not present a path leading to simultaneous and direct knowledge of all phenomena, they present the path of a Bodhisattva proceeding to Buddhahood when they relate how Shākyamuni Buddha, for instance, became enlightened. Similarly, the Great Vehicle schools——the Mind Only and Middle Way Schools—speak, not just about how Bodhisattvas proceed on the path but also about how Hearers and Solitary Realizers, who are Lesser Vehicle *practitioners*, proceed on the path. In the latter case, the Great Vehicle schools are not reporting how the Lesser Vehicle *schools* present the path but how the Great Vehicle schools themselves present the path for those beings—Hearers and Solitary Realizers—whose prime motivation, unlike that of Bodhisattvas, is, for the time being, not the welfare of others but their own liberation from cyclic existence. Therefore, it is said to be possible for someone who is, for instance, a Middle Way Consequentialist by tenet system to be a Lesser Vehicle practitioner by motivation, in that the person has decided for the time being to pursue his or her own liberation first before becoming primarily dedicated to the welfare of

---

[1] As is reported in Jam-ȳang-shay-b̄a's *Great Exposition of Tenets* (*kha* 7b.2), one of the eighteen subschools of the Great Exposition School, the One Convention School (*tha snyad gcig pa, ekavyavahārika*), uses the convention of one instant of a Buddha's wisdom realizing all phenomena. Jam-ȳang-shay-b̄a says that they employ this convention for a Buddha's one mind realizing all phenomena; he thereby suggests that this school did not actually hold that that a Buddha has such simultaneous knowledge. Jam-ȳang-shay-b̄a may be explaining away a discrepancy in a system that emerged for the sake of easy classification.

others. Also, it is possible for someone who is, for instance, a Proponent of the Great Exposition to be a Great Vehicle practitioner in terms of motivation, having become dedicated to achieving the enlightenment of a Buddha in order to be of service to all beings.

Fruits of the Paths. The three types of paths—Hearer, Solitary Realizer, and Bodhisattva—have different results or fruits. The first two reach fruition in liberation from cyclic existence, whereas the last reaches fruition in Buddhahood, a state free from both the obstructions to liberation from cyclic existence and from the obstructions to the all-knowingness of a Buddha, as described in the respective systems.

The map that a student gains through such a presentation ranging from the phenomena of the world through to the types of enlightenment provides a framework both for study and for practice. The world-view that emerges is of individuals bound by misconception in a round of suffering and mired in afflictive emotions counter-productive to their own welfare but also poised on a threshold of transformation. The uncontrolled course of cyclic existence is viewed as lacking a solid underpinning such that it is ready to be transformed into a patterned advance toward liberation. The starkness of the harrowing appraisal of the current situation of multi-layered pain stands in marked contrast to the optimistic view of the development that is possible. Such optimism stems from a perception that the afflictive emotions and obstructions that are the cause of misery are not endemic to the mind, but are peripheral to its nature and thus subject to antidotal influences that can remove them. The text is founded on a confidence in the mind's ability to overcome tremendous obstacles to the point where love, compassion, and altruism can be expressed in effective, continuous activity, and, therefore, it does more than just to structure Indian Buddhist systems; it structures practitioners' perception of their place in a dynamic world-view.

ABOUT THE AUTHOR

As mentioned earlier, the author of this presentation of tenets was recognized as the incarnation of Jam-ȳang-shay-b̄ay-dor-jay Ngak-w̄ang-d̄zön-drü (1648-1721) and thus is known as the second Jam-ȳang-shay-b̄a. His full name, as given in the table of contents of his Collected Works,[1] is Jam-ȳang-shay-b̄a-ḡön-chok-jik-may-w̄ang-b̄o-ye-s̄hay-d̄zön-drü,[2] but he is better known as Ḡön-chok-jik-may-w̄ang-b̄o. He was born in 1728 in the Am-do Province of Tibet at N̄ang-ra-s̄er-kang[3] near the birthplace of D̄zong-ka-b̄a, the founder of his sect, Ge-luk-b̄a.

The first Jam-ȳang-shay-b̄a had returned to Am-do from Central Tibet in 1707 at age fifty-nine and founded a monastic university to the southeast of Ḡum-bum, the monastic university built in 1588 at the site of D̄zong-ka-b̄a's birthplace. Jam-ȳang-shay-b̄a's new institution was called D̄ra-s̄hi-kyil (Auspicious Circle),[4] and his reincarnation, Ḡön-chok-jik-may-w̄ang-b̄o, became the presiding lama of that monastery. The latter's biography, written by his chief student Gung-tang Ḡön-chok-d̄en-

---

[1] Lokesh Chandra, ed., *Materials for a History of Tibetan Literature.* śata-piṭaka series, vol. 28-30 (New Delhi: International Academy of Indian Culture, 1963), Part One, p. 207.

[2] *'jam dbyangs bzhad pa dkon mchog 'jigs med dbang po ye shes brtson grus,* 1728-1791.

[3] *snang ra gser khang.* This information as well as the thirteen divisions of his biography is drawn from E. Gene Smith's preface to the first volume of Ḡön-chok-jik-may-w̄ang-b̄o's Collected Works (New Delhi: Ngawang Gelek Demo, 1971).

[4] *bkra shis 'khyil.* According to Geshe Thupten Gyatso of the Tibetan Buddhist Learning Center in New Jersey, the monastery was named after the place, which, in turn, was named after a spring in the area that had this name.

b̄ay-drön-may,[1] is divided into thirteen parts:

1 birth: 1728.
2 childhood: 1728-1732.
3 first vows: 1733-1741.
4 installation on Jam-ȳang-shay-b̄a's throne at D̄ra-s̄hi-kyil Monastic University: 1742-1744.
5 studies in eastern Tibet and final ordination: 1744-1752.
6 studies in Central Tibet at Go-mang College of Dre-b̄ung Monastic University: 1752-1759.
7 teaching in the monasteries of Am-do Province: 1759-69.
8 visit to China: 1769-1772.
9 travels in Eastern Tibet to propagate the Buddha's teaching: 1771-1784.
10 mission to Central Tibet: 1784-1786.
11 return from Central Tibet to Am-do Province and his contributions to the Buddha-Doctrine in summary form: 1786-1791.
12 death and funeral monuments: 1791.
13 reincarnation and recognition: 1792-1798.

J.F. Rock gives a brief biographical sketch from Chinese sources:[2]

---

[1] *gung thang dkon mchog bstan pa'i sgron me*, 1762-1823. This long biography is found in Ḡön-chok-jik-may-w̄ang-b̄o's Collected Works, Volume One. It is followed by a short verse biography by the same author. The two together fill the entire volume. See also Khetsun Sangpo, *Biographical Dictionary of Tibet and Tibetan Buddhism* (Dharamsala: Library of Tibetan Works and Archives, 1973), vol. V, pp.661-676. For other references and a two-page biography, see Katsumi Mimaki, Le *Grub mtha' rnam bźag rin chen phreṅ ba* de dKon mchog 'jigs med dbaṅ po (1728-1791), *Zinbun*, number 14 (The Research Institute for Humanistic Studies, Kyoto University), p. 56, and A.I. Vostrikov, *Tibetan Historical Literature*, Soviet Indology Series No. 4 (tr. H.C. Gupta), (Calcutta: 1970), p. 90 n. 294.

[2] *The Amney Ma-chhen Range and Adjacent Regions* (Rome: 1956), p. 41, as cited in Lokesh Chandra, ed., *Materials for a History of Tibetan*

> [The Emperor] Ch'ien-lung conferred on him the title Fu-fa Ch'an-shih Hu-t'u-k'u-t'u. He was born of an illustrious family in the Lang-jan village in the district of Jih-kung of the present T'ung-jen hsien of Ch'ing-hai [i.e., Am-do] Province. When he came to head the lamasery the latter began to prosper. He set up various regulations and institutions and the buildings were perfected. The relation between the lamasery and the population surrounding it was adjusted once for all. He visited Peking and Lhasa twice. He had political talent and was a diplomat. He had two brothers; one was loyal and brave, the other had the gift of eloquence; he depended on them and trusted them as his left and right hand, and they in turn helped him much. He was the author of eleven works [or, more accurately, seventy-eight works in eleven volumes]. Of him there is also a biography. He lived to reach sixty-four years.

Ḡön-chok-jik-may-w̄ang-b̄o was the chief student of the Mongolian scholar J̄ang-ḡya Röl-b̄ay-dor-jay who, residing in Beijing for most of his life, became the lama of the Ch'ien-lung Emperor—the latter being J̄ang-ḡya's classmate and friend during childhood in Beijing. J̄ang-ḡya conducted Ḡön-chok-jik-may-w̄ang-b̄o's ceremony for full ordination in 1749, and Ḡön-chok-jik-may-w̄ang-b̄o visited Beijing twice, receiving final ordination and teachings from J̄ang-ḡya Röl-b̄ay-dor-jay, whose high connections undoubtedly strengthened his student's effectiveness at D̄ra-s̄hi-kyil Monastic University.

Among the eleven volumes of Ḡön-chok-jik-may-w̄ang-b̄o's Collected Works, the first five and last two are mostly biographies—the two mentioned above of

---

Literature, Part One, p. 49. We have added the bracketed material.

himself by Gung-tang Ḡön-chok-d̄en-b̄ay-drön-may, two more esoteric biographies of himself by another of his students, two biographies of Jam-ȳang-shay-b̄a, brief biographies of the former incarnations of J̄ang-ḡya Röl-b̄ay-dor-jay, a biography of the Reincarnate Drak-ȳap Chung-tsang Ḡel-sang-tup-d̄en-w̄ang-chuk,[1] a biography of L̄ong-döl L̄a-ma Ngak-w̄ang-l̄o-sang,[2] a history of the Ḡum-bum Monastery, a two-volume biography of the Third Paṇ-chen Lama L̄o-sang-b̄el-den-ye-s̄hay,[3] an historical account of the J̄o-nay[4] Translation of the Treatises[5] beginning with Shākyamuni Buddha's appearance in the world and including presentations of the spread of Buddhism in India, Shambhala, China, Khotan, and Mongolia as well as an account of the House of J̄o-nay, an unfinished history of the Ge-luk-b̄a sect, and an unfinished biography of D̄zong-ka-b̄a's student Kay-drup Ḡe-lek-b̄el-s̄ang.

Ḡön-chok-jik-may-w̄ang-b̄o's philosophical works begin with volume six; first is a condensation of his predecessor's long treatise on Chandrakīrti's *Supplement to Nāgārjuna's 'Treatise on the Middle'*, which, despite being a condensation, is still lengthy (242 folios). Next is the brief work on tenets translated here; written in 1773, it is in the same general genre as Jam-ȳang-shay-b̄a's *Great Exposition of Tenets*, but it cannot be considered a condensation of the latter; rather, it belongs to a subgenre of short presentations of tenets for the sake of initial study. As will be pointed out in notes to the translation, Ḡön-chok-jik-may-w̄ang-b̄o evinces an independence of spirit, sometimes following neither his previous incarnation, Jam-ȳang-shay-b̄a, nor his teacher,

---

[1] *brag g.yab chung tsang sprul sku bskal bzang thub bstan dbang phyug*, 1741-1774.

[2] *klong rdol bla ma ngag dbang blo bzang*, 1719-1794.

[3] *blo bzang dpal ldan ye shes*, 1738/39-1780/81.

[4] *co ne*.

[5] *bstan 'gyur*.

J̄ang-ḡya Röl-b̄ay-dor-jay.

Other philosophical works include condensations of Jam-ȳang-shay-b̄a's texts on the four concentrations and four formless absorptions, on Maitreya's *Ornament for Clear Realization*,[1] and on Vasubandhu's *Treasury of Manifest Knowledge*. In addition to a commentary on Āryashūra's *Jātakamālā*, Ḡön-chok-jik-may-w̄ang-b̄o also authored several works on tantric topics, etc.

The general tenor of Ḡön-chok-jik-may-w̄ang-b̄o's works is one of simplification, providing access to a body of material, established by his predecessor, Jam-ȳang-shay-b̄a, that many have found inaccessible due to complicated detail and meticulous citation of sources. Just as these qualities of his predecessor's works make them valuable tools for scholars with the time to pursue such elaboration of detail, Ḡön-chok-jik-may-w̄ang-b̄o's works provide a more approachable avenue to gaining a broad picture which can then be filled in with details from other sources.

ABOUT THE EDITIONS OF THE TEXT USED

Seven editions of Ḡön-chok-jik-may-w̄ang-b̄o's *Presentation of Tenets, A Precious Garland* were used in making this translation:

1 A block-print edition from La-brang[2] in twenty-six folios reproduced by photo-offset in The Collected Works of dkon-mchog-'jigs-med-dbaṅ-po, Vol. 6, (New Delhi: Ngawang Gelek Demo, 1972), pp. 485-535. This is referred to as 'Collected Works'. It is a photographic reproduction of the D̄ra-s̄hi-kyil Monastic University xylographic prints, which were provided to Ngawang Gelek Demo by Ven. Kushok Bakula, member of parliament from Ladakh. It is pos-

---

[1] *mngon rtogs rgyan, abhisamayālaṃkāra.*

[2] *bla brang.*

sible that this edition represents the original edition in the author's Collected Works.

2 A block-print edition in thirty-two folios from the Lessing collection of the rare book section of the University of Wisconsin Library which is item 47 in Leonard Zwilling, *Tibetan Blockprints in the Department of Rare Books and Special Collections* (Madison; the University of Wisconsin-Madison Libraries, 1984). This is a Peking edition, item number 96 in the Catalogue of the University of Tokyo.[1] The colophon indicates that the publication was put together by A-ḡyā Ho-tok-tu[2] upon requests from members of the College of Philosophy of Yong-gön.[3] It is referred to as the 'Peking edition'. The text has Chinese in the right margins and has an extra colophon.

3 A fixed type edition in seventy-six pages printed in pamphlet form in South India (Mundgod: L̄o-s̄el-l̄ing Press, 1980. This is referred to as the 'Go-mang 1980 edition'. It was carefully prepared from three editions[4] in response to two error-laden editions made in India (the next two items).

4 A fixed type edition in seventy-eight pages prepared in pamphlet form in India that attempted to improve on Ḡön-chok-jik-may-w̄ang-b̄o's text without attribution of the changes (Ḍharamsala: Shes rig par khang, 1967). This is referred to as the 'Dharamsala 1967 edition'. Its successful and unsuccessful imaginative at-

---

[1] The identification is taken from Katsumi Mimaki, Le *Grub mtha' rnam bźag rin chen phreṅ ba* de dKon mchog 'jigs med dbaṅ po (1728-1791), *Zinbun*, number 14 (The Research Institute for Humanistic Studies, Kyoto University), p. 60.

[2] *a kyā ho thog thu.*

[3] *yongs dgon mtshan nyid grva tshang.*

[4] As given in the introduction to it (1.11), these are a Central Tibetan edition (*dbus kyi par ma*), the D̄ra-s̄hi-kyil edition (*mdo smad bkra shis 'khyil gyi par ma*), and an edition prepared at Ḡum-b̄um Monastic University (*rje sku 'bum gyi par ma*).

tempts to improve on the edition given in item 5 (most likely without the assistance of any other edition) are cited in the notes to the translation.

5 A photo-offset edition of a hand-written copy of seventy-nine pages reproduced in India in pamphlet form for use in teacher training (Dharamsala: Teaching Training, no date). This is referred to as the 'Teacher Training edition'; it was most likely printed in the early 1960's. It suffers greatly from miscopying but undoubtedly was useful to the refugee community during the early period after the escape to India in 1959.

6 A block-print edition in twenty-eight folios obtained in 1987 from Go-mang College on the outskirts of Hla-ṣa, printed on blocks that most likely pre-date the Cultural Revolution. It may be the Central Tibetan edition mentioned as one of the three from which item three was made, but the colophon is the same as item 1. It is referred to as the 'Tibet Go-mang 1987 edition'.

7 A critical edition by Katsumi Mimaki, Le *Grub mtha' rnam bźag rin chen phreṅ ba* de dkon mchog 'jigs med dbaṅ po (1728-1791), *Zinbun*, number 14 (The Research Institute for Humanistic Studies, Kyoto University), pp. 55-112. This is referred to as the 'Mimaki edition'.[1]

Given the difficulties with the fourth and fifth editions,

---

[1] Mimaki used eight editions, as listed on p. 60 of his edition; of these, four are found among our seven; the Collected Works edition (item 1) is the first in his list, the Peking edition (item 2) is the third in his list, the Dharamsala 1967 edition (item 4) is the fifth in his list, and the Teacher Training edition (item 5) is the sixth in his list. Mimaki's seventh text is an almost identical reprint of his sixth. Mimaki's edition is excellent even though he has given too much prominence to the Dharamsala 1967 edition (item 4) which contains within it many accretions that are clearly intended to improve the text but are not founded on any edition.

the translation mainly follows the texts of the other five editions, with the Collected Works edition and the Peking edition (i.e., the xylograph from the Lessing Collection at the University of Wisconsin), being the basis. Significant variations in readings of all seven editions are cited in the notes, as are significant emendations to the first three editions.

Annotated translation of Ḡön-chok-jik-may-w̄ang-b̄o's

Precious Garland of Tenets

Associate editor: Anne C. Klein

Material indented or within brackets is explanation added by the translators.

Guide to the Text

Prologue

OUR OWN AND OTHERS' PRESENTATIONS OF TENETS

[Obeisance]

The snowy mountain of [Buddha's] two marvellous collections of merit and wisdom was melted by the warmth of his compassion.
The stream gathered in a circle on the earth of the spontaneous Truth Body and split into the rivers of the four schools of tenets.
The successive waves of his deeds extended into space, and the childlike Forders[1] were frightened.
May the chief of Subduers, the great lake Manasarowar,[2] the harbor of millions of Conqueror Children[3] who are hooded dragons, prevail.

---

[1] *mu stegs pa, tīrthika.*

[2] As identified in Sarat Chandra Das, *A Tibetan-English Dictionary* (Calcutta, 1902), p. 947, this is 'one of a pair of large lakes lying at the foot of Kailas group of mountains, north of Lipu-lek Pass in West Purang.'

[3] I.e., Bodhisattvas.

Obeisance to the regent of the Conqueror, the undaunted protector ,[1]
To the union of all the wisdom of the Conquerors, Mañjughoṣha,[2]
To the honorable Nāgārjuna and Asaṅga who were prophesied by the Conqueror,
And to the second Conqueror, D̄zong-ka-b̄a[3] and his spiritual sons, Gyel-tsap and Kay-drup.[4]

[Promise of Composition and Exhortation to Listen]

If a presentation of tenets is understood, one sees all the different attributes of the outer [i.e., non-Buddhist] and inner [i.e., Buddhist] teachings
And takes on the aspect of the best of propounders among countless scholars.
What wise person would cast aside the effort to differentiate the principles of our own and others' tenets,
A white banner, known to be marvellous, raised by an unbiased being![5]

---

[1] Maitreya is the Buddha of the next era and thus the 'regent' of the 'Conqueror', or Buddha, of this era, Shākyamuni Buddha. Though many persons can achieve Buddhahood during any particular era, only one Buddha appears within the context of displaying the twelve deeds of a Buddha.

[2] Also known as Mañjushrī.

[3] *tsong kha pa blo bzang grags pa*, 1357-1419. For a short biography, see the *Life and Teachings of Tsong Khapa*, edited by Robert A. F. Thurman (Dharamsala: Library of Tibetan Works and Archives, 1982), pp. 4-39.

[4] Gyel-tsap-dar-ma-rin-chen (*rgyal tshab dar ma rin chen*, 1364-1432) and Kay-drup-gay-lek-b̄el-sang (*mkhas grub dge legs dpal bzang*, 1385-1438). For a short biography of the latter, see the introduction to Tenzin Gyatso and Jeffrey Hopkins, *The Kālachakra Tantra: Rite of Initiation for the Stage of Generation* (London: Wisdom Publications, 1985), pp. 139-145.

[5] The unbiased being is the author himself, Ḡön-chok-jik-may-w̄ang-b̄o.

Therefore, condensing all the good explanations of excellent beings,
I will briefly put forth a presentation of tenets
In order to provide for those whose lot is similar to mine.[1]
Those who seek clear understanding should listen respectfully.

Moreover, persons who are not looking for material goods and respect in this life, nor for poetry, but who seek liberation from the depths of their hearts must work at the means of understanding the correct view of selflessness. For, no matter how much you have internalized love, compassion, and the altruistic aspiration to enlightenment, if you are without the profound view of selflessness, you are unable to remove the root of suffering.

> Love is the wish that all sentient beings be joined with happiness. Compassion is the wish that all sentient beings be separated from suffering. The altruistic aspiration to enlightenment is the wish to attain Buddhahood in order to help all sentient beings. In order to carry out these three wishes, one must overcome the cause of suffering which is the ignorance that misconceives the nature of persons and of other phenomena.

The foremost venerable great D̄zong-ka-b̄a says [in his *Three Principal Aspects of the Path*]:[2]

If you do not have the wisdom realizing the way things are,

---

[1] The author humbly implies that those wiser than he is would not need such a book.

[2] *lam gtso rnam gsum*. This text forms the basis of the first part of this book.

Even though you have developed the thought
definitely to leave cyclic existence
As well as the altruistic intention, the root of
cyclic existence cannot be cut.
Therefore work at the means of realizing dependent-arising.

Hence, in order to remove faulty views and to delineate the gradation of coarse and subtle selflessnesses, I will give a brief explanation of our own and others' presentations of tenets. This explanation has two parts: a general teaching and a detailed explanation.

1 *Tenets in General*

OUR OWN AND OTHERS' TENETS IN GENERAL

The expression 'tenets' (*grub mtha'*, *siddhānta*) is not my own fabrication because it was mentioned in Buddha's scriptures. The *Descent into Laṅkā Sūtra*[1] says:

> My doctrine has two modes,
> Advice and tenets.
> To children I speak advice
> And to yogis, tenets.

Further, there are two types of persons: those whose minds have not been affected by tenets and those whose minds have been affected by tenets. Those

---

[1] *lang kar gshegs pa*, *laṅkāvatāra*. For an English translation of this sūtra, see D.T. Suzuki, *The Lankavatara Sutra* (London: Routledge, 1932). A Sanskrit edition is available in *Saddharmalaṅkāvatārasūtram*, P.L.Vaidya, ed. Buddhist Sanskrit Texts No.3. (Darbhanga: Mithila Institute, 1963); also: Bunyiu Nanjio, ed. Bibl. Otaniensis, Vol.I. (Kyoto: Otani University Press, 1923).

whose minds have not been affected by tenets seek only the pleasures of this life with an innate awareness that, since they have never studied a systematic presentation, neither investigates nor analyses. Those whose minds have been affected by tenets have studied some system such that within citing scripture and reasoning they propound a way of establishing a presentation of the three—bases, paths, and fruits—which is established for the perspective of their own understanding [though not necessarily true in fact].

Furthermore, the etymology for 'tenet' (*grub mtha'*, *siddhānta*) is as follows: a tenet [literally, an established conclusion] is a thesis decided upon and established in reliance upon scripture and/or reasoning and which, from the perspective of one's mind, will not be forsaken for something else. As Dharmamitra's *Clear Words, A Commentary on (Maitreya's) 'Ornament for Clear Realization'*[1] says:

> 'Tenet' [established conclusion] signifies one's own *established* assertion within being demonstrated by reasoning and scripture. Because one will not pass beyond this assertion, it is a *conclusion*.

Schools of tenets are divided into two types, Outsider [non-Buddhist] and Insider [Buddhist]. There is a difference between mere Outsiders and Insiders because persons who go for refuge to the Three Jewels from the depths of their hearts are Insiders, and persons who go for refuge from the depths of their hearts to a god of the transient world without turning their minds toward the Three Jewels are Outsiders.

> The Three Jewels are Buddha, the *dharma* or realizations of selflessness and abandonments of

---

[1] *shes rab kyi pha rol tu phyin pa'i man ngag gi bstan bcos mngon par rtogs pa'i rgyan gyi tshig le'ur byas pa'i 'grel bshad tshig rab tu gsal ba, abhisamayālaṃkārakārikāprajñāpāramitopadeśaśāstraṭīkāprasphuṭapadā.*

obstructions that protect one from suffering as well as the teachings of these, and the *saṅgha* or community of Buddha's followers. These are 'jewels'[1] because they are precious and difficult to find. The Tibetan term literally means 'superior rarity'; the three are *superior* because, possessing perfect attributes, they are similar to a wish-granting jewel; they are *rare* because these perfect attributes are seen only by one having a great mass of merit. Maitreya's *Sublime Continuum of the Great Vehicle*[2] explains the epithet 'jewel' thus:

> Because of appearing rarely, because of being without without defilement,
> Because of having power, because of being ornaments of the world,
> Because of being just superior, and because of being changeless,
> [They are called] Superior Rarities [Jewels].

The actual objects of refuge are the abandonments and realizations, specifically true cessations and true paths—the third and fourth noble truths—because these are what one practices in order to gain liberation and omniscience. The teacher of refuge is Buddha, and the friends helping one to refuge are the community, which here refers to at least four ordi-

---

1 *dkon mchog, ratna*.

2 *theg pa chen po rgyud bla ma'i bstan bcos, mahāyānottaratantraśāstra*; I.22. A Sanskrit edition is available in *The Ratnagotravibhāga Mahāyānottaratantraśāstra*, E.H. Johnston (and T. Chowdhury) ed., (Patna: Bihar Research Society, 1950). For English translations, see E. Obermiller, 'Sublime Science of the Great Vehicle to Salvation', *Acta Orientalia*, 9 (1931), pp. 81-306; and J. Takasaki, *A Study on the Ratnagotravibhāga*, (Rome: IS.M.E.O., 1966).

> nary monks or nuns or refers to one Superior.[1]
>
> The definition of Outsiders as 'persons who go for refuge from the depths of their hearts to a god of the transient world without turning their minds toward the Three Jewels' does not seem to be adequate since Chārvākas (Hedonists or Nihilists) are proponents of Outsider tenets (and hence Outsiders) but they do not necessarily go for refuge to a god of the transient world. The definition of a proponent of Outsiders' tenets given in the next chapter, however, appears to be adequate.

Also, there is a difference between Outsider and Insider proponents of tenets because they differ from three points of view: teacher, teaching, and view. Our own Buddhist schools have three distinguishing traits:

1 They have a teacher who has extinguished all faults and completed all good qualities.
2 Their teachings are not harmful to any sentient being.
3 They assert the view that the self is empty of being permanent, unitary, and independent.

The others' schools possess three distinguishing traits that are the opposite of those:

1 Their teachers have faults and have not completed their good qualities.
2 They have teachings that harm and injure sentient beings.
3 They assert the view that a permanent, unitary, independent self does exist.

> This indicates not that *all* the teachings of Outsiders are harmful to sentient beings, but that *some* teachings from each of their schools are harmful. For example, the teaching of animal

---

[1] *'phags pa, ārya.*

sacrifice is harmful to beings, as are extreme ascetic practices. Also, the teaching of a permanent, unitary, independent self fortifies the innate sense of self that prevents liberation from cyclic existence.

It is questionable whether Chārvākas (Hedonists or Nihilists) assert a permanent, unitary, independent self. Thus, the third qualification seems to refer not to all non-Buddhist schools but to those propounding an extreme of permanence. From the Buddhist perspective, the Chārvākas propound an extreme of nihilism.

2 *Short Explanation of Non-Buddhist Tenets*

The definition of a proponent of Outsiders' tenets is: a person who is a proponent of tenets, does not go for refuge to the Three Jewels, and asserts that there is a [perfect] teacher other than the Three Jewels. There are endless divisions of Outsiders; briefly, however, they are widely known to consist of five Schools of Philosophers—Vaishṇava, Aishvara, Jaina, Kāpila [Sāṃkhya], and Bārhaspatya [Chārvāka]. They are also set forth as the six fundamental schools, Vaisheṣhika, Naiyāyika, Sāṃkhya, Mīmāṃsaka, Nirgrantha [Jaina], and Lokāyata [Chārvāka]. The first five of these hold views of eternalism, and the last holds a view of nihilism.

VAISHEṢHIKA AND NAIYĀYIKA

The Vaisheṣhikas [Particularists] and the Naiyāyikas [Logicians] are followers of the sage Kaṇāda and the Brāhmaṇa Akṣhipāda respectively. Although these two schools differ a little in the features of some of their assertions, their general tenets do not differ.

Both the Vaisheṣhikas and the Naiyāyikas assert that all objects of knowledge[1] [i.e., all phenomena] are included among six categories of existents.[2]

> These are substance, quality, activity, generality, particularity, and inherence. The first category, substance, is divided into the nine types: earth, water, fire, air, space, time, direction, self, and mind.
>
> The second category, quality, has twenty-five types: (1) form, (2) taste, (3) smell, (4) touch, (5) sound, (6) number, (7) dimension, (8) separateness, (9) conjunction, (10) disjunction, (11) otherness, (12) non-otherness, (13) consciousness, (14) pleasure, (15) pain, (16) desire, (17) hatred, (18) effort, (19) heaviness, (20) moisture, (21) heat, (22) oiliness, (23) momentum, (24) merit, (25) demerit. A quality has four features: (1) it depends on a substance, (2) it does not possess other qualities, (3) it does not act either as a cause of inherence or as a cause of non-inherence, (4) it does not depend

---

[1] *shes bya, jñeya.*

[2] Five of the seven editions used (Collected Works, 490.2; Peking edition, 3b.6; Teacher Training edition, 7.1; Go-mang 1980 edition, 6.8; Tibet Go-mang 1987 edition, 3b.1) read *shes bya thams cad rdzas dgur 'dus par 'dod la,* 'assert that all objects of knowledge are included among the nine substances', whereas, more accurately, the text should read *shes bya thams cad tshig don drug tu 'dus par 'dod la,* 'assert that all objects of knowledge are included among the six categories of existents,' in accordance with the Dharamsala 1967 edition (6.2) and Mimaki 71.7. The nine substances are the first of the six categories. That five editions have the same reading here suggests, as elsewhere, that the Dharamsala 1967 edition was edited freely by a scholar who sought to improve the original; in this case, the editor succeeded in correcting a gross error, and thus we have accepted the correction.

on a sign, that is, a quality does not depend on another quality as a proof for its existence but is a proof for the existence of a substance.

The third category, activity, has five types; lifting up, putting down, contraction, extension, and going.

The fourth category, generality, is the common cause of designating terms and engaging the mind in a similar way with regard to a class of phenomena.

The fifth category, inherence, is a phenomenon which is the conjunction of a base and that which is based on it; it is a different entity from both the base and that which is based on it.

The sixth category, inherence, is a phenomenon which is the conjunction of a base and that which is based on it; it is a different entity from both the base and that which is based on it.[1]

---

[1] The sources are: Jam-ȳang-shay-b̄a, *An Explanation of 'Tenets', A Sun of the Land of Samantabhadra Brilliantly Illuminating All of Our Own and Others' Tenets and the Meaning of the Profound Emptiness, An Ocean of Scripture and Reasoning Fulfilling All Hopes of All Beings* (*grub mtha'i rnam bshad rang gzhan grub mtha' kun dang zab don mchog tu gsal ba kun bzang zhing gi nyi ma lung rigs rgya mtsho skye dgu'i re ba kun skong*) [known as the *Great Exposition of Tenets* (*grub mtha' chen mo*) and hereafter referred to that way], (Musoorie: Dalama, 1962), [modern blockprint, 310 folios], *ka* 48b. 7ff. Also: Ngak-w̄ang-b̄el-den (*ngag dbang dpal ldan*, 1797-?), *Annotations for (Jam-ȳang-shay-b̄a's) 'Great Exposition of Tenets', Freeing the Knots of the Difficult Points, Precious Jewel of Clear Thought* (*grub mtha' chen mo'i mchan 'grel dka' gnad mdud grol blo gsal gces nor*), [hereafter referred to as 'Ngak-w̄ang-b̄el-den's *Annotations*'], (Sarnath: Pleasure of Elegant Sayings Press, 1964) [modern blockprint, 416 folios], 101 b.2ff. That Jam-ȳang-shay-b̄a, who is identified as Ḡön-chok-jik-may-w̄ang-b̄o's previous incarnation, understood that all phenomena are included in the six categories of existents and not in the nine types of substance is clear in his *Great Exposition of Tenets*.

They assert that ablutions, initiations, fasts, sacrifice, burnt offerings, and so forth are the paths of liberation. Through having meditatively cultivated yoga in accordance with the quintessential instructions of a guru, yogis come to know the self as a factuality other than the senses and so forth and thereby see reality,[1] understanding the nature of the six categories of existents. At that time, they know the self to be an all-pervasive entity but lacking activity. They do not accumulate any virtuous or non-virtuous actions or the predispositions those establish.[2] Because they do not accumulate new actions and extinguish old ones, the self separates from the body, senses, awareness, pleasure, pain, desire, hatred, and so forth, and does not assume a new body and senses. Thereby, the continuum of births is severed like a fire that has consumed its fuel. When the self is alone [without any of its nine qualities—desire, hatred, effort, pleasure, pain, consciousness, virtue, non-virtue, and activity]—this is said to be the attainment of liberation.

SĀṂKHYA

The Sāṃkhyas [Enumerators] are followers of the sage Kapila. They assert that all objects of knowledge are enumerated in twenty-five categories.[3]

According to Bhāvaviveka's *Blaze of Reasoning*[4]

---

[1] *de kho na nyid, tattva;* this term often is also translated as 'suchness' or 'thatness'.

[2] *Karma (las)* has the two senses of actions themselves and the predispositions that those actions establish in the mind.

[3] Whether those Sāṃkhyas who assert that the deity Īshvara supervises the creation assert only twenty-five objects of knowledge or whether they assert that Īshvara is a twenty-sixth is unclear.

[4] *Blaze of Reasoning, a Commentary on the 'Heart of the Middle Way' (dbu ma'i snying po'i 'grel pa rtog ge 'bar ba, madhyamakahṛdayavṛttitarkajvālā)*, as cited in Ngak-w̄ang-b̄el-den's *Annotations, stod* 63b.3.

they maintain that one is liberated through understanding the ramifications of this enumeration.

The twenty-five categories are the self, principal, the great one, I-principle, five subtle objects, eleven faculties, and five elements. The five subtle objects are visible forms, sounds, odors, tastes, and tangible objects. The eleven faculties are the five mental faculties, the five action[1] faculties, and intellectual faculty. The five mental faculties are those of the eye, ear, nose, tongue, and skin. The five action faculties are speech, arms, legs, anus, and genitalia. The five elements are earth, water, fire, wind, and space.

In chart form, the twenty-five categories are:[2]

1. person (*bdag, puruṣa*) [or self, consciousness, conscious self, mind, sentience, knower of the field]
2. fundamental nature (*gtso bo, prakṛti*) [or nature, principal, universality, general principal]
3. intellect (*blo, buddhi*), or great one (*chen po, mahat*)
4. I-principle (*nga rgyal, ahaṃkāra*)
   (a) I-principle dominated by motility (*rajas*)
   (b) I-principle dominated by darkness (*tamas*)
   (c) I-principle dominated by lightness (*sattva*)

---

[1] Five editions (Collected Works, 490.6; Peking edition, 4a; Teacher Training edition, 8.3; Go-mang 1980 edition, 7.12; and Tibet Go-mang 1987 edition, 3b.5) read ***las kyi dbang po*** 'action faculties' whereas the Dharamsala 1967 edition (7.6) reads ***lus kyi dbang po*** 'physical faculties'. The former reading is preferred.

[2] This list is adapted from Jeffrey Hopkins, *Meditation on Emptiness*, (London: Wisdom Publications, 1983), pp. 322-323.

Five subtle objects or potencies of objects which evolve from the I-principle dominated by darkness:

5. visible forms (*gzugs, rūpa*)
6. sounds (*sgra, śabda*)
7. odors (*dri, gandha*)
8. tastes (*ro, rasa*)
9. tangible objects (*reg bya, spraṣṭavya*).

Eleven faculties which evolve from the I-principle dominated by lightness:

Five mental faculties

10. eye (*mig, cakṣus*)
11. ear (*rna ba, śrota*)
12. nose (*sna, ghrāṇa*)
13. tongue (*lce, rasana*)
14. body or skin (*pags pa, sparśana*).

Five physical faculties or action faculties

15. speech (*ngag, vāc*)
16. arms (*lag pa, pāṇi*)
17. legs (*rkang pa, pāda*)
18. anus (*rkub, pāyu*)
19. genitalia (*'doms, upastha*).

One intellectual faculty

20. Intellectual faculty (*yid, manaḥ*) the nature of which is both mental and physical.

Five elements:

21. earth (*sa, pṛthivī*) which evolves from the odor potency
22. water (*chu, āp*) which evolves from the taste potency
23. fire (*me, tejas*) which evolves from the visible form potency
24. wind (*rlung, vāyu*) which evolves from the tangible object potency

25. space (*nam mkha', ākāśa*) which evolves from the sound potency.

From among these twenty-five categories, the person or self is asserted to be [just] consciousness [because it is not an aggregation of particles].[1] The remaining twenty-four are asserted to be matter because they are aggregations [of particles].[2] The person and the principal [or fundamental nature] are ultimate truths[3] [because they are non-manifest objects of knowledge].[4] The others are asserted to be conventional truths.[5]

Furthermore, these twenty-five categories are included in only four types: that which is a cause but not an effect; that which is both a cause and an effect; that which is an effect but not a cause; and that which is neither a cause nor an effect.

> 'Cause' here has the sense of a source, an evolvent, or, as it is called in the citation below, a nature. An 'effect' is a transformation, an evolute.

The fundamental nature is a cause but not an effect. The intellect, the I-principle, and the five subtle objects are both causes and effects. The remaining sixteen [the eleven faculties and the five elements] are effects but not causes. The person is neither a cause nor an effect. Moreover, this is as is explained in Īshvarakṛṣṇa's *Tantra*:[6]

---

[1] Ngak-w̄ang-b̄el-den's *Annotations, stod* 65a.3.
[2] Ngak-w̄ang-b̄el-den's *Annotations, stod* 64b.2.
[3] *don dam bden pa, paramārthasatya.*
[4] Ngak-w̄ang-b̄el-den's *Annotations, stod* 65a.3.
[5] *kun rdzob bden pa, saṃvṛtisatya.*
[6] This is the third stanza of the *Sāṃkhyakārikā* by Īshvarakṛṣṇa (third century, C.E.). The Sanskrit text is available in the *Sāṃkhyakārikā of Īśvara Kṛṣṇa,* edited and translated by S.S. Suryanarayana Sastri (Madras: University of Madras, 1935). 'Transformations' are evolutes; 'natures' are evolvents. The entire citation is missing from the

The fundamental nature is not a transformation.
The seven—the great one and so forth—are natures and transformations.
Sixteen are transformations.
The person is not a nature and not a transformation.

'Fundamental nature', 'general principal', and 'principal' are synonyms. The fundamental nature is asserted to be an object of knowledge that possesses six distinguishing characteristics.

1. It is the *agent of actions* because it is the agent of virtue and non-virtue.
2. It is *unborn and permanent* because it does not disintegrate or dissolve into anything else.
3. It is *unitary* because it is partless.
4. It is *only an object* and not an object-possessor, i.e., subject, because it is without realization and consciousness and because it is the object of enjoyment of the person.
5. It *pervades all animate and inanimate objects*, such as cause and effect, because it pervades all transformations.
6. It is *unmanifest* and is an *equilibrium* of the three qualities: activity, lightness, and darkness.[1]

Person, self, consciousness, and basic mind are mutually inclusive and synonymous.

The mode of production of the remaining twenty-three is the following. Whenever the person generates a desire to enjoy objects, the fundamental nature [recognizes this desire, unites with the person,[2] and] cre-

---

Dharamsala 1967 edition (8.5).

[1] Ngak-w̄ang-b̄el-den's *Annotations*, *stod* 64b.2 and *stod* 51b.2; Jam-ȳang-shay-b̄a's *Great Exposition of Tenets*, 30b.5.

[2] J̄ang-ḡya Röl-b̄ay-dor-jay (*lcang skya rol pa'i rdo rje*, 1717-86), *Pre-*

ates manifestations such as sounds.

According to the non-theistic Sāṃkhyas all manifest objects whatsoever are transformations of the fundamental nature. The theistic Sāṃkhyas assert that the varieties of environments and animate beings are not produced from the fundamental nature alone because it is mindless and that which is mindless is not capable of overseeing production. For, without an overseer, the initiation of an effect is not possible. The person is not suitable to be the overseer because at that time, before the transformation of the fundamental nature, there is no knowledge since the intellect has not yet been produced, and without determination by the intellect there is no realization of objects. Therefore, through the mutual dependence of the great god Īshvara and the fundamental nature, the varieties of effects are produced. When, from among the three qualities that dwell in the entity of the fundamental nature, the quality of activity increases in strength, this acts as the cause of Īshvara's issuing forth all animate beings and environments. When lightness increases in strength, this acts as the cause of their duration. When darkness increases in strength, this acts as the cause of their disintegration. Therefore, although Īshvara and the

---

sentation of Tenets/ Clear Exposition of the Presentations of Tenets, Beautiful Ornament for the Meru of the Subduer's Teaching (*grub mtha'i rnam bzhag/ grub pa'i mtha'i rnam par bzhag pa gsal bar bshad pa thub bstan lhun po'i mdzes rgyan*), (Varanasi: Pleasure of Elegant Sayings Printing Press, 1970), [referred to hereafter as J̄ang-ḡya's *Presentation of Tenets*], 32.8. The author of our text, Ḡön-chok-jik-may-w̄ang-b̄o, was the principal student of J̄ang-ḡya Röl-b̄ay-dor-jay, whom Jam-ȳang-shay-b̄a, Ḡön-chok-jik-may-w̄ang-b̄o's previous incarnation, helped find as the incarnation of the previous J̄ang-ḡya.

> fundamental nature, which are the two causes that produce all manifest phenomena, always exist, serial production, duration, and disintegration of effects are admissible because the three—activity, lightness, and darkness—increase and diminish serially.[1]

The great one arises from the principal [i.e., the fundamental nature]. 'Intellect' and 'great one' are synonyms. The intellect is considered to be like a two-sided mirror which reflects the images of objects from the outside and the image of the person from the inside.

> The intellect 'empowers' the senses, and it apprehends the objects that the senses apprehend; these objects are then known by the person. The person is consciousness, and the intellect is a material entity wherein consciousness mixes with the senses, which are matter.[2] The person is then mistakenly confused with the senses; this error must be corrected in order to attain liberation.

From the intellect, the I-principle is produced; it has three divisions: the activity dominated I-principle, the lightness dominated I-principle, and the darkness dominated I-principle. From the first [the activity dominated I-principle] the five subtle objects are produced, and the five elements are produced from these [see chart, pp. 159-161]. From the second [the lightness dominated I-principle] the eleven faculties are produced. The third [the darkness dominated I-principle] is said to be the motivator of the other two.

> This presentation accords with that of D̄zong-ka-b̄a and his student Gyel-tsap; however,

---

[1] Ngak-w̄ang-b̄el-den's *Annotations, stod* 65a.4.

[2] Ngak-w̄ang-b̄el-den's *Annotations, stod* 64b.4.

> Avalokitavrata, an Indian scholar known for his *Explanatory Commentary on (Bhāvaviveka's) 'Lamp for (Nāgārjuna's) "Wisdom"'*,[1] names the darkness dominated I-principle as the producer of the five subtle objects and the activity dominated I-principle as the motivator of the other two I-principles.[2]

The Sāṃkhyas assert that one cycles in cyclic existence[3] through the force of ignorance that mistakes the fundamental nature, which is like a blind man with good legs, and the person, which is like a cripple with good eyesight, to be one and thereupon does not understand that transformations are manifested by the fundamental nature. When, in dependence on hearing the quintessential instructions of a guru, one fully generates definite knowledge that the transformations are only manifestations of the fundamental nature, one gradually separates from attachment to objects. At that time, through relying on the concentrations, the clairvoyance of the divine eye is generated. The fundamental nature, when it is seen by this clairvoyant consciousness, is flushed with shame like another's wife [that is, like a mistress when seen by the wife]; it gathers its transformations [and disappears]. The fundamental nature then dwells alone [separate from the self] with the result that all appearances of conventional phenomena disappear for the mind of the yogi. The person then abides without enjoying objects and without action; at that time, liberation is attained.

---

1 *prajñāpradīpaṭīkā, shes rab sgron ma'i rgya cher 'grel pa*; P5259, Vol. 96-7.

2 Ngak-w̄ang-b̄el-den's *Annotations, stod* 64b.8. Avalokitavrata's explanation seems the more likely, although the source of the other opinion needs to be investigated.

3 In the Dharamsala 1967 edition (9.9) read *dbang gis 'khor bar 'khor bar 'dod* for *dbang gis 'khor bar 'dod* in accordance with the Collected Works edition (492.3), etc.

MĪMĀṂSAKA

The Mīmāṃsakas [Analyzers or Ritualists] are followers of Jaimini. They maintain that whatever appears in the *Vedas* is self-produced [because the *Vedas* were not made by anyone].

> In explaining why the Mīmāṃsakas hold the *Vedas* to be valid, Bhāvaviveka's *Heart of the Middle Way*[1] says:
>
> > Because of degeneration [which occurs on account of] the faults of desire and so forth,
> > The words of persons are always false.
> > Because the *Vedas* were not made by persons,
> > They are held to be valid sources of knowledge.
>
> Thus, from their point of view, the scriptures of the Sāṃkhyas, Vaisheṣhikas, Nirgranthas, Nihilists, Buddhists, and so forth are false because they were made by persons.[2]

They make the exaggeration that what appears in the *Vedas* is reality, and, thereupon, they assert that sacrifices and so forth [which are revealed in the *Vedas*] are the only way to attain a high condition of life [in the future].

This high condition of life is asserted to be liberation only from bad transmigrations [not liberation from all transmigrations in cyclic existence]. Moreover, there is no liberation that extinguishes all suffering; this is because defilements subsist in the nature of the mind [and, therefore, to eliminate defilements would be to eliminate the mind]. Also, there is no omniscience because

---

[1] *dbu ma'i snying po'i tshig le'ur byas pa, madhyamakahṛdayakārikā.*
[2] Jam-ȳang-shay-b̄a's *Great Exposition of Tenets, ka* 42b.8.

objects of knowledge are limitless. Hence, the Mīmāṃsakas also propound that there is no true speech [of persons; only the *Vedas* are true].

> Buddhists assert the true speech of one who has abandoned all defilements and become omniscient.

NIRGRANTHA

The Nirgranthas [Jainas] are followers of Ṛṣhabha Jina. They assert that all objects of knowledge are included in nine categories: life, contamination, restraint, wearing down, bond, action, sin, merit, and liberation.[1]

Life is self; it is the same size as a person's body. Its nature is such that its entity is permanent, but its states are impermanent. *Contamination*[2] is virtuous or non-virtuous action[3] because on account of actions one falls into cyclic existence. *Restraint* is what ceases contaminations because [on account of it] actions are not newly accumulated. *Wearing down* is exhaustion of previously accumulated actions [i.e., karmic matter] by way of asceticism, such as not drinking liquids, physical hardships, and so forth. A *bond* is a wrong view. *Actions* are

---

[1] According to Ngak-w̄ang-b̄el-den's *Annotations* (*stod* 118b.4-119.4), Jam-ȳang-shay-b̄a calls the nine categories as listed here the system of the Nirgranthas of India and another set of nine the system of the Nirgranthas of Shambhala. The latter are: life, the lifeless, contamination, restraint, abandonment of non-virtue, bonds of bad views, liberation, going from this to the next transient life, and coming from the last life to this.

[2] The word translated as 'contamination' is *āsrava* (*zag pa*) which, in a Buddhist context, is etymologized as 'flowing downward' or 'falling'; hence, 'contamination' is to be identified as virtuous and non-virtuous actions since these cause one to *fall* into cyclic existence. However, in a Jaina context, it is etymologized as 'flowing into' in the sense that karmic matter flows into and weighs down the person.

[3] *las, karma.*

of four types: [the determiners of the general] experience in a later life, of name, of lineage, and of life-span. *Sin* is non-virtue. *Merit* is virtue.

Liberation is the following: By resorting to deeds of asceticism such as going naked, not speaking, the five fires [fires in front, back, on both sides, and the sun above] and so forth, all previous actions [accretions of karmic material] are consumed [and liberation, a state that lacks all contaminations of good and bad actions, is attained]. Because actions are not newly accumulated, one goes to a place that is at the top of all worlds, called Consummation of the Worlds.[1] It is like a white umbrella held upside down, white like yogurt and the esculent white water lily, the size of four million five hundred thousand *yojanas*. Because this place has life, it is a thing;[2] because it is free from cyclic existence, it is also a non-thing.[3] This place is called liberation.

Ṛṣhabha Jina said:

Jina explains that liberation
Has the color of snow, the incense flower,
Cow's yogurt, frost, and pearl,
The shape of a white umbrella.

LOKĀYATA

The Lokāyatas [or Chārvākas (Hedonists)] say that one does not come to this life from a previous life because no one perceives previous lives.

> Since among Lokāyatas there are also Meditators[4] who clairvoyantly perceive a limited

---

[1] A synonym of Īsipabbārā.
[2] *dngos po, bhāva.*
[3] *dngos po med pa, abhāva.*
[4] *snyoms 'jug pa, samāpattika.*

number of past lives, the reference here is to the Dialectician[1] Lokāyatas.

From an adventitious body a mind is adventitiously established, just as light is adventitiously established from the adventitious existence of a lamp.

Also, one does not go to a future life from this life because body and mind are one entity and, therefore, when the body perishes, the mind also perishes. For example, when a stone is destroyed, a design on the stone is likewise destroyed.

Thus, this [system] maintains that all objects of comprehension [all existents] are necessarily specifically characterized [i.e., directly perceived] phenomena and all valid cognitions are necessarily direct valid cognitions. This is because they do not accept that generally characterized [i.e., only inferentially perceived] phenomena or inferential valid cognitions exist.

Some Āyatas assert that all phenomena [whose causes cannot be directly perceived] arise from their own nature, causelessly. They say:

The rising of the sun, the running downwards of a
 river,
The roundness of peas, the sharpness of thorns,
The 'eyes' of peacock feathers and so forth—all phenomena

---

[1] *rtog ge pa, tārkika.* See Jeffrey Hopkins, *Meditation on Emptiness*, p. 328. Ḡön-chok-jik-may-w̄ang-b̄o's failure to mention the Meditators is a deviation from the presentation of this school by Jam-ȳang-shay-b̄a, his previous incarnation, who, in his *Great Exposition of Tenets*, makes a clear differentiation between the two types of Nihilists (ka 21b.4):

> Because it is explained that some assert and some do not assert cause and effect, gods, and so forth,
> It is mistaken [to hold that all Nihilists] say that former and future lives are totally non-existent and that there are only three transmigrations, and so forth.

Arise from their own nature, without being made
by anyone.

* * *

Stanza between sections:

A rung on the ladder to the city of liberation
Is the understanding and abandoning
Of all types of Outsiders' tenets,
Which are fords to extremes of bad views.[1]

---

[1] The author is making a pun based on the term 'Forders' (*mu stegs pa, tīrthika*), which is another name for non-Buddhists. They call themselves 'Forders' because, from their own viewpoint, they have a ford (*stegs*) to the end (*mu*), i.e., to liberation; the author, however, identifies the end (*mu*) as an extremist view.

3 *General Exposition of Buddhist Tenets*

The King of the Shākyas, a peerless teacher, initially generated an attitude of dedication to attaining highest enlightenment for the sake of all sentient beings. Then, [in order to actualize this wish] he amassed the collections of merit and wisdom for three countless aeons. Finally, in the vicinity of Bodhgayā, he became perfectly enlightened.

At Varaṇāsi he turned the wheel of doctrine of the four noble truths for the five good ascetics [who had previously practiced asceticism with him]. Then, on Vulture Peak [so called because it is shaped like a heap of vultures] he turned the wheel of doctrine of characterlessness [that is, phenomena's not possessing establishment by way of their own character]. Then, at Vaishālī and other places, he extensively turned the wheel of doctrine of good differentiation.

> The third wheel is called the wheel of good differentiation because it differentiates well be-

tween what is and is not established by way of its own character. The fundamental idea of the first wheel was that all phenomena without exception are established by way of their own character as the referents of conceptual consciousnesses and that in this respect there is no cause for differentiation among them. The fundamental idea of the second wheel was that all phenomena without exception are not established by way of their own character and that in this respect there is no cause for differentiation among them. When Buddha was questioned about the apparent conflict between these two teachings, he taught the third wheel in which he explained that thoroughly established natures,[1] that is, emptinesses, and other-powered natures,[2] such as houses, trees, and persons, are established by way of their own character, but that imputational natures,[3] such as uncompounded space, cessations, and phenomena's being the referents of conceptual consciousnesses, are not established by way of their own character. Thus, the third wheel is the teaching that differentiates well what is and is not established by way of its own character.

This way of categorizing the three wheels of doctrine is found in the *Sūtra Unravelling the Thought*.[4] It says that the first wheel consists of teachings of the four noble truths and the like,

---

[1] *yongs grub, pariniṣpanna.*
[2] *gzhan dbang, paratantra.*
[3] *kun btags, parikalpita.*
[4] *dgongs pa nges par 'grel pa'i mdo, saṃdhinirmocanasūtra.* For an edited Tibetan text and translation into French, see Étienne Lamotte, *Saṃdhinirmocanasūtra: l'explication des mystères,* (Louvain, Paris, 1935). The topic of the three wheels of doctrine is found in chapter seven of that sūtra, the 'Questions of Paramārthasamudgata'.

which were taught for the sake of trainees of the Lesser Vehicle; that the second wheel consists of the Perfection of Wisdom Sūtras and the like, which were taught for the sake of trainees of the Great Vehicle; and that the third wheel, which includes the *Sūtra Unravelling the Thought* itself, was taught for the sake of both Lesser Vehicle and Great Vehicle trainees. The *Sūtra Unravelling the Thought* teaches that the third wheel is the highest and most direct. However, this teaching is for Proponents of Mind Only; the Consequence School, which is considered by most Tibetan orders to be the highest system of tenets and which follows the second wheel, holds that this presentation of the three wheels itself requires interpretation.

All inferior proponents of tenets, the six teachers of the Forders[1] and so forth were quelled by Buddha's magnificence; and his precious teaching, a source of help and happiness, flourished and spread widely. Later on, commentators explained individually the thought of the three wheels, and thus the four schools of tenets arose. Of these four, the two schools that propound [truly existent external] objects [the Great Exposition School and the Sūtra School] follow the first wheel. The Proponents of Non-Entityness[2] [Proponents of the Middle Way School] follow the second wheel; and the Yogic Practitioners[3] [Proponents of Mind Only] follow the third wheel. All four schools make definitive presentations of the three—basis, paths, and fruits—following their respective wheels.

The number of schools of tenets that follow our teacher is definitely four: the two Lesser Vehicle

---

1 *mu stegs pa, tīrthika.*

2 *ngo bo nyid med par smra ba, niḥsvabhāvavādin.*

3 *rnal 'byor spyod pa ba, yogācāra.*

schools, Great Exposition School and Sūtra School, and the two Great Vehicle schools, Mind Only School and Middle Way School.

> The order of the schools, as presented by almost all orders of Tibetan Buddhism, is, from top to bottom:

Great Vehicle

- Middle Way School
  - Consequence School
  - Autonomy School
- Mind Only School
  - Followers of Reasoning
  - Followers of Scripture

Lesser Vehicle

- Sūtra School
  - Followers of Reasoning
  - Followers of Scripture
- Great Exposition School – eighteen subschools

This is so because it is said that there is no fifth system of tenets apart from these four and that there is no fourth vehicle apart from the three vehicles [Hearer, Solitary Realizer, and Bodhisattva vehicles]. Vajragarbha's *Commentary on the Condensation of the Hevajra Tantra*[1] says:

> It is not the Subduer's thought that a fourth [vehicle]

---

[1] *kye'i rdo rje bsdus pa'i don gyi rgya cher 'grel pa, hevajrapiṇḍārthaṭīkā.* The *Hevajra Tantra* itself has been translated by David L. Snellgrove in *The Hevajra Tantra, A Critical Study*, (London: Oxford University Press, 1959), Parts 1 and 2.

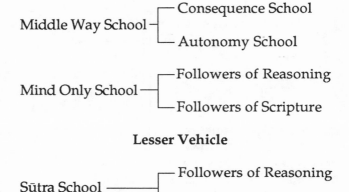

Or a fifth [school of tenets] exists for Buddhists.

When the [other] Buddhist schools—the Autonomy, Mind Only, Sūtra, and Great Exposition Schools—are weighed by the Consequence School, they are all found to fall to extremes of permanence and annihilation. However, the Autonomists and below each maintain that their own system is a middle [way school] because they claim that they assert a middle free from the two extremes of permanence and annihilation. Moreover, each of the four schools of tenets has a different way of avoiding the extremes of permanence and annihilation.

> To hold an extreme of permanence is to superimpose existence on what actually does not exist, as in holding that a unitary and independent self exists. To hold an extreme of annihilation is to deny the existence of something that actually does exist, as in holding that there is no liberation from cyclic existence or that phenomena do not exist at all.

The Proponents of the Great Exposition maintain that they avoid the extreme of permanence because [they assert that] when an effect is produced, its causes cease. They say that they also avoid the extreme of annihilation because [they assert that] an effect arises after the termination of a cause.

The Proponents of Sūtra say that they avoid the extreme of annihilation through asserting that the continuum of a compounded phenomenon exists continuously.

> For example, they assert that when a table is burned, even though the continuum of similar type of the compounded phenomenon—namely the continuum of a specific table—is severed, a continuation of the substance is not severed because ashes remain.

The Proponents of Sūtra maintain that they are also free from the extreme of permanence because [of their assertion that] compounded phenomena disintegrate from moment to moment.

The Proponents of Mind Only say that they avoid the extreme of permanence by [asserting that] imputational natures do not truly exist. They say that they also avoid the extreme of annihilation through [asserting] the true existence of dependent natures.

The Proponents of the Middle Way School maintain that they are free from the extreme of annihilation because [they assert] the conventional existence of all phenomena. They consider that they are free from the extreme of permanence because [they assert that] all phenomena whatsoever are without ultimate existence.

Although those tenets of the lower schools that are not shared by the higher schools are refuted by the higher schools of tenets, an understanding of the lower views is an excellent method for gaining an understanding of the higher views. Therefore, you should not despise the lower tenets just because you hold the higher tenets to be superior.

The definition of a proponent of Buddhist tenets is: a person who asserts the four seals which are the views testifying that a doctrine is Buddha's. The four seals are:

1 All compounded phenomena are impermanent.
2 All contaminated things are miserable.
3 All phenomena are selfless.
4 Nirvana is peace.

> Each of the Buddhist schools has its own particular interpretation of these four. The following interpretation is accepted by all four schools: Compounded phenomena are things such as chairs and tables that are produced in dependence on an aggregation of major and

minor causes. Uncompounded phenomena are phenomena such as space that are not produced in dependence on major or minor causes. Contaminated things are those phenomena that are under the influence of contaminated actions and afflictive emotions. Phenomena are selfless in the sense that they are empty of being a permanent, unitary, independent self or of being the objects of use of such a self. Nirvana is peace because peace is not bestowed by Indra, or anyone else, but is achieved by one's own individual passing beyond the afflictions of desire, hatred, and ignorance.

Objection: In that case, the Vātsīputrīyas [a subschool of the Great Exposition School] would not be proponents of Buddhist tenets because they assert a self of persons.

Answer: There is no such fallacy because the self that they assert is a self-sufficient, substantially existent self whereas the selflessness of the four seals refers to the absence of a permanent, unitary, independent self and that [selflessness] is asserted even by the five Saṃmitīya schools [—the Vātsīputrīyas being one of the five—although they do assert an inexpressible self].

In his *Great Exposition of Tenets*[1] Jam-ȳang-shay-b̄a, who is identified as Ḡön-chok-jik-may-w̄ang-b̄o's previous incarnation, does not accept that the Vātsīputrīyas assert a self-sufficient, substantially existent person because they, like the other Proponents of a Person,[2] hold that the person is inexpressible as either substantially existent or imputedly existent, or as the same as or different from the aggre-

[1] *kha* 8b.8-10b.1.

[2] *gang zag smra ba, pudgalavādin.*

gates, whereas a self-sufficient, substantially existent person is necessarily able to stand by itself separate from the aggregates. Thus, although Ḡön-chok-jik-may-w̄ang-b̄o agrees with Jam-ȳang-shay-b̄a that the selflessness mentioned in the four seals refers to 'the absence of a permanent, unitary, independent self', he does not agree with Jam-ȳang-shay-b̄a's position that the Vātsīputrīyas do not assert a substantially existent person. In holding that the Vātsīputrīyas assert a substantially existent person, Ḡön-chok-jik-may-w̄ang-b̄o is probably following his teacher, J̄ang-ḡya Röl-b̄ay-dor-jay, who, in his *Presentation of Tenets*,[1] gives a long refutation of Jam-ȳang-shay-b̄a on this topic. However, Ḡön-chok-jik-may-w̄ang-b̄o does not accept J̄ang-ḡya's conclusion[2] that the Vātsīputrīyas, though Buddhist, are not actual proponents of Buddhist tenets. Ḡön-chok-jik-may-w̄ang-b̄o maintains that they are actual proponents of Buddhist tenets by holding—as does Jam-ȳang-shay-b̄a, as mentioned above—that the selflessness indicated in the four seals refers to 'the absence of a permanent, unitary, independent self'. In this way, Ḡön-chok-jik-may-w̄ang-b̄o does not agree completely with either his previous incarnation, Jam-ȳang-shay-b̄a, or with his teacher J̄ang-ḡya; his critical stance devoid of partisan allegiance is typical of much of his and many others' scholarship and stands in contrast to the work of some scholars whose main aim, it seems, is to uphold their own College's assertions.

---

[1] 77.5-84.12.
[2] 84.4.

4 The Great Exposition School

The presentation of the tenets of the Proponents of the is in four parts: definition, subschools, etymology, and assertions of tenets.[1]

DEFINITION

The definition of a Proponent of the Great Exposition is: a person propounding Lesser Vehicle tenets who does not accept self-cognizing consciousness[2] and who asserts external objects as being truly established.

> This definition must be qualified because it does not exclude Proponents of Sūtra Following Scripture, who also do not assert self-cognizing consciousness but assert truly established external objects. A self-cognizing consciousness is, roughly speaking, a mind's awareness of itself simultaneous with its awareness of an object.

---

[1] Herbert V. Guenther also has translated this and the remaining chapters in *Buddhist Philosophy in Theory and Practice* (Baltimore: Penguin, 1972).

[2] *rang rig, svasaṃvedana.*

SUBSCHOOLS

There are three groups of Proponents of the Great Exposition: Kashmiris, Aparāntakas, and Magadhas.

> There are generally renowned to be eighteen subschools divided, according to various accounts, from two, three, or four basic subschools.[1]

ETYMOLOGY

There is reason for calling the master Vasumitra a 'Proponent of the Great Exposition' [or a 'Proponent of the Particularist School'][2] because he propounds tenets following the *Great Detailed Exposition*[3] and because he propounds that the three times [past, present, and future objects] are particulars [or instances] of substantial entities.[4]

> Their assertions on the three times are discussed in more detail below.

ASSERTIONS OF TENETS

This section has three parts: their assertions on the basis,[5] paths,[6] and fruits.[7]

---

[1] For an excellent discussion of the subschools, see André Bareau, *Les sectes bouddhiques du Petit Véhicule* (Saigon: 1955). For a brief presentation of the modes of division, see Jeffrey Hopkins, *Meditation on Emptiness*, pp. 713-719.

[2] In accordance with the second etymology about to be given.

[3] *bye brag bshad mtsho chen mo, mahāvibhāṣā*. This text was not translated into Tibetan but was translated into Chinese.

[4] *rdzas, dravya*.

[5] *gzhi, sthāpana*.

[6] *lam, mārga*.

[7] *'bras bu, phala*.

ASSERTIONS ON THE BASIS

This section has two parts: assertions regarding objects[1] and assertions regarding object-possessors[2] [subjects].

> A subject (or object-possessor) can be an object of another consciousness, and thus all phenomena, including subjects, are included within objects.

Assertions Regarding Objects

This system asserts that all objects of knowledge[3] are included within five basic categories: appearing forms,[4] main minds,[5] accompanying mental factors,[6], compositional factors not associated [with either minds or mental factors],[7] and uncompounded phenomena.[8]

> Forms are of eleven types: the five sense objects, the five sense powers, and non-revelatory forms. The five sense objects are: (1) colors and shapes, (2) sounds, (3) odors, (4) tastes, and (5) tangible objects. The five sense powers are: (6) eye sense, (7) ear sense, (8) nose sense, (9) tongue sense, and (10) body sense. Non-revelatory forms are, for example, the subtle form of the absence of a vow as in the case of the subtle form of non-virtuous deeds that a butcher would always possess even when not actually engaged in killing.
>
> A main mind is a consciousness apprehend-

---

[1] *yul, viṣaya.*
[2] *yul can, viṣayin.*
[3] *shes bya, jñeya.*
[4] *gzugs, rūpa.*
[5] *sems, citta.*
[6] *sems byung, caitta.*
[7] *ldan pa ma yin pa'i 'du byed, viprayuktasaṃskāra.*
[8] *'dus ma byas, asaṃskṛta.*

> ing the general object, such as an eye consciousness apprehending a table. Mental factors accompany main minds and apprehend the particulars of an object, for example, the pleasantness or unpleasantness of a table. Ten mental factors accompany all main minds: feeling, intention, discrimination, aspiration, contact, intelligence, mindfulness, mental engagement, interest, and stabilization.
>
> Illustrations of compounded phenomena that are not associated with minds or mental factors are the four characteristics of compounded phenomena: production, aging, duration, and disintegration. Etymologically speaking, these are phenomena that are not associated (*ldan min, viprayukta*) with minds or mental factors; more specifically, they are neither form nor consciousness and thus are a separate category.

Moreover, these five objects are 'things'.[1] The definition of a thing is: that which is able to perform a function. Existent,[2] object of knowledge,[3] and thing[4] are mutually inclusive [i.e., whatever is the one is the other].[5] Uncompounded phenomena are considered to be permanent things; forms, consciousnesses, and non-associated compositional factors [which are neither form nor consciousness] are considered to be impermanent things.

---

[1] *dngos po, bhāva.*

[2] *yod pa, sat.*

[3] *shes bya, jñeya.*

[4] *dngos po, bhāva.*

[5] *don gcig, ekārtha.* 'Mutually inclusive' does not indicate that these are necessarily just different names for the same thing, as would be the case with synonyms (*ming gi rnam grangs*); rather, it indicates that whatever is the one is necessarily the other—they are mutually pervasive.

> Among the four Buddhist tenet systems, only this system asserts that a permanent phenomenon such as uncompounded space is able to perform a function and thus is a thing. For instance, the lack of obstructing contact that space affords performs the function of allowing movement to take place. Since both permanent and impermanent phenomena are asserted to be 'things' in this system, functionality is not limited to producing causal sequences; instead, as with uncompounded space, functionality can refer to *allowing* or *opening the way* for something to happen.

All things are necessarily substantially established,[1] but they are not necessarily substantially existent.[2]

> It is clear that if something is substantially existent, this does not necessitate that it is a substance, since impermanence is substantially existent but not a substance. Rather, to be substantially existent means (in accordance with the definition of an ultimate truth given below) that when the object is either broken physically or mentally divided into parts, the awareness of that object is not cancelled.

This is so because they assert that ultimate truths[3] and substantial existents are mutually inclusive and that conventional truths[4] and imputed existents[5] are mutually inclusive.

There are divisions of objects into the two truths and

---

[1] *rdzas grub, dravyasiddha.*
[2] *rdzas yod, dravayasat.*
[3] *don dam bden pa, paramārthasatya.*
[4] *kun rdzob bden pa, saṃvṛtisatya.*
[5] *btags yod, prajñaptisat.*

into the contaminated[1] and uncontaminated.[2] Also [with regard to this discussion of objects] there is a teaching of other ancillary topics.

The two truths

The definition of a conventional truth is: a phenomenon which is such that when it is broken up or mentally separated into individual parts, the awareness apprehending that object is cancelled. A clay pot and a rosary are illustrations[3] of conventional truths because, if a clay pot is broken with a hammer, the awareness apprehending that object as a clay pot is cancelled; and, if the beads of a rosary are separated, the awareness apprehending that object as a rosary is cancelled.

> With respect to the term 'illustration', the Sanskrit term *lakṣya* also translates into Tibetan as *mtshon bya*, 'definiendum'. In the triad of definition, definiendum, and illustration, the definition of a thing (*dngos po, bhāva*), for example, is: that which is capable of performing a function.[4] The definiendum is thing. An illustration is a pot. As can readily be seen, the definiendum and an illustration are markedly different. Technically speaking:[5]
>
> > An illustration is defined as: that which serves as a basis for illustrating the appropriate definiendum by way of its defini-

---

[1] *zag bcas, sāsrava.*
[2] *zag med, anāsrava.*
[3] *mtshan gzhi, lakṣya.*
[4] *don byed nus pa, arthakriyāśakti/ arthakriyakāritva.*
[5] Daniel Perdue, *Debate in Tibetan Buddhist Education* (forthcoming from Snow Lion Publications), Part 3, pp. 12ff.

> tion.[1] ... [An illustration] cannot be such that understanding [it] ...effectively serves as understanding all of the essential characteristics of the illustrated object. That is, in order to be a valid illustrator (*mtshon byed*) of something, a phenomenon must be such that although someone might have realized the illustration, that person would not necessarily have realized that which it illustrates. For instance, a gold pot is a proper illustration of a functioning thing because it is a functioning thing and merely through having ascertained a gold pot with valid cognition, one would not necessarily have ascertained functioning thing itself with valid cognition. ... A gold pot indicates functioning thing by way of being able to perform a function; thus, it *illustrates* or *demonstrates* the meaning of functioning thing.
>
> On the other hand, a gold pot is not a proper illustration of a pot because, although it is a pot, if someone has ascertained a gold pot with valid cognition, that person must have ascertained pot with valid cognition. It is not possible for one to know the meaning of a gold pot and not know the meaning of pot.

Thus, it is clear that an illustration not only is not the definiendum itself but also is not constituted merely by instances of an object. This distinction was a Tibetan development, and thus, when *mtshan gzhi* refers to an illustration and not to the definiendum, it is clearly not

---

[1] *mtshan nyid kyis skabs su bab pa'i mtshon bya mtshon pa'i gzhir gyur pa.*

suitable to translate it as 'definiendum' by referring back to the Sanskrit which does not make this distinction.[1]

The definition of an ultimate truth is: a phenomenon which is such that when it is broken up or mentally separated into individual parts, the consciousness apprehending that object is not cancelled. Illustrations of ultimate truths are directionally partless particles, temporally partless moments of consciousness, and uncompounded space.

In this system, the smallest units of matter are asserted to be directionally partless, but this does not mean that they are partless in general; even the smallest particle has factors relating to its production, duration, and cessation and factors relating to the production of effects, and so forth. Similarly, the smallest temporal unit of consciousness is temporally partless but is not partless in general; for example, one instant of an eye consciousness can have many parts that apprehend the various colors of a tile floor.

For, Vasubandhu's *Treasury of Manifest Knowledge* says:[2]

---

[1] Dzong-ka-ba speaks to this issue in his *Ocean of Reasoning, Explanation of (Nāgārjuna's) 'Treatise on the Middle Way'* (*dbu ma rtsa ba'i tshig le'ur byas pa shes rab ces bya ba'i rnam bshad rigs pa'i rgya mtsho*), (Sarnath, India: Pleasure of Elegant Sayings Printing Press, no date), 141.14-141.20.

[2] *chos mngon pa'i mdzod, abhidharmakośa*; VI.4: *yatra bhinnena tadbuddhiranyāpohe dhiyā ca tat/ ghaṭāmbuvat saṃvṛtisat paramārthasadanythā//*. For a Sanskrit edition, see *Abhidharmakośa & Bhāṣya of Ācārya Vasubandhu with Sphuṭārtha Commentary of Ācārya Yaṣomitra*, Swami Dwarikadas Shastri, ed., Bauddha Bharati Series no.5. (Banaras: Bauddha Bharati, 1970). For a translation into French, see Louis de La Vallée Poussin, *L'Abhidharmakośa de Vasubandhu* (Paris: Geuthner, 1923-31). Vasubandhu flourished around 360 C.E.

A thing which is such that, if broken or mentally separated into others [i.e. parts],
An awareness of it no longer operates,
Such as a pot or water, is conventionally existent.
[All] others are ultimately existent.

> Since a single minute particle of water is an ultimate truth, Vasubandhu's reference must be to a quantity of water, such as in a cup or even a river.

Therefore, it is asserted that conventional truths are not ultimately established,[1] although they are truly established.[2] This is because this system asserts that all things are necessarily truly established.

The contaminated and the uncontaminated

The definition of a contaminated object is: a phenomenon that is amenable to the increase of contaminations from the point of view of being either an object of observation[3] or an [afflicted] concomitant. The five mental and physical aggregates[4] are illustrations of contaminated objects.

> However, not all phenomena included in the five mental and physical aggregates are illustrations of contaminated phenomena because, for instance, true paths—the fourth of the four noble truths—are included in the five aggregates but are not contaminated objects.
>
> A table, for example, is a contaminated phenomenon not because it possesses the afflictive

---

[1] *don dam par grub pa, paramārthasiddha.*
[2] *bden par grub pa, satyasiddha.*
[3] *dmigs pa, ālambana.*
[4] *phung po, skandha.*

> emotions[1] of desire, hatred, or ignorance but because it can act as an object of observation that increases those afflictive emotions, especially desire, in the perceiver. An afflicted concomitant can be an afflicted main mind that accompanies afflicted mental factors or an afflicted mental factor that accompanies an afflicted main mind or other afflicted mental factors. An illustration is the mental factor of desire that accompanies the perception of an attractive object and could increase the afflictive emotions of the main mind and other mental factors accompanying it.
>
> All phenomena that are contaminated objects from the viewpoint of being afflicted concomitants are also contaminated from the viewpoint of being objects of observation because they can increase afflictive emotions in other beings who take cognizance of them, or they can increase one's own afflictive emotions if one should take cognizance of them at a later time, as in the case of desire. However, all phenomena that are contaminated objects from the viewpoint of being objects of observation are not necessarily contaminated from the viewpoint of being afflicted concomitants, such as an attractive table which could never be an afflicted concomitant because it is not a mind or a mental factor.

The definition of an uncontaminated object is: a phenomenon that is not amenable to the increase of contaminations from the viewpoint of being either an object of observation or a mental concomitant. True paths and uncompounded phenomena are illustrations, for,

---

[1] *nyon mongs, kleśa.*

Vasubandhu's *Treasury of Manifest Knowledge* says,[1] 'Except for true paths, all compounded phenomena are contaminated'; and,[2] 'The uncontaminated consists of true paths and the three uncompounded phenomena.'

> When true paths are objects of observation or mental concomitants, they destroy contamination and do not increase it. Uncompounded space as an object of observation cannot destroy contamination, but does not increase it. The three uncompounded phenomena are: non-analytical cessations, analytical cessations, and uncompounded spaces. A non-analytical cessation is a cessation that occurs as a result of the incompleteness of the conditions for its production, such as the lack of hunger at the time of intensely concentrating on conversation. Once the moment has passed, the fact that one had no desire for food at that time will never change, and for this reason, its cessation is said to be permanent. An analytical cessation is an eradication of an obstruction such that it will never occur again, as in the case of a complete cessation forever of a particular type of desire through meditation on the four noble truths.

All contaminated objects are to be abandoned, for [even] the two paths of accumulation and preparation,[3] are to be abandoned.

> The paths of accumulation and preparation are not actual antidotes to afflictive emotions and

---

[1] I.4b-c1; *saṃskṛtā mārgavarjitāḥ sāsravāḥ.*

[2] I.5a-b: *anāsravā mārgasatyaṃ trividhaṃ cāpyasaṃskṛtam.*

[3] *tshogs lam, saṃbhāramārga; sbyor lam, prayogamārga.* More literally, the latter is translated as 'path of connection' or 'path of linking' since it connects or links the practitioner to the path of seeing.

> thus do not eliminate them; they are virtues of common beings and, therefore, suitable to increase desire.

The path of seeing[1] is completely uncontaminated.

> The path of seeing consists solely of direct contemplation of the four truths and occurs only in one meditative session; thus, it is only uncontaminated.

Paths of meditation[2] and paths of no more learning[3] both have instances of contaminated and uncontaminated paths.

> On both the path of meditation and the path of no more learning there are instances when yogis cultivate worldly paths, such as the eight absorptions, for the sake of increasing their mental capacity. These worldly paths are paths of meditation. They are contaminated from the viewpoint of being objects of observation because, through taking cognizance of them, afflictive emotions not only are not eliminated but also are suitable to increase in the sense that someone could become desirous of these states. One who has attained the path of no more learning no longer has any afflictive emotions; therefore, training in the eight absorptions could not increase afflictive emotions for that person, but these worldly paths could increase the desire of others who notice them. Worldly paths in the continuum of one who has attained the path of no more learning are, therefore, contaminated from the viewpoint of

---

[1] *mthong lam, darśanamārga.*
[2] *sgom lam, bhāvanāmārga.*
[3] *mi slob lam, aśaikṣamārga.*

being objects of observation but not from the viewpoint of being afflicted concomitants because they themselves are not afflicted in the sense that desire, for instance, is afflicted.

All superior[1] paths are necessarily uncontaminated, but the paths in the continuum of a Superior are not necessarily uncontaminated. This is because a path that is in the continuum of one on the path of meditation and has the aspect of reflecting on the peacefulness [of higher levels] and the coarseness [of the present level] is contaminated [as in the case of generating the eight absorptions in their mundane form].

All Buddhist schools, except the Great Exposition School and the Sūtra School Following Scripture, maintain that a superior path and a path in the continuum of a Superior are mutually inclusive—whatever is the one is the other. The Great Exposition School, however, states the example of one who meditates on the advantages of the First Concentration, such as peacefulness and long life, and on the disadvantages of the Desire Realm, such as coarseness, ugliness, and short life, in order to do away with manifest desire for the objects of the Desire Realm. By meditating thus, a yogi can attain a higher state of concentration and can suppress manifest afflictive emotions, but cannot get rid of the seeds of the afflictive emotions. Many non-Buddhists attain their 'liberation' through this means; however, because of the fault of not destroying the seeds of desire by means of analytical cessation, such 'liberation' is only temporary. In the specific case mentioned in the text, the meditator is a

1 *'phags pa, ārya.*

> Superior on the path of meditation. On this path, those of greater intelligence simultaneously rid themselves of the afflictive emotions together with their seeds, level by level in nine stages (see chart p. 213). However, the Superiors being discussed here are of duller faculties and suppress manifest afflictive emotions first by means of a worldly path, which can serve to increase afflictive emotions in the ways mentioned earlier. Only afterwards do they go on to rid themselves of the seeds of those afflictive emotions.

Other ancillary topics

The three times [past, present, and future objects] are asserted to be substantial entities because the Proponents of the Great Exposition maintain that a pot exists even at the time of the past of a pot and that a pot exists even at the time of the future of a pot.

> Yesterday's pot exists today as a past pot. The past of a thing occurs after its present existence, that is, after its present existence has passed. Tomorrow's pot exists today as a future pot. The future of a thing occurs before its present existence, that is, when its present existence is yet to be. Today's pot exists as a present pot today.

Although they assert that both negative phenomena[1] and positive phenomena[2] exist, they do not accept the existence of non-affirming negatives[3] because they

---

[1] *dgag pa, pratiṣedha.*
[2] *sgrub pa, vidhi.*
[3] *med dgag, prasajyapratiṣedha.*

assert that all negatives are necessarily affirming negatives.[1]

> A positive phenomenon such as a table does not require the explicit negation of its being non-table in order for that table to appear to a conceptual consciousness, but a negative phenomenon such as non-table entails an explicit negation of table in order for it to appear to a conceptual consciousness. The Proponents of the Great Exposition consider that there is always something affirmative about a negative because their system always deals with substantially established entities. This emphasis on substantiality sets in relief the tendency of the higher schools to become less and less substance oriented, and these variations are especially significant as regards the schools' different modes of arriving at their interpretations of emptiness.

The Kashmiri Proponents of the Great Exposition accord with the Proponents of Sūtra in asserting that the continuum of consciousness is the base that connects actions (*las, karma*) with their effects.

> Every Buddhist system has to deal with the issue of providing for an uninterrupted base to connect karmic cause with karmic fruit. The Kashmiris say that the continuum of the mental consciousness[2] is the base that allows the continued chain of actions and their fruits to prevail from life to life. This is because the mental consciousness, unlike the other five consciousnesses, functions even in deep sleep and in the meditative absorption of cessation.

---

[1] *ma yin dgag, paryudāsapratiṣedha.*
[2] *yid kyi rnam shes, manovijñāna.*

All Proponents of the Great Exposition, except for the Kashmiris, assert that a compositional phenomenon that is neither form nor consciousness is the base that connects actions with their fruits. This is an obtainer[1] and a 'non-wastage'[2] which is like a seal that guarantees a loan [preventing the loan from becoming a loss to the lender].

Both this system and the Consequence School assert that actions of body and speech have form.

> The other Buddhist systems assert physical and verbal actions (*las, karma*) to be mental. Proponents of the Great Exposition and Consequentialists reason that speech is sound and that sound is form; therefore, speech is form. Also, there is coarse and subtle form. Speech that has coarse form is, for example, that heard when a person speaks. Speech that has subtle form is, for example, the pure speech manifested by a monk who, even when silent, is keeping a vow not to speak lies and so forth. Although unheard by either himself or others, it nevertheless exists. Examples of bodily actions that have subtle form are the ethical deeds of a Superior in meditative equipoise. These would not be seen by others, but could be seen by someone with high clairvoyance, such as a Buddha.
>
> The Proponents of Sūtra, Proponents of Mind Only, and Autonomists maintain that actions of body and speech are actually mental factors of intention.[3]

All compounded phenomena are necessarily imperma-

---

[1] *thob pa, prāpti.*
[2] *chud mi za ba, avipraṇāśa.*
[3] *sems pa, cetanā.*

nent but do not necessarily disintegrate moment by moment, for the Proponents of the Great Exposition assert that following production there is the activity of duration, and then the activity of disintegration occurs.

> All Buddhist schools agree that coarse impermanence is the production of a thing such as a table, its lasting for a period of time, and finally its disintegration such as its being consumed by fire. Buddhist schools also assert a subtle impermanence that, except for developed yogis, is not accessible to direct experience. For example, death, which is an instance of coarse impermanence, is clearly experienced, but the momentary aging of a person, which is a subtle impermanence, is not.
>
> The Proponents of the Great Exposition differ from the other Buddhist schools in asserting that the factors of production, abiding, aging, and disintegration are external to the entity that undergoes these. All other systems hold that production itself is a cause or sufficient condition for disintegration; disintegration begins *with,* and not after, the very first moment of production. In all systems except the Great Exposition School, that which is produced is that which abides and that which disintegrates. This is because production is understood to be the arising of a new entity due to certain causes; abiding is the continued existence of that type of entity; disintegration is its quality of not lasting a second moment; and aging is the factor of its being a different entity from the entity of the previous moment. In this way, the four can occur simultaneously. The Great Exposition School, however, asserts that the factors of production, duration, aging,

and disintegration act on the object and occur in series, one after the other.

Assertions Regarding Object-Possessors [Subjects]

This section has three parts: [the Great Exposition School's] assertions regarding persons, consciousnesses, and terms.

Every consciousness has an object and thus is an object-possessor. Every name or term expresses a meaning that is its object, and thus is an object-possessor. Every person possesses objects and is an object possessor in this sense.

Persons

The mere collection of the mental and physical aggregates[1] that are its basis of imputation is an illustration of a person.

'Illustration of a person'[2] refers to what is found upon analyzing what a person is. Thus, even the subschools of the Great Exposition School which hold that there is no substantially existent person assert that the mere collection of mind and body is the person.

Some of the five Saṃmitīya subschools assert that all five aggregates are an illustration of a person.

There is controversy on whether this means that they assert that *each* of the five aggregates individually can be an illustration of a person or whether only all five *together* can.

---

1 *phung po, skandha.*
2 *gang zag gi mtshan gzhi.*

The Avantakas assert that the mind alone is an illustration of a person.

Consciousnesses

This section has two parts: the [Great Exposition School's] assertions regarding prime cognitions[1] and assertions regarding non-prime consciousnesses.[2]

> 'Consciousness' is used here as a general term referring both to minds and mental factors.

PRIME COGNITIONS

There are direct prime cognitions[3] and inferential prime cognitions.[4]

> Buddhist psychological terms that signify a consciousness that perceives an object are often rendered in English by words such as 'perception' or 'cognition' which tend to indicate either the act or object of perception and cognition rather than the agent. Therefore, it is important to remember that these terms are understood as referring to the perceiving consciousness, the cognizing consciousness as agent.

With regard to direct prime cognitions, they assert sense direct perceptions, mental direct perceptions, and yogic direct perceptions [such as direct cognitions of the four noble truths and their sixteen attributes, impermanence and so forth]. They do not accept self-cognition as

---

[1] *tshad ma, pramāṇa.* As will be explained in the next chapter, the *pra* of *pramāṇa* is taken to mean 'new' and thus has been translated as 'prime'.

[2] *tshad min gyi shes pa, apramāṇabuddhi.*

[3] *mngon sum gyi tshad ma, pratyakṣapramāṇa.*

[4] *rjes su dpag pa'i tshad ma, anumānapramāṇa.*

a direct perception.

> Sense direct perceptions are the five sense consciousnesses. For a brief discussion of mental direct perceptions, see the next chapter. Self-cognition refers to a consciousness that is non-dualistically aware of a consciousness. Roughly speaking, it is that part of a consciousness which is aware of its own cognizing activity; all systems that accept this type of consciousness assert that it is the same entity as the consciousness that it knows and that it cognizes the consciousness in a non-dualistic manner. For this reason, self-cognition is rejected by the Proponents of the Great Exposition, Proponents of Sūtra Following Scripture, Sūtra Autonomists, and Consequentialists, for they maintain that agent and object would be confused if such existed. The other schools assert the existence of self-cognition mainly on the basis of common experience in which the seer of an object is remembered as well as the object that was seen, thus showing that the subjective element is registered in awareness. For, if the subjective element were not experienced, there would be no memory of the subjective side of a cognition.

[Unlike the other schools] the Proponents of the Great Exposition assert that a sense direct prime cognition is not necessarily a consciousness because a physical eye sense is a common locus of being matter [not consciousness], of being a perception, and of being a prime cognition.

> They do not assert that a sense power[1] alone can perceive an object, nor do they assert that

[1] *dbang po, indriya.*

> a sense consciousness alone is capable of doing so. They maintain that the two together perceive an object; and consequently they, unlike all other Buddhist schools, assert that both sense powers and sense consciousnesses are perceivers.

They assert that a sense consciousness comprehends its object nakedly, without taking on the aspect of that object. Also, they assert that even a physical eye sense power which is the base [of an eye consciousness] perceives form, for they say that if a consciousness alone were the seer, then one would see forms that are obstructed by walls and so forth.

> Because a consciousness does not have form, it is not obstructed by form; however, because the support of the eye consciousness is a physical sense power, the seer also incorporates form and so is obstructed by form.

A mind and its mental factors are asserted to be different substantial entities.

> A mind and its accompanying mental factors are each instances of consciousness and possess five similar qualities. An example of this is an inferential consciousness cognizing that a sound is an impermanent thing. Here the main mind is a mental consciousness, and the accompanying mental factors include the ten omnipresent factors: feeling, intention, discrimination, aspiration, contact, intelligence, mindfulness, mental engagement, interest, and stabilization. The five qualities that this mind and its accompanying mental factors share are: (1) they have the same basic object, the sound; (2) they have the same 'aspect object', the impermanent sound; (3) they have the same sense as

their base, namely, the mental sense which is a previous moment of the mental consciousness; (4) they are simultaneous; (5) their entities are the same in number—the mental consciousness is only one and the feeling, for instance, that accompanies it is only one. Only the Proponents of the Great Exposition say that a mind and its mental factors are different substantial entities; the other schools assert that they are the same entity.

[NON-PRIME CONSCIOUSNESSES

Non-prime consciousnesses are wrong consciousness and so forth.][1]

There are five types of consciousness that are not new and/or incontrovertible cognitions: wrong consciousness, doubt, subsequent cognition, correctly assuming consciousness, and a consciousness to which an object appears without being noticed (see the next chapter).

Terms

Mere sounds in general are divided into two types, sounds arisen from elements conjoined with consciousness and sounds arisen from elements not conjoined

---

[1] This line (*gnyis pa ni tshad min gyi shes pa la log shes sogs yod do*) is missing in the Collected Works edition (501.4), the Peking edition (10a.5), the Go-mang 1980 edition (23.14), and the Tibet Go-mang 1987 edition (8b.4) but is in the Dharamsala 1967 edition (23.10) and the Teacher Training edition (23.7), from which it is incorporated into Mimaki (80.10). The Go-mang 1980 edition (2.6) reports that the line has unnecessarily been added and does not appear in any of the three editions that they used. We agree that the line is a later addition for the sake of symmetry and completeness, and thus we have included it but in brackets since it clearly was not in the original.

with consciousness. An example of the first is the voice of a sentient being. An example of the second is the sound of a river.

Sounds arisen from elements conjoined with consciousness and sounds arisen from elements not conjoined with consciousness are each divided into two types: sounds that intentionally indicate meaning to sentient beings and sounds that do not intentionally indicate meaning to sentient beings.

> An example of a sound arisen from elements conjoined with consciousness that intentionally indicates meaning is the spoken expression 'house'. An example of a sound arisen from elements conjoined with consciousness that does not intentionally indicate meaning is the sound of a spontaneous hiccup. An example of a sound arisen from elements not conjoined with consciousness that intentionally indicates meaning is the sound of the great drum in the Heaven of the Thirty-Three which conveys the message of impermanence and so forth to its listeners. An example of a sound arisen from elements not conjoined with consciousness that does not intentionally indicate meaning is the sound of an ordinary running brook.

Sound that intentionally indicates meaning to sentient beings, sound that reveals meaning through speech, and expressive sound are mutually inclusive. Sound that does not intentionally indicate meaning, sound that does not reveal meaning through speech, and non-expressive sound are mutually inclusive.

> This requires qualification because there are sounds that intentionally indicate meaning to sentient beings, such as the sound of the drum in the Heaven of the Thirty-Three, but do not

reveal meaning through speech.

The word of Buddha and the treatises[1] are both asserted to be entities that are collections of letters, stems, and words.[2] They are accepted as generic images of sounds[3] and as non-associated compositional factors.[4] Therefore, one wonders whether in this system matter and non-associated compositional factors are not mutually exclusive.

> About the word of Buddha, Vasubandhu's *Treasury of Manifest Knowledge*[5] says:
>
> Those eighty thousand bundles of doctrine
> Which were spoken by the Subduer
> Are names and are included among [non-associated] compositional factors.
>
> Since names are sounds and sounds are material forms, it appears that the Proponents of the Great Exposition assert that the words of Buddha are both material and non-associated compositional factors.[6]

---

[1] *bstan bcos, śāstra.*

[2] 'Stems' (*ming, nāma*) are uninflected, whereas 'words' (*tshig, pāda*) are inflected.

[3] *sgra spyi, śabdasāmānya*; literally, sound-generalities.

[4] *ldan min 'du byed, viprayuktasaṃskāra.* In the other systems, generic images are not asserted to be non-associated compositional factors, which are impermanent, but instead are asserted to be permanent; for discussion, see the next chapter.

[5] I.25: *dharmaskandhasahasrāṇi yānyaśītiṃ jagau muniḥ/ tāni vāṅ nāma ve'tyeṣāṃ rūpasaṃskārasaṃgrahaḥ//.*

[6] As Ngak-w̄ang-b̄el-den's *Annotations for (Jam-ȳang-shay-b̄a's) 'Great Exposition of Tenets'* (*dngos*, 48.1) says, it is difficult to posit that something could be both obstructive (*thogs bcas*) due to being material and unobstructive (*thogs med*) due to being a non-associated compositional factor. Ḡön-chok-jik-may-w̄ang-b̄o is most likely taking his lead from Jam-ȳang-shay-b̄a's *Great Exposition of Tenets* (*kha* 13b.1) where he indicates just such an assertion.

An apparent complication is that Ḡön-chok-jik-may-w̄ang-b̄o has interpreted Vasubandhu's reference to 'names' as generic images of sounds, which are not material. Also, if 'names' are merely generic images of sounds, it could be asked whether the Proponents of the Great Exposition assert that the sounds heard from the mouth of Buddha, which are forms and thus material phenomena, are not the word of Buddha, for the word of Buddha would be comprised of the generic images of the sounds that appeared to Buddha's mind before he expressed the particular sounds. For instance, before one says the word 'tree' the generic image of the sound 'tree' first appears, and then the sound is spoken. This image of the sound 'tree' is asserted to be a non-associated compositional factor and thus neither form (matter) nor consciousness. One might then wonder whether the Proponents of the Great Exposition would say that the sounds heard from the mouth of Buddha are not the word of Buddha.

ASSERTIONS ON THE PATHS

This section has three parts: the Great Exposition School's assertions regarding the objects of observation of the paths, objects abandoned by the paths, and the nature of the paths.

Objects of Observation of the Paths

The objects of observation are the sixteen attributes of the four truths, impermanence and so forth.

There are four attributes to each of the four truths. The attributes of the first, true sufferings, are impermanence, misery, emptiness,

> and selflessness. The attributes of the second, true origins, are cause, origin, strong production, and condition. The attributes of the third, true cessations, are cessation, pacification, auspiciousness, and definite emergence from a portion of the obstructions. The attributes of the fourth, true paths, are path, suitability, achievement, and deliverance.

Subtle selflessness and subtle selflessness of persons[1] are asserted to be mutually inclusive.

> All selflessnesses are either of persons or of phenomena, and since the Proponents of the Great Exposition do not assert a selflessness of phenomena,[2] for them a subtle selflessness is necessarily a selflessness of persons.

The subtle selflessness of persons is asserted to be a person's emptiness of being substantially existent in the sense of being self-sufficient. From among the eighteen subschools of the Great Exposition School, the five Saṃmitīya subschools do not assert that a person's emptiness of being substantially existent in the sense of being self-sufficient is the subtle selflessness because they consider that a substantially existent or self-sufficient person exists.[3]

The Proponents of the Great Exposition do not assert a presentation of coarse and subtle selflessnesses of phenomena because they hold that all established bases [i.e., such as mind, body, house, and so on] have a self of phenomena [that is, they truly exist and have a difference of entity of subject and object].

---

[1] *gang zag gi bdag med, pudgalanairātmya.*
[2] *chos kyi bdag med, dharmanairātmya.*
[3] See the end of the previous chapter (pp. 177-178) for discussion of the author's partial agreement and partial disagreement with Jam-ȳang-shay-b̄a on this issue.

> When the Proponents of the Great Exposition speak of a subtle self of persons, they mean a person that is seen as having a character different from the mental and physical aggregates. This definition of 'self' applies only to persons because phenomena are not conceived this way. Therefore, within the context of their own perspective, it is possible for the Proponents of the Great Exposition to maintain the existence of a self of phenomena, such as their true existence, and to deny the existence of a self of persons.

Objects Abandoned by the Paths

There are two types of ignorance to be abandoned through the path: afflictive ignorance and non-afflictive ignorance. The first, afflictive ignorance, mainly prevents the attainment of liberation. Illustrations of afflictive ignorance are a consciousness conceiving a self of persons and the three poisons [desire, hatred, and ignorance] which arise on account of this conception, as well as their seeds.

Non-afflictive ignorance mainly prevents the attainment of all-knowingness. Illustrations of non-afflictive ignorance are the four causes of non-knowingness, such as the non-afflictive obstruction that is the ignorance of the profound and subtle qualities of a Buddha.

> The other three causes of non-knowingness are ignorance due to the distant place of the object, ignorance due to the distant time of the object, and ignorance due to the nature of the object, such as the subtle details of the relationship of karmic causes with their effects.
>
> The all-knowingness mentioned here is not a Buddha's quality of omniscience as it is under-

> stood by the Great Vehicle tenet systems. All-knowingness here simply means that if a Buddha thinks about objects, seen or unseen, a Buddha will know those things one by one. The Great Vehicle tenet systems, however, assert that a Buddha can know all things simultaneously and instantaneously, without exerting any effort of thought. The Proponents of the Great Exposition do not accept such omniscience, and, therefore, they do not assert obstructions to omniscience; they merely distinguish between afflictive and non-afflictive ignorance. The Great Vehicle tenet systems distinguish between an ignorance that is an afflictive obstruction and a non-afflictive ignorance that is an obstruction to omniscience.

With respect to the obstructions, aside from obstructions to liberation and non-afflictive ignorance, the Proponents of the Great Exposition do not accept the designation 'obstructions to omniscience'.[1]

Nature of the Paths

With respect to the paths of the three vehicles [Hearer,[2] Solitary Realizer,[3] and Bodhisattva[4]] they assert a presentation of the five paths—path of accumulation,[5] path of preparation,[6] path of seeing,[7] path of meditation,[8] and path of no more learning.[9] However, they do not

---

[1] *shes sgrib, jñeyāvaraṇa.*
[2] *nyan thos, śrāvaka.*
[3] *rang rgyal/ rang sangs rgyas, svajina/pratyekabuddha.*
[4] *byang chub sems dpa', bodhisattva.*
[5] *tshogs lam, sambhāramārga.*
[6] *sbyor lam, prayogamārga.*
[7] *mthong lam, darśanamārga.*
[8] *sgom la, bhāvanāmārga.*
[9] *mi slob lam, aśaikṣamārga.*

accept the exalted wisdoms of the ten [Bodhisattva] grounds.[1]

They assert that the first fifteen of the sixteen moments of forbearance and knowledge constitute the path of seeing, and that the sixteenth moment, which is called subsequent knowledge of the path, is [the beginning of] the path of meditation [see chart, next page].[2]

> The path of seeing is the time when direct cognition of the four noble truths first occurs. The paths of forbearance are so called because one develops facility, or non-fear, with respect to the object of meditation; they are also called uninterrupted paths[3] because they lead without interruption into paths of release[4] in the same meditative sitting. These paths of release are the paths of knowledge, or the knowledge that certain afflictive emotions have been abandoned.

They assert that the generation [of these sixteen moments] occurs no other way than serially [one step at a time], like a goat walking over a bridge.

---

[1] *sa, bhūmi*. These are ten stages or levels that, according to the Great Vehicle tenet systems, begin with the path of seeing. They are called 'grounds' because, just as the earth or ground is the basis of all the forests and so forth that depend on it, they serve as bases for the production of a Bodhisattva's increasingly marvelous qualities.

[2] Among the seven editions of the text used, five (Collected Works, 503.2; Peking edition, 11a.4; Go-mang 1980 edition, 26.5; Tibet Go-mang 1987 edition, 9b.1; and Mimaki, 81.20) read *sgom lam yin la* whereas two (Teacher Training edition, 25.17 and Dharamsala 1967 edition, 26.3) read *sgom lam yin pas*. Both make sense since the latter would mean that *since* they hold that the sixteenth moment marks the beginning of the path of meditation, the sixteen *must* be serially generated. The former, however, most likely represent the original reading.

[3] *bar chad med lam, ānantaryamārga.*

[4] *rnam grol lam, vimuktimārga.*

They envision the process in this way: The four noble truths are the objects contemplated on the path of seeing. For each noble truth there is a path of forbearance and a path of knowledge in relation to the Desire Realm;[1] there is also a path of subsequent forbearance and a path of subsequent knowledge in relation to the higher

Sixteen Moments of Forbearance and Knowledge
(read from bottom to top)

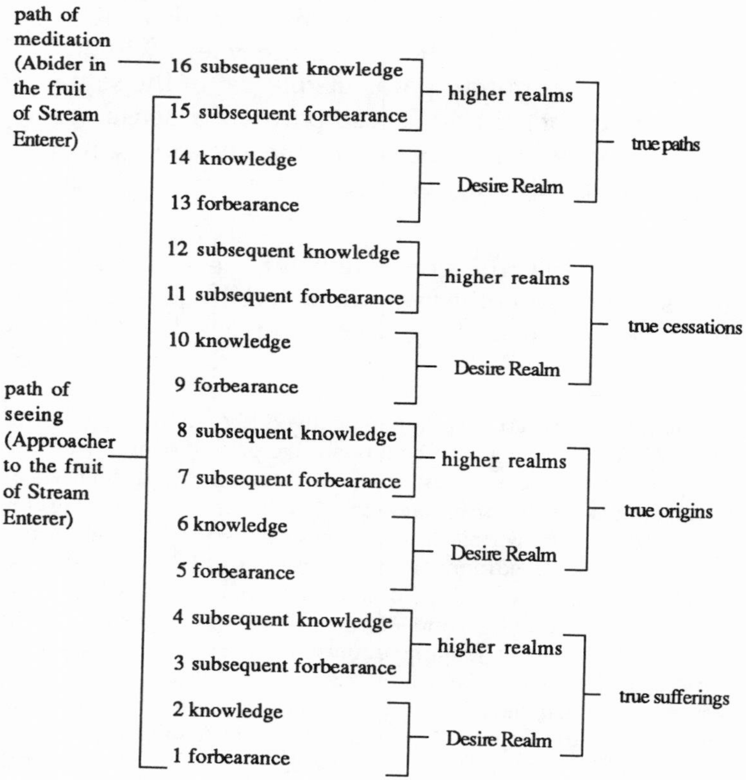

[1] *'dod khams, kāmadhātu.*

realms, the Form and Formless Realms[1] which are here included in one category. When meditators complete the paths of the first truth in relation to the Desire Realm, they then pass on to the paths of the first truth in relation to the Form and Formless Realms. The sixteenth moment is the time of entering the path of meditation. Other schools say that the eight forbearances can occur simultaneously and that the eight knowledges can occur simultaneously.

True paths are not necessarily consciousnesses because the Proponents of the Great Exposition maintain that the five uncontaminated mental and physical aggregates are true paths.

Except for the Great Exposition School and the Sūtra School Following Scripture, all schools assert that true paths are consciousnesses. The Proponents of the Great Exposition include within true paths the five mental and physical aggregates at, for example, the time of the fifteenth moment of the path of seeing. However, it is not the case that every instance of the five aggregates included within a Superior's continuum is a true path and hence uncontaminated. The point is that there *are* instances of each of the aggregates that are true paths and thus uncontaminated. These uncontaminated phenomena are those associated with a Superior's uncontaminated path. Illustrations are a Superior's mental consciousness, the accompanying mental factors of feeling and discrimination, the subtle forms which restrain certain faults and which naturally arise whenever a

---

[1] *gzugs khams, rūpadhātu; gzugs med khams, ārūpyadhātu.*

> Superior is in meditative equipoise in an uncontaminated path, and the predispositions established by this path. All these are uncontaminated objects and are truth paths.

ASSERTIONS ON THE FRUITS OF THE PATHS

Those of the Hearer lineage become familiar with the sixteen attributes [of the four noble truths], impermanence and so forth, during three lifetimes or more. By relying on the vajra-like meditative stabilization[1] of the Hearer path of meditation, they finally abandon the afflictive obstructions by ceasing their obtaining causes [the potentialities that cause one to have those afflictive emotions].

> A 'vajra' (*rdo rje*, literally, 'foremost of stones') is a diamond which, being viewed as unbreakable, is a suitable metaphor for a meditative state that is able to overcome the final object of abandonment.

They then manifest the fruit of becoming a Foe Destroyer.

On the great path of accumulation[2] and below, rhinoceros-like Solitary Realizers practice the realization that the person is empty of substantial existence in the sense of being self-sufficient. They do this in conjunction with amassing a collection of merit for one hundred great aeons and so forth; and then, in one sitting, they actualize the stages from the heat level of the path of preparation through to and including the path of no more learning.

> Solitary Realizers are those who have met with

---

[1] *rdo rje lta bu'i ting nge 'dzin, vajropamasamādhi.*
[2] The path of accumulation is divided into three periods—small, middling, and great.

> teachers and listened to their teaching of the doctrine in previous lives but in their final life live in the Desire Realm peacefully and by themselves, like a rhinoceros. They do not meet with teachers or study doctrine in that life. Great Vehicle tenet systems also assert another type of Solitary Realizers who meet and study with a teacher early in their final lifetime but later achieve their goal alone.
>
> According to the Great Exposition School, Solitary Realizers, having accumulated merit for one hundred great aeons over the path of accumulation, pass in one meditative sitting through the four levels of the path of preparation—heat, peak, forbearance, and supreme mundane qualities—and then the paths of seeing, meditation, and no more learning.

Furthermore, the Proponents of the Great Exposition assert the existence of types of Foe Destroyers who degenerate, etc., because there are Lesser Vehicle Foe Destroyers who fall from their abandonment [of the obstructions] and their realizations [of the four truths], whereupon they become Stream Enterers.[1]

> The Proponents of the Great Exposition maintain that there are five types of fallible Foe Destroyers and a sixth type who is not capable of degeneration. Only this sixth type would be considered an actual Foe Destroyer by the other schools.

With respect to Hearers, they enumerate a presentation of the twenty members of the spiritual community[2] along with the eight Approachers and Abiders; however, they do not assert that anyone simultaneously

---

[1] *rgyun zhugs, śrotāpanna.*
[2] *dge 'dun, saṅgha.*

[abandons the afflictive emotions].

The twenty members of the spiritual community represent a classification of the location and number of lives remaining for practitioners on the way to attaining the fruits of Stream Enterer, Once Returner,[1] Never Returner,[2] and Foe Destroyer.

The Eight Approachers and Abiders are beings who are approaching to or abiding in the fruits of Stream Enterer, Once Returner, Never Returner, or Foe Destroyer. The four Abiders refer to persons who have fully accomplished, or who abide in, these fruits. A Stream Enterer is one who will never again be reborn as a hell-being, hungry ghost, or animal. A Once Returner will be reborn once more in the Desire Realm. A Never Returner will never be born again in the Desire Realm. A Foe Destroyer has overcome the afflictive emotions and thus is completely liberated from cyclic existence.

Cyclic existence is divided into three realms and nine levels. The first level is the Desire Realm. The next four levels are the four divisions of the form realm, called the Four Concentrations. The last four levels are divisions of the Formless Realm. Each level has nine series of obstacles that are to be abandoned; big big, middle big, and small big; big middle, middle middle, and small middle; big small, middle small, and small small (see chart next page). Thus, if trainees proceed serially, they have to pass through eighty-one steps, that is, through a series of nine steps on each of the nine levels.

---

[1] *lan gcig phyir 'ong, sakṛdāgamin.*
[2] *phyir mi 'ong, anāgamin.*

Path of Meditation
(read from bottom to top)

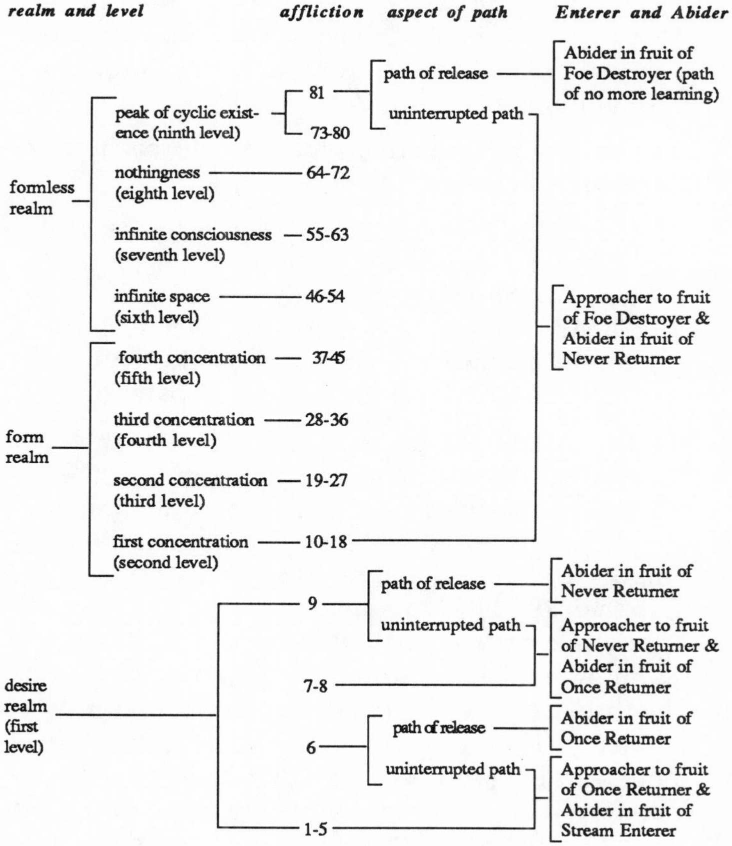

> Simultaneous abandonment refers to the simultaneous overcoming or abandoning of, for example, each of the big big of the nine levels. Thus, one who passes through the path of meditation with simultaneous abandonment has only nine steps to accomplish instead of eighty-one. The Proponents of the Great Exposition do not accept any such simultaneous abandonment.

They maintain that the eight types of Approachers and Abiders are necessarily Superiors.

> This means that even Approachers to the fruit of Stream Enterer have attained the path of seeing, from which point they are no longer ordinary beings but Superiors. Other systems maintain that an Approacher to the fruit of Stream Enterer is on the path of preparation.

Bodhisattvas [such as Shākyamuni] complete their collections [of merit and wisdom] over three periods of countless great aeons during the path of accumulation. Having done this, they achieve the causes of the excellent marks [of a Buddha] over one hundred aeons, and then, in their final life vanquish the array of demons[1] at twilight while seated beside the tree of enlightenment. At midnight, while in meditative equipoise, they actualize the three paths of preparation, seeing, and meditation. Later, just prior to dawn, they actualize the path of no more learning [and become a Buddha].

Therefore [from among the twelve deeds of a Buddha] they consider that the taming of the demons at twilight and the preceding deeds are performed when a common being and that the three Bodhisattva paths of preparation, seeing, and meditation are all only medita-

---

[1] *lha'i bu'i bdud, devaputamāra*; literally, demons that are children of gods.

tive equipoise [because they occur only during meditative sitting]. Of the twelve deeds, the first nine are asserted to be the deeds of a Bodhisattva, and the last three are asserted to be the deeds of a Buddha.

> The twelve deeds are: descent from the Joyous Pure Land,[1] conception, birth, mastery of the arts, sporting with the retinue, renunciation, asceticism, meditation under the tree of enlightenment, conquest of the array of demons, becoming a Buddha, turning the wheel of doctrine, and nirvana (death).

The Proponents of the Great Exposition assert that a wheel of doctrine[2] is necessarily a path of seeing and that a verbal wheel of doctrine is necessarily a wheel of doctrine of the four truths.

The Proponents of the Great Exposition assert that the Seven Treatises of Manifest Knowledge[3] were spoken by Buddha [and written down by Foe Destroyers]. They say that Buddha's word is always literal.[4] Apart from the eighty thousand bundles of doctrine, they do not assert a presentation of eighty-four thousand bun-

---

[1] *dga' ldan, tuṣita.*

[2] The Go-mang 1980 edition (2.15) points out that the word *rtogs pa'i* ('realizational'), as found in the Dharamsala 1967 edition (28.2), does not appear in any of the three editions that they used and is a later addition. Following the Dharamsala 1967 edition, the clause would read, 'a realizational wheel of doctrine is necessarily a path of seeing.' Mimaki (82.19) accepts this new reading, duly noting its origin, but we think it best to avoid incorporating into Gön-chok-jik-may-wang-bo's text what are clearly modern accretions by an editor who thought to improve the text. The phrase appears in none of the other editions used by Mimaki or us.

[3] *mngon pa, abhidharma.*

[4] Again, Gön-chok-jik-may-wang-bo disagrees with his previous incarnation, Jam-yang-shay-ba, who cogently holds (*Great Exposition of Tenets, kha* 13b.2) that this is true only of *some* Proponents of the Great Exposition and that others hold that there are both definitive and interpretable passages among Buddha's word.

dles of doctrine. This is because Vasubandhu's *Treasury of Manifest Knowledge* says:[1]

> Those eighty thousand bundles of doctrine
> Which were spoken by the Subduer ...

> The doctrine is arranged into bundles like wheat that has been cut and bound at harvest time. A bundle signifies a teaching of variable length which, if thoroughly realized, is capable of overcoming one affliction. Those schools asserting eighty-four thousand bundles say that there are twenty-one thousand bundles for each of the three afflictive emotions—desire, hatred, and ignorance—and a fourth bundle of twenty-one thousand for the three of these together.

The place where Bodhisattvas actualize enlightenment during their last lifetime is definitely just the Desire Realm; therefore, the Proponents of the Great Exposition do not assert a presentation of a Heavily Adorned Highest Pure Land[2] or an Enjoyment Body.[3]

> According to the Great Vehicle systems, a Highest Pure Land is where an immortal Enjoyment Body resides and preaches the Great Vehicle path to Bodhisattvas on the path of seeing and above. Ordinary beings are not found in this type of pure land although they do exist in the pure lands of Emanation Bodies.[4] Most Great Vehicle systems also hold that Bodhisattvas attain full enlightenment in a Highest Pure Land.

---

[1] I.25.

[2] *'og min stug po bkod pa, akaniṣṭaghanavyūha.*

[3] *longs sku, saṃbhogakāya.*

[4] *sprul sku, nirmāṇakāya.*

Not only this, but they also do not accept omniscience [because they only assert all-knowingness, as mentioned above].

All Foe Destroyers of the three vehicles have a nirvana with remainder[1] because they assert that when one attains a nirvana without remainder[2] there is a severing of the continuum of consciousness, like the extinction of a flame.[3] Hence, they assert that there are three final vehicles.

Some propound that the Teacher [Buddha] merely withdrew a creation of his body from the sight of certain trainees when he passed from suffering [entered *parinirvāṇa,* that is, at the time of his 'death'] and did not actually pass from suffering [or completely vanish]. This is similar to a confusion of fish and turnips.

> Fish and turnips are both long and white but clearly different. For this reason, they are used metaphorically to indicate an absurd state of confusion. The author appears to hold that it is inconsistent for proponents of a system—that asserts a complete severance of the continuum of consciousness in a nirvana without remainder—to assert that such did not actually happen upon Shākyamuni Buddha's death. Jam-ȳang-shay-b̄a[4] speaks of just such an assertion as being reported by a transmission stemming from Atīsha. Ḡön-chok-jik-may-w̄ang-b̄o seems to question even the existence of such an assertion, as does Jam-ȳang-shay-b̄a's annotator, Ngak-w̄ang-b̄el-den,[5] but Jam-

---

[1] *lhag bcas myang 'das, sopadhiśeṣanirvāṇa.*

[2] *lhag med myang 'das, nirupadhiśeṣanirvāṇa.*

[3] The simile is of an flame that goes out because of the exhaustion of it fuel; the comparison is not made to blowing out a flame.

[4] See Jam-ȳang-shay-b̄a's *Great Exposition of Tenets, kha* 12b.5.

[5] *Annotations, dngos* 47.8.

> ȳang-shay-b̄a cogently makes reference, albeit briefly, to the mere fact of the eighteen subschools (and thus a wide variety of opinion) and to the presence of supportive scripture, but he does not cite it.

Buddha Superiors have abandoned all sufferings and their origins without exception, and yet, it is not contradictory that true sufferings exist within their continuum. This is because when all afflictive emotions that take true sufferings as their objects are abandoned, this is posited as the abandonment of true sufferings.

> When all afflictive emotions have been removed, even if one still possesses true sufferings in one's continuum, they do not give rise to afflictive emotions, and thus from this perspective it is said that all true sufferings have been abandoned.

A Buddha's physical body is included in the same lifetime as the physical base of a Bodhisattva on the path of preparation. Therefore, they assert that this body is not a Buddha Jewel [an object of refuge] although it is Buddha.

> In this system Bodhisattvas are said to pass from the path of preparation to the path of no more learning in one meditative sitting; therefore, when they achieve Buddhahood, their body is the same body with which they, as Bodhisattvas, began the path of preparation. Since it is still an ordinary body, it cannot be an immaculate Buddha Jewel. Many scholars also say that a Buddha's body is not Buddha because it is a true suffering.[1]

---

[1] This is the opinion of Jam-ȳang-shay-b̄a, whose *Great Exposition of Tenets* (*kha* 15a.7) says, 'The form aggregate [of a Buddha] is not that

The Buddha Jewel is asserted to be the wisdom of extinction [of the obstructions] and the wisdom [that the obstructions] will never be produced again which exist in the mental continuum of a Buddha.

> When one takes refuge or bows down to the Buddha Jewel, one bows not to the Buddha's body but to the Buddha's wisdom. With regard to the two wisdoms, the degenerating types of Foe Destroyer attain only the wisdom of extinction of afflictive emotions; they do not attain the wisdom of the future non-production of the afflictive emotions.

Similarly, because Learner Superiors [those on the paths of seeing and meditation] are beings who have contamination, they are not considered to be the Community Jewel although they are of the spiritual community. It is the true paths in the mental continuum of[1] Learner Superiors which are asserted to be the Community Jewel. There also is a presentation of the Doctrine Jewel because nirvanas and true cessations in the continuums of Hearers, Solitary Realizers, and Buddhas are all Doctrine Jewels.

> A nirvana refers to the true cessation of all afflictive emotions, whereas a true cessation can be a cessation of any affliction, such as any one of the eighty-one abandonments on the path of meditation.

[i.e., Buddha]; Buddha is only the qualities of non-learning,' (*gzugs phung de min sangs rgyas mi slob chos*).

[1] In the Peking edition (12b.5) read *rgyud kyi* for *rgyud kyis* in accordance with the other six editions used—Collected Works (505.4), Teacher Training edition (29.11), Go-mang 1980 edition, 29.13, the Dharamsala 1967 edition (29.16), the Tibet Go-mang 1987 edition (10b.4), and Mimaki (83.13).

*   *   *

Stanza between sections:

May the youthful with clear minds enjoy
This festival of fresh ambrosia of eloquence,
Taken from the ocean of the system of the Great Exposition
With the golden vessel of my mind's analysis.

5 The Sūtra School

The presentation of the tenets of the Proponents of Sūtra is in four parts: definition, subschools, etymology, and assertions of tenets.

DEFINITION

The definition of a Proponent of Sūtra is: a person propounding Lesser Vehicle tenets who asserts the true existence of both external objects and self-cognizing consciousness.

> This definition must be qualified because it does not take into account Proponents of Sūtra Following Scripture, who do not assert self-cognizing consciousness. Also, the definition is perhaps subject to a more general fault. According to Jam-ȳang-shay-b̄a, external objects are not limited to material objects or even to impermanent phenomena but include permanent phenomena such as uncompounded space. Since permanent phenomena are not

> held, in the Sūtra School Following Reasoning, to be truly established and since, when a category contains both permanent and impermanent phenomena, permanence predominates, external objects in general cannot be said to be truly established according to the system of the Sūtra School Following Reasoning.[1] Still, there is general agreement in all branches of the Sūtra School that impermanent external objects are truly established.

Proponents of Sūtra and Exemplifiers[2] are mutually inclusive [i.e., whoever is the one is the other].

SUBSCHOOLS

There are two types of Proponents of Sūtra—Proponents of Sūtra Following Scripture and Proponents of Sūtra Following Reasoning. The former are [mainly] Proponents of Sūtra who follow Vasubandhu's *Treasury of Manifest Knowledge* and the latter are [mainly] Proponents of Sūtra who follow Dharmakīrti's Seven Treatises on Prime Cognition.[3]

---

[1] A-ku Lo-drö-gya-tso (*a khu blo gros rgya mtsho*), a follower of Jam-ȳang-shay-b̄a, finds fault with the definition from both of these points of view. A-ku Lo-drö-gya-tso says that Ḡön-chok-jik-may-w̄ang-b̄o, in setting the definition of a Proponent of Sūtra this way, is following the old textbook literature of the Go-mang College of Dre-b̄ung Monastic University by Gung-ru Chö-jung (*gung ru chos 'byung*) whose works were supplanted by Jam-ȳang-shay-b̄a's. For this discussion, see A-ku Lo-drö-gya-tso, *Commentary on the Difficult Points of (Dzong-ka-b̄a's) 'The Essence of the Good Explanations, Treatise Differentiating Interpretable and Definitive Meanings': A Precious Lamp (drang ba dang nges pa'i don rnam par 'byed pa'i bstan bcos legs bshad snying po'i dka' 'grel rin chen sgron me)*, (Delhi: Kesang Thabkhes, 1982), 105.4 and 104.1.

[2] *dpe ston pa, dārṣṭāntika.*

[3] Dharmakīrti lived during the seventh century; for a listing of this set of seven renowned works, see the Bibliography.

ETYMOLOGY

There are reasons for their being called Proponents of Sūtra and Exemplifiers. They are called 'Proponents of Sūtra' because they propound tenets chiefly in reliance on the Supramundane Victor's sūtras without following the *Great Detailed Exposition*. They are called 'Exemplifiers' because they teach all doctrines by way of examples.

ASSERTIONS OF TENETS

This section has three parts: their assertions on the basis, paths, and fruits.

ASSERTIONS ON THE BASIS

This section has two parts: assertions regarding objects and assertions regarding object-possessors.

Assertions Regarding Objects

The definition of an object[1] is: that which is suitable to be known by an awareness. The definition of an object of knowledge[2] is: that which is suitable to be an object of an awareness. Object, existent,[3] object of knowledge, and established base[4] are mutually inclusive.

Objects are divided into the two truths; into specifically characterized and generally characterized phenomena; into negative phenomena and positive phenomena; into manifest phenomena and hidden phenomena; into the three times; and into the single and the different.

---

1 *yul, viṣaya.*
2 *shes bya, jñeya.*
3 *yod pa, sat.*
4 *gzhi grub, *vastu.*

The two truths

The definition of an ultimate truth is: a phenomenon that is able to bear reasoned analysis from the point of view of whether it has its own mode of subsistence without depending on imputation by terms or conceptual consciousnesses. [Functioning] thing,[1] ultimate truth, specifically characterized phenomenon,[2] impermanent thing,[3] compounded phenomenon,[4] and truly existent phenomenon[5] are mutually inclusive.

The definition of a truth-for-an-obscured[-awareness][6] is: a phenomenon that only exists through being imputed by a conceptual consciousness. Non-functioning phenomenon,[7] truth-for-an-obscured[-awareness], generally characterized phenomenon,[8] permanent phenomenon,[9] uncompounded phenomenon,[10] and false existent[11] are mutually inclusive.

There are etymologies for the two truths. Uncompounded space is called a truth-for-the-obscured because it is a truth for an obscured awareness. 'Obscured' here refers to a conceptual consciousness, which is called obscured because it is obstructed from the direct perception of specifically characterized phenomena.

> An uncompounded space, i.e., an absence of obstructive contact, cannot be cognized di-

---

[1] *dngos po, bhāva.*
[2] *rang mtshan, svalakṣaṇa.*
[3] *mi rtag pa, anitya.*
[4] *'dus byas, saṃskṛta.*
[5] *bden grub, satyasiddha.*
[6] *kun rdzob bden pa, saṃvṛtisatya.*
[7] *dngos med kyi chos, abhāvadharma.*
[8] *spyi mtshan, sāmānyalakṣaṇa.*
[9] *rtag pa, nitya.*
[10] *'dus ma byas kyi chos, asaṃskṛtadharma.*
[11] *brdzun par grub pa.*

> rectly; it is cognized only by a conceptual consciousness. A conceptual consciousness is said to be obscured because it cannot perceive impermanent things directly; it can perceive them only through the medium of conceptual images.

However, this is only an etymology [and not a definition, because it is too wide]. Everything that is a truth for a conceptual consciousness, that is, for an obscured awareness, is not necessarily a truth-for-the-obscured. This is because a pot, for example, which is an illustration of an ultimate truth, is also a truth for a conceptual consciousness, that is, for an obscured awareness. Furthermore, although a self of persons and a permanent sound, for instance, are truths for conceptual consciousnesses, that is, for obscured awarenesses, these do not exist even conventionally.

A pot is called an ultimate truth because it is a truth for an ultimate awareness. This ultimate awareness is a consciousness that is not mistaken with regard to its appearing object.[1]

> A conceptual consciousness is always mistaken with respect to its appearing object, i.e., a generic image, because a generic image of a house, for instance, appears to be an actual house. Hence, even an inferential conceptual consciousness, such as a consciousness that realizes the impermanence of a house, is mistaken with regard to its appearing object, the image of a house; however, it is not mistaken

---

[1] *snang yul, *pratibhāsaviṣaya*. An 'appearing object' is not just the object that appears to a consciousness because it is asserted that a pot, for instance, appears to a conceptual consciousness apprehending a pot but a pot is not the appearing object of that consciousness. The 'appearing object' of a conceptual consciousness is a 'meaning-generality' (or conceptual generic image) of the object.

with regard to its conceived object[1] or object of engagement,[2] which is the impermanence of the house and which it conceives correctly. A direct prime cognition, however, is not mistaken with regard to either its appearing object or its object of engagement. Direct prime cognitions are the ultimate consciousnesses that are referred to by the word 'ultimate' in the term 'ultimate truth'.

The *appearing object* of a conceptual consciousness is a generic image, an image from memory, an imaginary construct, or in some cases an after-image of an object apprehended by a sense consciousness. This generic image is the same entity as the conceptual consciousness itself.

The *conceived object* of an inferential cognition is not a generic image of an object, but the actual object itself. For example, when one realizes the subtle impermanence of a chair, the appearing object is a generic image of the impermanence of a chair, and the conceived object is the actual impermanence of a chair, but it is apprehended or gotten at through the medium of a generic image. When one perceives the image of the horns of a rabbit, the appearing object is a generic image of the horns of a rabbit; however, the conceived object, actual horns of a rabbit, does not exist. This distinction between 'appearing object' and 'conceived object' is made only with regard to conceptual consciousnesses.

The generic image of fire, for instance, in a given person's mind operates in the identifica-

---

1 *zhen yul.*
2 *'jug yul, pravṛttiviṣaya.*

tion of the many fires that the person perceives; therefore, that image is 'generic'. Another person would have a different image of fire, the form of which might depend on the initial identification of fire made in the present life. Thus, generic images are not general or universal in the sense that one image serves for all beings. Also, a person's generic image might shift during his or her lifetime. Thus, a generic image is an imputation by a conceptual consciousness; it does not exist in and of itself and, therefore, is not a specifically characterized phenomenon and not impermanent. Though permanent, a generic image does not eternally exist, available for occasional usage by beings, nor does it exist eternally in individual minds, sometimes noticed and sometimes unnoticed. Rather, a generic image which represents the elimination of everything that is not a particular object is formed at some time and then dwells in latency until the proper conditions are assembled, such as a person's catching sight of a fire. At that time, a conceptual consciousness is produced with a generic image as its appearing object. The generic image *seems* to be the actual object even if it is understood not to be the actual object, much as a mirror image of a face can be said to *seem* to be a face even if one continuously understands that it is not a face. In this sense, consciousnesses that have generic images as their appearing objects are said to be mistaken.

Generic images are permanent, have parts, and are individual for each sentient being. They should not be confused with the permanent, partless, independent universals of other philosophical systems. The permanence of a generic image is that of occasional permanence. Another example of an occasional permanence is the space associated with a physical object. When the object is destroyed, the space is no longer suitable to be designated. Also, the space associated with the object does not change moment by moment and thus cannot be called impermanent. It is an occasional permanence because it does not exist forever and yet it does not disintegrate momentarily as do all impermanent phenomena.

Generic images are not just images of memory that are used for the identification of objects. They are also after-images. For instance, it is said that when one actually sees an object, the object manifest before one is a specifically characterized phenomenon. An eye consciousness is produced in the image of the object, much as if a tiny mirror inside the orb of the eye were reflecting an object. The object—for example, a table—exists one moment previous to the eye consciousness that is produced in its image; nevertheless, the table of the preceding moment is the object of the eye consciousness because nothing intervened between the moment of the object and the moment of the eye consciousness that apprehends the object. The specifically characterized phenomenon, table, is therefore perceived directly. If a mental consciousness is produced through the influence of that eye consciousness, the mental consciousness has one moment of direct perception of the object and thus for that moment is a mental direct perception. In all succeeding moments

> the appearing object is a generic image that is an after-image.

This way of presenting the two truths is the system of the Sūtra School Following Reasoning. The Sūtra School Following Scripture asserts a presentation of the two truths that accords with that of the Great Exposition School.

Specifically and generally characterized phenomena

The definition of a specifically characterized phenomenon is: a phenomenon that is ultimately able to perform a function. A pot is an illustration of a specifically characterized phenomenon. The definition of a generally characterized phenomenon is: a phenomenon that is ultimately unable to perform a function. Uncompounded space is an illustration of a generally characterized phenomenon. Imputed phenomena, such as generality and instance, one and different, mutually exclusive and related, and so forth, are generally characterized phenomena; however, something that is any of these is not necessarily a generally characterized phenomenon. This distinction should be made.

> For example, one itself is a generally characterized object, but one pot is a specifically characterized object because it exists by way of its own specific nature. When we refer to a pot and say, 'It is one,' that oneness is not a phenomenon that exists by way of its own specific nature because from another point of view the designation 'different' can be applied as, for example, when we refer to the pot as being different from a table. The designations 'one' and 'different' are dependent on imputation by conceptuality; and, therefore, although they might have their base in a specifically charac-

terized phenomenon, they themselves are generally characterized phenomena.

The terms *svalakṣaṇa* and *sāmānyalakṣaṇa*, which here mean 'specifically characterized phenomenon' and 'generally characterized phenomenon', are also sometimes used with a different meaning. They then refer to 'exclusive characteristic' and 'general characteristic'. An example of an exclusive characteristic is the definition of consciousness—that which is luminous and knowing; impermanence, on the other hand, is a general characteristic of consciousness that is shared with other compounded phenomena which are not consciousnesses, such as forms.

Negative and positive phenomena

The definition of a negative phenomenon[1] is: an object that is realized through the explicit elimination of an object of negation.

Because objects of knowledge are being divided into the negative and the positive, 'negative' here does not refer to the act of negation. It refers to an object that is the negative, or absence, of an object of negation. For example, a negative object such as non-cow is not an act of negation nor either a statement of negation or what is negated. Non-cow is known through explicitly eliminating cow and thus is a negative phenomenon. Non-cow includes all phenomena other than cow—house, fence, person, and so forth. (Although cow is not non-cow, when one says or thinks 'cow', conceptuality does not need *explicitly* to elimi-

---

[1] *dgag pa, pratiṣedha.*

nate non-cow, and thus cow is a positive phenomenon.)

Negative object and exclusion-of-the-other[1] are mutually inclusive.

In 'exclusion-of-the-other, the 'other' is the object negated.

There are two types of negative phenomena, non-affirming negatives[2] and affirming negatives.[3] The definition of a non-affirming negative is: an object realized by an awareness that explicitly realizes [that negative object] within the context of only eliminating its negated element. An example is Brahmins' not drinking beer.

The statement that Brahmins should not drink beer indicates a non-affirming negative because only the negated element, drinking beer, is eliminated, and nothing, no other type of food or drink, for example, is affirmed in its place. Though Brahmins, being humans, must drink something, Brahmins' not drinking beer does not imply this in place of the negation of drinking beer. Also, Brahmins, though existent, are not implied in place of the negation of the object of negation; Brahmins are the base of the negation.[4]

The definition of an affirming negative is: [a negative

---

[1] *gzhan sel, anyāpoha.*

[2] *med dgag, prasajyapratiṣedha.* The two types of negations seem to have their origin among the Mīmāṃsakas, who used the terms to refer to types of injunctions—when something was just forbidden and when something positive was implied in place of what was forbidden. See J.F. Staal, 'Negation and the Law of Contradiction in Indian Thought' (London, *Bulletin of the School of Oriental and African Studies*, Vol. XXV: Part 1, 1962), especially pp. 56-66.

[3] *ma yin dgag, paryudāsapratiṣedha.*

[4] *dgag gzhi.*

that] implies some other phenomenon, whether a positive phenomenon or another affirming negative [or both], in place of the negation of its own negated element by the awareness that explicitly realizes it. An example is the fat Devadatta's not eating food during the daytime.

> In this case, the negation of eating food *during the daytime* implies that Devadatta, given his corpulence, eats at night.

The definition of a positive phenomenon is: a phenomenon that is not realized through the explicit elimination of its own negated element by the awareness explicitly realizing it. An example is a pot.

> When a conceptual consciousness knows or identifies a pot, it is not necessary for it *explicitly* to eliminate non-pot.

Manifest and hidden phenomena

The definition of a manifest phenomenon[1] is: an object that is explicitly realized by a direct prime cognition.

> In all systems except the Consequence School, a prime cognition is both new and non-delusive. The second moment of prime cognition is no longer new, and thus is a subsequent cognition, a non-prime cognition.

Manifest phenomenon and [functioning] thing[2] are mutually inclusive.

> From the point of view of direct cognition all functioning things are manifest phenomena.

---

[1] *mngon gyur, abhimukhī.*
[2] *dngos po, bhāva.*

The definition of a hidden phenomenon[1] is: an object that is explicitly realized by an inferential prime cognition. Hidden phenomenon and object of knowledge are mutually inclusive.

> From the point of view of conceptuality, all objects of knowledge, including functioning things, are hidden phenomena because conceptuality cannot perceive them directly; it can perceive them only through the medium of a generic image. Therefore, in this system, manifest phenomenon and hidden phenomenon are not mutually exclusive. All manifest phenomena are hidden phenomena, but all hidden phenomena are not manifest phenomena; for example, uncompounded space can only be cognized conceptually by sentient beings (i.e., non-Buddhas) and thus is not a manifest phenomenon.

The three times

The definition of a pastness [of an object] is: that state of destructedness [which exists] in the next period after the time of an object—the object being a [functioning] thing that is other [than its own pastness].

> For example, the time of the existence of a pencil—which is an existent that is other than the phenomenon of the state of destruction of the pencil—is its own time of existing as a pencil, say for three months. Let us say that at the end of the three months it was burned. The pencil's next period begins with its burning, its destruction. The destructedness of the pencil is then unchangeable, and since it does not disinte-

[1] *lkog gyur, parokṣa.*

grate moment by moment, the destructedness, or pastness, of the pencil is said to be permanent.

The definition of the futureness of an object is: that state of non-production of a [functioning] thing—which is other [than its future]—in some time and place, due to the non-completion of subsidiary causes, although the main cause for its production is present.

The futureness of an object comes into being when that object's main cause is present but the object itself is not present; therefore, the futureness of an object exists prior to the present of that object. The futureness of an object is a mere absence that is due to the non-completion of contributing causes; hence, the Sūtra, Mind Only, and Autonomy Schools hold that a futureness—as well as a pastness—are not functioning things but are permanent, non-disintegrating. For the Consequence School, they are functioning things and impermanent.

The definition of a present object is: that which has been produced and has not ceased.

A pastness and a futureness are both permanent [because they are mere absences and do not undergo momentary change].

There are two types of permanence, occasional permanence and non-occasional permanence. An occasional permanence, such as the pastness of a table, depends upon the destruction of the table, but once the destruction occurs, the pastness of the table—which is the state of its having ceased—exists unchangeably. General uncompounded space, which is a lack of obstructive contact, is a non-occasional permanence; it exists forever unchangeably without a

> beginning, although the uncompounded space associated with a specific object comes into existence with that object and goes out of existence with its destruction.

Present object and [functioning] thing are mutually inclusive. Moreover, these features should be known: the pastness of a thing occurs after that thing; the futureness of a thing occurs prior to that thing.

The single and the different

The definition of the single is: a phenomenon that is not diverse. An example is a pot. The definition of the different is: those phenomena that are diverse. An example is pillar and pot.

> The single is what appears as single to a conceptual consciousness. For example, pot is single; also pot and pot are single because the term is the same and the meaning is the same. The different are what appear to a conceptual consciousness to be different. Pillar and pot are obviously different, from the point of view of both the terms and their meanings. However, dog and its Tibetan equivalent *khyi* are different, even though their meaning is the same because the terms themselves are different. The mention of 'dog' does not necessarily evoke '*khyi*' for a conceptual consciousness; therefore, the two are different, but not different entities. Similarly, product and impermanent thing are mutually inclusive—whatever is the one is the other—but different.
>
> Dog and pot are different and mutually exclusive because there is no one thing that is both a pot and a dog. However, dog and pot are not a dichotomy, that is, a set that includes

> all phenomena, because if something is not a pot, it is not necessarily a dog. Permanent phenomenon and impermanent phenomenon are a dichotomy because, if something exists, it must be either one or the other.
>
> Product and pot are different, are not mutually inclusive, i.e., whatever is the one is not necessarily the other, are not mutually exclusive (since something such as a copper pot can be both a product and a pot), and are not a dichotomy.
>
> The mutually inclusive are always the same entity, but they are different within this sameness of entity. Mutually exclusive phenomena such as a table and its color can be the same entity but different within this sameness of entity. Mutually exclusive phenomena such as dog and pot are simply different entities.

Phenomena that are different entities are necessarily different isolates.[1]

> For example, dog and pot are different entities and different isolates. 'Isolates' are conceptually isolatable factors.

However, different isolates are not necessarily different entities because product[2] and impermanent thing [which are mutually inclusive] are one entity but different isolates.

> The isolate of product is identified as opposite from being one with product, and the isolate of impermanent thing is identified as opposite from being one with impermanent thing. Prod-

---

[1] *ldog pa*. The Teacher Training edition (35.9) should be corrected to *kyis khyab* from *kyis ma khyab* in accordance with the Ngawang Gelek Collected Works edition (509.3), etc.

[2] *byas pa, kṛta*.

uct and impermanent thing are the same entity, since they are mutually inclusive, but are different isolates, since for a conceptual consciousness the one term does not evoke the other.

Furthermore, they assert directionally partless particles and temporally partless moments of consciousness in accordance with the Proponents of the Great Exposition.

Proponents of the Great Exposition and Proponents of Sūtra Following Scripture assert these as ultimate truths because they are irreducible, whereas the Proponents of Sūtra Following Reasoning assert them as ultimate truths because they are ultimately capable of performing the function of creating effects.[1]

However, the Proponents of Sūtra are not similar to the Proponents of the Great Exposition in all respects because the Proponents of the Great Exposition assert that all existents are substantially established [as having their own autonomous entity that is not dependent on conceptuality] whereas the Proponents of Sūtra do not accept this. Also, both the Proponents of the Great Exposition and the Consequentialists assert that non-revelatory forms[2] are fully qualified forms, but the Proponents of Sūtra, Proponents of Mind Only, and Autonomists do not accept these as fully qualified forms.

[1] This comment has been added in accordance with the thought of the author, Ḡön-chok-jik-may-w̄ang-b̄o. Some contemporary followers of Jam-ȳang-shay-b̄a, however, hold that, within the Sūtra School, only the Sūtra School Following Scripture asserts that directionally partless particles and temporally partless moments of consciousness exist; they maintain that the Sūtra School Following Reasoning, being followers of Dignāga and Dharmakīrti, refute the existence of such partless phenomena.

[2] *rnam par rig byed ma yin pa'i gzugs, avijñaptirūpa.*

> Certain forms are called non-revelatory because their presence does not affect ordinary communication. An example is the subtle form of a monk's speech that is the opposite of lying and so forth but cannot be heard by others. It could, however, be perceived by those with special auditory clairvoyance.

This is not the only difference between the Proponents of the Great Exposition and the Proponents of Sūtra because the Proponents of the Great Exposition assert [some] cause and effect as being simultaneous, whereas the Proponents of Sūtra and above do not assert this.

> According to the Proponents of the Great Exposition, a main mind and its accompanying mental factors are simultaneously and mutually supportive, like the legs of a tripod, and thus simultaneously each other's causes and effects. The Proponents of Sūtra and above do not assert this to be a case of simultaneous cause and effect because, for them, a cause must precede its effect. They maintain that the previous moment of one mental factor aids the later moment of another mental factor.

Assertions Regarding Object-Possessors [Subjects]

This section has three parts: persons, consciousnesses, and terms.

Persons

The Followers of Scripture assert that the continuum of the aggregates is an illustration of a person [i.e., the continuum of the aggregates is the person]. The Followers of Reasoning assert that the mental consciousness is an illustration of a person.

The Followers of Reasoning assert that the actual person is a subtle neutral type of mental consciousness because this consciousness exists continuously—through deep sleep, during meditative equipoise, and from lifetime to lifetime.

Consciousnesses

Prime cognitions and non-prime awarenesses are the two types of consciousnesses.

> A prime cognition is defined as a new and incontrovertible knower.[1] A prime cognition, therefore, must be *both* new and valid; later moments of cognition after the initial period of a prime cognition, which are called 'subsequent cognitions', are, therefore, not prime cognitions. Despite being valid, they are not new and thus are not prime cognitions.

There are two types of prime cognitions, direct prime cognitions[2] and inferential prime cognitions.[3]

Direct prime cognitions are of four types: direct prime cognitions that are sense direct perceptions,[4] mental direct perceptions,[5] self-cognizing direct perceptions,[6] and yogic direct perceptions.[7]

---

[1] *gsar du mi slu ba'i rig pa.* See Lati Rinbochay and Elizabeth Napper, *Mind in Tibetan Buddhism* (London: Rider and Company, 1980; Ithaca: Snow Lion, 1980), pp. 31 and 116. The requirement of both newness and incontrovertibility (non-delusiveness) is based on Dharmakīrti's *Commentary on (Dignāga's) 'Compendium of [Teachings on] Valid Cognition'*, II.2.

[2] *mngon sum gyi tshad ma, pratyakṣapramāṇa.*

[3] *rjes su dpag pa'i tshad ma, anumānapramāṇa.*

[4] *dbang po'i mngon sum, indriyapratyakṣa.*

[5] *yid kyi mngon sum, mānasapratyakṣa.*

[6] *rang rig mngon sum, svasaṃvedanapratyakṣa.*

> The Followers of Scripture do not accept that there are self-cognizing consciousnesses.

The physical senses [such as an eye sense] are not suitable to be prime cognitions because, lacking being luminous and knowing, they are incapable of comprehending their objects.

There are five types of non-prime awarenesses: subsequent cognition,[1] wrong consciousness,[2] doubt,[3] correct assumption,[4] and an awareness to which an object appears without being noticed.[5]

> Non-prime awarenesses are either not new or not valid or both. Subsequent cognitions are moments of direct or conceptual cognition of an object that follow the moment in which that object was newly cognized by a direct or inferential cognition; they are valid but not new and thus are not prime cognitions (*tshad ma, pramāṇa*).[6]
>
> A wrong consciousness is any consciousness that is mistaken as to its object of engagement; for example, due to a fault of the eye, a wrong consciousness that perceives the moon as double is produced. A wrong consciousness should not be confused with a mistaken consciousness,[7] which is so called because it is a consciousness that is mistaken with respect to its appearing object. The appearing object of an

---

7 *rnal 'byor mngon sum, yogipratyakṣa.*

1 *bcad shes / dpyad shes, *paricchinnajñāna.*

2 *log shes, viparyayajña.*

3 *the tshom, vicikitsā / saṃśaya.*

4 *yid dpyod, *manaḥparīkṣā.*

5 *snang la ma nges pa'i blo, *aniyatapratibhāsabuddhi.*

6 For more on this topic, see the chapter on the Consequence School.

7 *'khrul shes, bhrāntijñāna.*

inferential cognition that realizes a sound to be impermanent is a generic image of impermanent sound; its conceived object is impermanent sound. All inferences are mistaken with regard to their appearing object because the generic image of their object *appears* to be the actual object. However, an inferring consciousness does not *conceive* that the generic image and the actual object are one; it does not expressly determine, 'This generic image of impermanent sound is actual impermanent sound.' The generic image merely *appears* to an inferring consciousness to be actual impermanent sound. Therefore, although an inferential consciousness is mistaken in the sense that an image appears to it to be the actual object, it is not mistaken with respect to its object of engagement or conceived object, as in the case of understanding a sound to be impermanent. A wrong consciousness, on the other hand, is mistaken with respect to its object of engagement in the sense that, for instance, it sees a single moon as double or conceives sounds to be permanent.

Doubt, the third of the five non-prime awareness, is of three types. The first is doubt tending toward what is wrong—for example, a consciousness that has not decided whether sound is permanent or not but tends toward the wrong view that sound is permanent. The second is doubt that is equally divided between what is right and what is wrong—for example, a consciousness that tends toward both the wrong view that sound is permanent and the right view that it is impermanent. The third is doubt tending toward what is right, such as a consciousness that has no certainty as to

> whether sound is permanent or impermanent but tends toward the right view that sound is impermanent. These three stages of doubt are often experienced successively in the process of passing from wrong views, or ignorance, to correct views, or wisdom.
>
> A correct assumption is a conceptual consciousness (not a sense consciousness, for instance) which 'decides' that, for instance, sound is impermanent but does not have unshakeable conviction. Usually, even when many proofs demonstrating the subtle impermanence of compounded phenomena are given, a valid and unshakeable inference of the momentary impermanence of sound is not immediately generated. Most persons first gain only a correct assumption, which is not entirely unshakeable, and later, after familiarization with correct reasoning, gain an inference.
>
> The fifth non-prime awareness is an awareness to which an object appears without being noticed. This refers to a consciousness which, due to lack of interest and so forth, does not have sufficient power to draw the mental consciousness into noticing the perception. For example, when one has great interest in seeing a beautiful object, the conversation of someone close by might not be noticed. Technically, the conversation is heard, but it is not noticed and cannot be remembered.

Among these, two—direct perceptions and awarenesses to which an object appears but is not noticed—are necessarily devoid of conceptuality and are unmistaken, and three—inferential, correctly assuming, and doubting awarenesses—are only conceptual consciousnesses [because they never perceive their objects directly].[1]

> Subsequent cognitions and wrong consciousnesses can be either conceptual or non-conceptual awarenesses.

When a consciousness comprehends an object, it realizes it within the context of having been generated in the image of its object. Also, minds and mental factors are asserted to be one substantial entity.[2]

Terms

The definition of a term is: an object of hearing that causes the meaning that is its own object of expression to be understood. If terms are divided from the viewpoint of their objects of expression, there are two types, terms that express types and terms that express collections. An example of the first is the term 'form'; an example of the second is the term 'pot'.

---

[1] The Dharamsala 1967 edition (37.11) mistakenly reads *snang la ma nges pa'i blo dang lnga yod pa las the tshom dang yid dpyod gnyis ni rtog pa kho na yin no*, whereas it should read *snang la ma nges pa'i blo dang* ***lnga'o// de dag las mngon sum dang snang la ma nges pa'i blo gnyis la rtog bral ma 'khrul bas khyab cing/ rjes dpag/ yid dpyod/ the tshom gsum ni*** *rtog pa kho na yin no* in accordance with the Collected Works edition (510.3), the Go-mang 1980 edition (37.5), the Peking edition (15b.3), the Tibet Go-mang 1987 edition (12b.6), and Mimaki (87.16). The Teacher Training edition (37.2) has an even more confused reading that starts in the previous sentence: *tshad min gyi blo la/ bcad shes/ log shes/ the tshom/ yid dpyod/ the tshom gsum ni rtog pa kho na yin no.*

[2] For more reading on the topic of consciousness in the system of the Sūtra School Following Reasoning, see Lati Rinbochay and Elizabeth Napper, *Mind in Tibetan Buddhism* (London: Rider and Company, 1980; Ithaca: Snow Lion, 1980). For a more historical presentation, see Leonard van der Kuijp, *Contributions to the Development of Tibetan Buddhist Epistemology* (Wiesbaden: Franz Steiner Verlag, 1983).

> Terms that express types and terms that express collections are not mutually exclusive. For, the term 'pot' expresses both a type and a collection since pot is a type and is a collection composed of parts. 'Table and vase' is a term that expresses a collection but not a type.

Again, if terms are divided from the viewpoint of their manner of expression, there are two types: terms that express qualities and terms that express qualificands. An example of the first type is the term 'impermanence of sound';[1] an example of the second type is the term 'impermanent sound'.[2]

ASSERTIONS ON THE PATHS

This section has three parts: objects of observation of the paths, objects abandoned by the paths, and nature of the paths.

Objects of Observation of the Paths

The sixteen aspects of the four truths, impermanence and so forth,[3] are the objects of observation of the paths. The Proponents of Sūtra assert that the subtle selflessness and the subtle selflessness of persons are mutually inclusive.

> These are mutually inclusive because the Proponents of Sūtra do not assert a selflessness of phenomena as do the Great Vehicle schools.

A person's emptiness of being a self that is permanent [non-disintegrating], unitary [partless], and independent [not depending on the mental and physical aggre-

---

[1] *sgra'i mi rtag pa.*

[2] *sgra mi rtag pa.*

[3] For a listing of these sixteen aspects, see pp. 203-204.

gates] is asserted to be the coarse selflessness of persons. A person's emptiness of being substantially existent in the sense of being self-sufficient [i.e., able to exist by itself] is asserted to be the subtle selflessness of persons.

Objects Abandoned by the Paths

Like the Proponents of the Great Exposition, the Proponents of Sūtra [when referring to the objects abandoned by the path] use the vocabulary of the conception of a self of persons, afflictive ignorance [which obstructs liberation from cyclic existence], and non-afflictive ignorance [which obstructs the all-knowingness of a Buddha]. Aside from merely those, the Proponents of Sūtra and the Proponents of the Great Exposition do not assert a conception of a self of phenomena, nor do they assert obstructions to omniscience, etc.

Nature of the Paths

They make a presentation of the five paths of the three vehicles. They assert that all sixteen moments of the eight paths of forbearance and the eight paths of knowledge[1] are the path of seeing.

Because the appearing object of direct perception must be a specifically characterized object, the Proponents of Sūtra do not assert that the subtle selflessness of persons is the object of the mode of apprehension by an uninterrupted path of a Hearer's [or anyone's] path of seeing. This is because they assert that the subtle selflessness of persons is realized *implicitly* by Hearers [and so forth] through *explicit* comprehension of compositional phenomena [the mental and physical aggregates] that are devoid of a self of persons.

---

[1] For discussion of these, see pp. 207-209.

The object comprehended by an uninterrupted path belonging to a path of seeing or a path of meditation must be perceived directly. Whatever is perceived directly must be a specifically characterized phenomenon, and such are always compounded phenomena. An emptiness, however, is an uncompounded phenomenon and, therefore, not a specifically characterized phenomenon. Since an emptiness cannot be cognized directly, it is asserted that a yogic direct perception does not *explicitly* cognize selflessness. Rather, it cognizes the mind and body as no longer qualified with such a self. Thus, it is compounded phenomena, the mental and physical aggregates, that are directly cognized, and thereby the emptiness of a self of persons is *implicitly* realized. This fact greatly distinguishes the Proponents of Sūtra from the Great Vehicle schools, which assert direct cognition of emptiness itself.

ASSERTIONS ON THE FRUITS OF THE PATHS

The Proponents of Sūtra assert that there is no Foe Destroyer who falls from abandonment [of all afflictions] or from realization [of the subtle personal selflessness]. They also assert that the form aggregate of a Buddha is Buddha. Other than this, the Sūtra School's assertions on the ways of actualizing the fruits of the three vehicles and so forth are similar to those of the Great Exposition School.

In the chapter on the Great Exposition School, Ḡön-chok-jik-may-w̄ang-b̄o said, 'A Buddha's physical body is included in the same lifetime as the physical base of a Bodhisattva on the path of preparation. Therefore, they assert that

> this body is not a Buddha Jewel [an object of refuge] although it is Buddha.' Hence, he seems to contradict himself here by saying that the assertion by the Proponents of Sūtra that the form aggregate of a Buddha is Buddha is not shared with the Proponents of the Great Exposition.

Both the Proponents of the Great Exposition and the Proponents of Sūtra maintain that the scriptural collections [i.e., discipline,[1] sets of discourses,[2] and manifest knowledge][3] of the Great Vehicle are not the word of Buddha. However, it is said that there are later Proponents of the Great Exposition and later Proponents of Sūtra who do assert them to be the word of Buddha.[4]

* * *

Stanza between sections:[5]

A festival of delight should be had by those propounding reasoning
In this expression of the secret words of reasoning
Of the Exemplifiers Following Reasoning,
Accurate from having trained well in the texts of reasoning.

---

[1] *'dul ba, vinaya.*

[2] *mdo sde, sūtrānta.*

[3] *chos mngon pa, abhidharma.*

[4] For more reading on the tenets of the Sūtra School, see Anne C. Klein, *Knowing, Naming, and Negation*. Ithaca: Snow Lion, 1989; and Anne C. Klein, *Knowledge and Liberation: A Buddhist epistemological analysis in support of transformative religious experience: Tibetan interpretations of Dignaga and Dharmakirti* (Ithaca: Snow Lion, 1986).

[5] The author uses the word 'reasoning' (*rigs pa*) in all four lines to indicate the emphasis on reasoning in the Sūtra School Following Reasoning.

6 The Mind Only School

The presentation of the tenets of the Proponents of Mind Only is in four parts: definition, subschools, etymology, and assertions of tenets.

DEFINITION

The definition of a Proponent of Mind Only is: a person propounding Buddhist tenets who asserts the true existence of other-powered natures but does not assert external objects.[1]

> Other-powered natures are phenomena that are under the influence of causes and conditions that are other than themselves; therefore, other-powered natures are impermanent. They are held to be truly established by this system but not by the Middle Way School. External objects are objects that are different entities from the consciousness apprehending

[1] *phyi don, bāhyārtha.*

them. That the Mind Only School refutes external objects means that they refute that a form, for instance, and the valid cognition apprehending it are different entities; still, this school holds that forms are the same entity as the consciousness that perceives them—both the form and the consciousness apprehending it being produced from a single predisposition contained within the mind. This school is, nevertheless, not solipsistic; it accepts that there are other beings who are different entities from oneself.

SUBSCHOOLS

Proponents of Mind Only are of two types, True Aspectarians[1] and False Aspectarians.[2] Differences exist between these two groups because (1) an appearance of a blue [patch] as blue to an eye consciousness perceiving blue is the 'aspect' that is the basis of debate between the True and False Aspectarians and (2) True Aspectarians assert that an appearance of blue as blue to an eye consciousness apprehending blue exists as it appears whereas False Aspectarians maintain that an appearance of blue as blue does not exist as it appears to an eye consciousness apprehending blue .

It is important to determine just what 'aspect' (*rnam pa, ākāra*) is being discussed in a passage, for there are many meanings to this word. In general, 'object-aspect' (*yul rnam, viṣaya-ākāra*) means the object itself; 'that which has (taken on) the aspect of the apprehended' (*gzung rnam, grāhya-ākāra*) means the perceiving subject; 'apprehending aspect' (*'dzin rnam, grāhaka-*

---

1 *rnam bden pa, satyākāravādin.*
2 *rnam brdzun pa, alīkākāravādin.*

ākāra) means the perceiver of the apprehending subject, that is, a self-cognizing consciousness. However, sometimes 'that which has the aspect of the apprehended' (*gzung rnam*, *grāhya-ākāra*) refers to the object rather than the subject. Here, 'aspect' refers to a mode of appearance of the object.

The True Aspectarians hold that a blue patch that appears as a gross or coalesced object does in fact exist as a gross or coalesced object in the manner in which it appears, whereas the False Aspectarians say it does not. Being Proponents of Mind Only, the True Aspectarians agree with the False Aspectarians that the appearance of a blue patch as an external object is false. However, unlike the False Aspectarians, the True Aspectarians maintain that, within the context of this false appearance, the portion of the appearance as a gross object is correct. The False Aspectarians, on the other hand, hold that there is a sense of grossness beyond what is actually there.

The above presentation is correct because:

1 Both the True and False Aspectarians are similar in asserting that blue appears as blue to an eye consciousness apprehending blue.

This means that both accept that there are eye consciousnesses that perceive blue as blue and not as yellow, for there are objects that are the same entity as a perceiving consciousness even though there are no external objects. Similarly, both agree that there are eye consciousnesses that perceive blue as yellow, due to some fault in the eye.

2 They are also similar in asserting that blue appears as

a gross object[1] to an eye consciousness apprehending blue and that blue [falsely] appears to be an external object.

Both True and False Aspectarians agree on the undeniable point that a patch of blue appears to be a gross object—something composed of many particles and not just a single particle—and that even to valid sense consciousnesses objects appear falsely as if they were entities external to the perceiving consciousness.

3 However, the True Aspectarians assert that an appearance of blue as an external object to an eye consciousness apprehending blue is polluted by ignorance, but that an appearance of blue as blue and an appearance of blue as a gross object are not polluted by ignorance, whereas the False Aspectarians assert not only that an appearance of blue as an external object is polluted by ignorance, but also that an appearance of blue as blue[2] and an appearance of blue as a gross object is polluted by ignorance.

Therefore, the definition of a True Aspectarian Proponent of Mind Only is: a Proponent of Mind Only who asserts that an appearance of a gross object to a sense consciousness exists as it appears. The definition of a False Aspectarian Proponent of Mind Only is: a Proponent of Mind Only who asserts that an appearance of a

---

[1] In the Dharamsala 1967 edition (41.6), read *dang/ sngon po* ***rags par snang ba dang/*** *sngon po phyi* for *dang/ sngon po phyi* in accordance with the Collected Works edition (512.5), etc. This misprint (or editorial 'correction') is pointed out in the Go-mang 1980 edition (3.8).

[2] In the Dharamsala 1967 edition (41.11), read *zad/ sngon po* ***sngon por snang ba dang/*** *sngon po rags* for *zad/ sngon po rags* in accordance with the Collected Works edition (512.5), etc. This misprint (or editorial 'correction' by the publisher of the Dharamsala 1967 edition) is pointed out in the Go-mang 1980 edition (3.8).

gross object to a sense consciousness does not exist as it appears.

There are three types of True Aspectarians: Proponents of an Equal Number of Subjects and Objects,[1] Half-Eggists,[2] and Non-Pluralists.[3]

> Only in the Mind Only and Yogic Autonomy systems do object and subject exist simultaneously. One latency[4] or seed[5] simultaneously produces both object and subject. For instance, one latency would produce the mottle of colors on the wing of a butterfly as well as the eye consciousness that apprehends these colors. Since the object appears to the perceiving consciousness, there is a question of whether just one aspect of the object, the mottle, appears to the subject, or whether many aspects of the object, such as the blue, yellow, red, and so forth, appear to the subject. Also, every school except the Great Exposition School asserts that the perceiving subject, such as an eye consciousness, comes to be like its object, much as a mirror comes to be like an object set before it. Thus, a similar question is asked: does an eye consciousness come to be produced in the many aspects of the object, an aspect of red, an aspect of blue, an aspect of yellow, and so forth? The question is this: at any one moment are there many eye consciousnesses that perceive the individual aspects of the object or is there one eye consciousness that perceives the object in general?

---

1 *gzung 'dzin grangs mnyam pa.*

2 *sgo nga phyed tshal pa.*

3 *sna tshogs gnyis med pa.*

4 *bag chags, vāsanā.*

5 *sa bon, bīja.*

If there are many eye consciousnesses each moment, it would seem to contradict scripture which says that a plurality of consciousnesses of *similar type* does not occur at the same moment, even though an eye consciousness, an ear consciousness, a nose consciousness, a tongue consciousness, a body consciousness, and a mental consciousness may exist at the same moment. On the other hand, if there is only one eye consciousness every moment, how are all the individual aspects of the object perceived?

A few possible 'solutions' are:

(1) there are many eye consciousnesses each moment equal in number to the number of aspects belonging to the object;
(2) there is one general eye consciousness that apprehends the mottle, and there are many parts of this eye consciousness that individually apprehend the individual colors;
(3) there is only one eye consciousness each moment, and moment by moment the various aspects are serially apprehended.

All three of these are represented in the Sūtra School where external objects are asserted. The Proponents of Mind Only offer another set of three which are given below in accordance with three different sets of interpretations by Tibetan scholars. The amount of attention that Ḡön-chok-jik-may-w̄ang-b̄o devotes to this topic suggests that despite the supposedly decisive analysis of this topic in the *Great Exposition of Tenets* by his previous incarnation, Jam-ȳang-shay-b̄a, he was not convinced. Perhaps, Ḡön-chok-jik-may-w̄ang-b̄o found the various

> interpretations a convenient means for stimulating interest in issues of perception.

The assertions of scholars with regard to the differences between these three do not agree. Gung-ru Gyel-tsen-sang-b̄o[1] explains in his *Distillation of the Middle Way*[2] that:

1 Proponents of an Equal Number of Subjects and Objects are so called because they assert that when an eye consciousness apprehending the mottled colors on the wing of a butterfly apprehends that mottle, from the side of the object, aspects of each of the different colors—blue, yellow, and so forth—are cast [to the perceiving consciousness] and also from the subject's side, aspects of the each of the different colors—blue, yellow, and so forth—are produced in the manner of being true aspects.

> It is doubtful that any Proponent of Mind Only would assert that an object is known through its 'casting its aspect' toward the perceiving consciousness. This is the language of schools that assert external objects. In the Mind Only School, objects are known through the activation of internal predispositions for perception.

2 Half-Eggists are so called because they assert that, when the mottled colors on the wing of a butterfly are apprehended, from the side of the object, aspects

---

[1] *gung ru rgyal mtshan bzang po*; Herbert Guenther (*Buddhist Philosophy in Theory and Practice*, n.5 p. 220) gives his dates as 1350-1425 and identifies him as associated with S̄e-ra Monastic University. 'Gung-ru' is the name of a house unit both in S̄e-ra Monastic University and in Dre-b̄ung Monastic University.

[2] *dbu ma'i stong mthun*. The term *stong mthun*, also spelled *stong 'thun*, is a frequently used as a title for texts; more properly, it should be spelled *stong thun*, which has the sense of a distillation of the manifold into something more manageable.

of each of the different colors—blue, yellow, and so forth—are cast [to the perceiving consciousness] and from the subject's side, aspects of the each of the different colors—blue, yellow, and so forth—are produced in an aspectless manner.

3 Non-Pluralists are so called because they assert that, when the mottled colors on the wing of a butterfly are apprehended, from the side of the object, aspects of each of the different colors—blue, yellow, and so forth—are not cast [to the perceiving consciousness] but the aspect of only the mottle is cast, and from the subject's side, aspects of the each of the different colors—blue, yellow, and so forth—are not produced in an aspectless manner but the aspect of only the mottle is produced in an aspectless manner.

Drung-chen Lek-b̄a-sang-b̄o,[1] Paṇ-chen S̄ö-nam-drak-b̄a,[2] and so forth explain that:

1 Proponents of an Equal Number of Subjects and Objects are so called because they assert that just as the blue and the yellow, which appear to a sense consciousness apprehending a mottle, are different substantial entities, so within the eye consciousness apprehending the mottle there are many eye consciousnesses that are different substantial entities.

2 Half-Eggists are so called because they assert that, although in general a [patch of] blue and an eye consciousness apprehending the blue are of the entity of consciousness, they are different substantial entities.

It would seem that in this interpretation they are called Half-Eggists because they are one

---

[1] *drung chen legs pa bzang po.*

[2] *paṇ chen bsod nams grags pa,* 1478-1554. He is the author of the textbook literature of the L̄o-s̄el-l̄ing College of Dre-b̄ung Monastic University and of the S̄har-d̄zay College of Gan-den Monastic University.

half like the Proponents of Sūtra in that they maintain that subject and object are different entities and one half like the Proponents of Mind Only since in general they hold that subject and object are one entity. It is highly doubtful that any Proponent of Mind Only would assert that subject and object are different entities.

3 Non-Pluralists are so called because they assert that just as the blue and yellow of a mottle are one substantial entity, so the sense consciousnesses that apprehend the blue and the yellow and are within the eye consciousness apprehending the mottle are one substantial entity.

Jam-ȳang-shay-b̄a's *Great Exposition of Tenets*[1] explains that:

1 Proponents of an Equal Number of Subjects and Objects are so called because they assert that when an eye consciousness apprehending the mottle [of colors on the wing of a butterfly] looks at the mottle, consciousnesses of similar type equal in number to the number of colors—blue, yellow, and so forth of the mottle—are produced simultaneously.

2 Half-Eggists are so called because they assert that although the blue and an eye consciousness apprehending the blue are serial in terms of the time of their coming into existence, they are one substantial entity

---

1 Jam-ȳang-shay-b̄a's *Great Exposition of Tenets, nga* 52a.5ff. Jam-ȳang-shay-b̄a is the author of the textbook literature the Go-mang College of Dre-b̄ung Monastic University and the previous incarnation of the author of this text, Ḡön-chok-jik-may-w̄ang-b̄o. It is particularly interesting that, despite Jam-ȳang-shay-b̄a's supposedly having settled this issue in a decisive way, Ḡön-chok-jik-may-w̄ang-b̄o does no more than list it as the third of three possibilities, after which he advises his readers to choose whatever seems most suitable to them.

in terms of the time of their observation.

> They maintain that the object exists before and helps to produce the perceiving consciousness, but they hold that at the same time that the object is observed by the eye consciousness, the eye consciousness is observed by a self-cognizing consciousness.

3 Non-Pluralists are so called because they assert that it is not the case when an eye consciousness apprehending a mottle looks at its object, consciousnesses of similar type equal in number to the number of colors—blue, yellow, and so forth of the mottle—are produced simultaneously. Rather, they assert that the mere eye consciousness apprehending the mottle is the sense consciousness apprehending the blue, yellow, and so forth of the mottle.

Since [there are these different interpretations], one should hold whatever is most appealing.

Proponents of an Equal Number of Subjects and Objects are of two types: those who assert eight consciousnesses [the five sense consciousnesses, a mental consciousness, an afflicted mind,[1] and a mind-basis-of-all];[2] and those who assert six consciousnesses [the five sense consciousnesses and the mental consciousness]. Non-Pluralists are said to be of two types, proponents of six consciousnesses and proponents of a single consciousness.

It is said that the False Aspectarians are of two types, Tainted False Aspectarians and Non-Tainted False Aspectarians. It is said that Tainted False Aspectarians are so called because they assert that the nature of the mind is polluted by the latencies of ignorance and that Non-Tainted False Aspectarians are so called because they as-

---

[1] *nyon mongs can gyi yid, kliṣṭamanas.*
[2] *kun gzhi rnam par shes pa, ālayavijñāna.*

sert that the entity of the mind is not in the least polluted by the latencies of ignorance. Or [according to another interpretation] it is said that the Tainted False Aspectarians are so called because they assert that although there is no ignorance at Buddhahood, there are mistaken appearances and that Non-Tainted False Aspectarians are so called because they assert that because there is no ignorance at Buddhahood, there are also no mistaken appearances.

> The great Mongolian savant, J̄ang-ḡya Röl-b̄ay-dor-jay[1] rejects both interpretations of Tainted False Aspectarians saying that there is no Buddhist system which asserts that the nature of the mind itself is polluted or that a Buddha perceives false appearances.

Further, Proponents of Mind Only can be divided into two types: Followers of Scripture and Followers of Reasoning. The former are followers of Asaṅga's Five Treatises on the Grounds,[2] and the latter are followers of Dharmakīrti's Seven Treatises on Prime Cognition.

ETYMOLOGY

Why are they called 'Proponents of Mind Only'? They are called 'Proponents of Mind Only'[3] and 'Proponents of Cognition'[4] because they propound that all phenomena are of the mere entity of the mind. Also, because they settle the practice of the deeds of the path from the

---

1 J̄ang-ḡya, *Presentation of Tenets,* 212.17.

2 Asaṅga lived during the fourth century; for a list of these texts, see the Bibliography.

3 *sems tsam pa, cittamātrin.*

4 *rnam rig pa, vijñaptika/vijñaptivādin.*

yogic point of view,[1] they are also called 'Yogic Practitioners'.[2]

ASSERTIONS OF TENETS

This section has three parts: their assertions on the basis, paths, and fruits.

ASSERTIONS ON THE BASIS

This section has two parts: assertions regarding objects and assertions regarding object-possessors.

Assertions Regarding Objects

The Proponents of Mind Only assert that all objects of knowledge are included in the three characters.[3]

> These are other-powered characters,[4] thoroughly established characters,[5] and imputational characters.[6] The three characters are also called the three natures.[7]

This is so because they assert that all compounded phenomena are other-powered characters, that the real natures of all phenomena [emptinesses] are thoroughly established characters, and that all other objects of knowledge are imputational characters.

> Except for emptinesses, all permanent phe-

---

[1] In the Go-mang 1980 edition (45.5), read *rnal 'byor pa'i gzhi'i* for *rnal 'byor pa'i bzhi'i* in accordance with Collected Works (515.4), Peking (18b.4), the Dharamsala 1967 (45.15), the Teacher Training (46.8), the Tibet Go-mang 1987 (15a.6), and Mimaki (91.18).
[2] *rnal 'byor spyod pa pa, yogācāra.*
[3] *mtshan nyid gsum, trilakṣaṇa.*
[4] *gzhan dbang, paratantra.*
[5] *yongs grub, pariniṣpanna.*
[6] *kun btags, parikalpita.*
[7] *rang bzhin gsum/ ngo bo nyid gsum, trisvabhāva.*

nomena such as uncompounded space are imputational natures. All emptinesses are thoroughly established natures. All impermanent phenomena are other-powered natures. In this way, all phenomena are included within the three natures.

Imputational natures are of two types, existent and non-existent. Except for emptinesses, all permanent objects of knowledge, such as uncompounded space, are included in the category of existent imputational natures. Non-existent imputational natures are not objects of knowledge, and thus they are not phenomena. For example, a permanent self or a table that is a separate entity from the consciousness perceiving it do not exist at all; these are non-existent imputational natures.

They assert that the three natures exist in their own right[1] and exist inherently.[2]

If a class has both existent and non-existent members, the class itself is considered to be existent. Thus, imputational natures in general are existent even though some imputational natures, such as a permanent self, do not exist. Since in the Mind Only School whatever exists necessarily inherently exists—i.e., can be found when sought among its bases of designation, even imputational natures, as a class, exist inherently.

However, there are differences with regard to whether the natures truly exist or not, because the Proponents of Mind Only assert that imputational natures do not truly exist and that both other-powered natures and thor-

---

1 *rang ngos nas grub pa, svarūpasiddha.*
2 *rang bzhin gyis grub pa, svabhāvasiddha.*

oughly established natures are truly established.

The definition of an imputational nature is: that which does not ultimately exist but exists for a conceptual consciousness. When divided, imputational natures are of two types, enumerated [or existent] imputational natures and imputational natures whose character is nihil [i.e., non-existent imputational natures]. An example of an existent imputational nature is object of knowledge.

> As generalities, object of knowledge, one, different, and so forth are permanent because their instances are both permanent and impermanent. In determining the classification of a category, existence predominates over non-existence and permanence predominates over impermanence.

Examples of non-existent imputational natures are the two selves.

> The two selves are a self of persons and a self of phenomena. Persons are empty of being self-sufficient, substantial entities, and phenomena are empty of being subjects and objects that are different entities. Thus, a non-existent imputational nature is something that exists for a conceptual consciousness, such as a substantially existent person, but does not actually exist at all. Existent imputational natures, on the other hand, do actually exist but only in dependence on a conceptual consciousness, as in the case of uncompounded space which can only be realized through conceptually eliminating obstructive contact.

The definition of an other-powered nature is: that which arises in dependence upon the power of others, that is, causes and conditions, and which is a base of a thoroughly established nature [an emptiness].

> All compounded phenomena are other-powered natures because they arise in dependence on the major and minor causes that produce them. An other-powered nature is a base of a thoroughly established nature because it is empty of being a separate entity from a consciousness that perceives it and hence is a substratum of the quality of that emptiness. Thus every product is a base of emptiness.

When divided, there are two types of other-powered natures, pure and impure. Pure other-powered natures are, for instance, the wisdom of Superiors subsequent to meditative equipoise and the major and minor marks of a Buddha.

> Superiors (those who have attained a path of seeing) directly cognize emptiness during meditative equipoise. Their wisdom at that time is a pure other-powered nature. When they rise from meditation, they have a second type of wisdom; this is the knowledge that although subject and object appear to be different entities, they are not different entities. This knowledge is indirect or conceptual, whereas during meditative equipoise they had direct cognition of emptiness.

Impure other-powered natures are, for instance, the mental and physical aggregates that are appropriated through contaminated [actions and afflictive emotions].

The definition of a thoroughly established nature is: a suchness that is an emptiness of either of the two selves [a self of persons or of phenomena].

> There is controversy among Ge-luk-b̄a colleges as to whether a selflessness of persons is a thoroughly established nature. Jam-ȳang-shay-b̄a, who is the author of the textbook literature

> of the Go-mang College of Dre-b̄ung Monastic University and the previous incarnation of the author of this book, holds that it is.

When divided, there are two types of thoroughly established natures, non-perverse and immutable. An example of the first is a Superior's wisdom during meditative equipoise. An example of the second is the real nature of phenomena. Although non-perverse thoroughly established natures are stated as a division of thoroughly established natures, they [actually] are not thoroughly established natures. This is because they are not final objects of observation of a path of purification through observation of which obstructions are extinguished.

> A Superior's wisdom consciousness of meditative equipoise is not an emptiness simply because it is a consciousness; it is a cognition of emptiness in the mode of being fused with emptiness. The two are fused like fresh water in fresh water, but they are nevertheless different for a conceptual consciousness. Therefore, it cannot be said that this wisdom itself is an emptiness, and thus it cannot serve as an object of meditation that would remove obstructions.

Again, objects of knowledge can be divided into the two, conventional truths and ultimate truths. The definition of a conventional truth is: an object found by a prime cognition that is a correct consciousness distinguishing a conventionality. Falsity,[1] conventional truth,[2] and nominal truth[3] are mutually inclusive.

All objects except emptinesses are falsities be-

---

[1] *brdzun pa, mṛṣā.*
[2] *kun rdzob bden pa, saṃvṛtisatya.*
[3] *tha snyad bden pa, vyavahārasatya.*

> cause they do not exist the way they appear, that is, as separate entities from a perceiving consciousness. However, in this system, impermanent phenomena and emptinesses truly exist, because the Proponents of Mind Only maintain that if these phenomena exist, they necessarily truly exist.

The definition of an ultimate truth is: an object found by a prime cognition that is a correct knower distinguishing an ultimate. Emptiness,[1] element of [a Superior's] qualities,[2] thoroughly established [nature],[3] ultimate truth,[4] limit of reality,[5] and thusness[6] are asserted to be mutually inclusive.

Ultimate truths necessarily exist by way of their own character, but conventional truths do not necessarily exist by way of their own character. This is because other-powered natures exist by way of their own character, but imputational natures [which are also conventional truths] do not exist by way of their own character [although they inherently exist and exist in their own right].

> Existent imputational natures, such as uncompounded space, are conventional truths, but non-existent imputational natures, such as a permanent self or a table that is a separate entity from a perceiving consciousness, are not even conventional truths because they do not exist.

---

1 *stong pa nyid, śūnyatā.*

2 *chos dbyings, dharmadhātu.* Because emptiness is that through meditation on which the qualities of a Superior are generated, it is called the 'element of [a Superior's] qualities'.

3 *yongs grub, pariniṣpanna.*

4 *don dam bden pa, paramārthasatya.*

5 *yang dag mtha', bhūtakoṭi.*

6 *de bzhin nyid, tathatā.*

Falsities do not necessarily falsely exist, for, although other-powered natures are falsities, they do not falsely exist.

> In the Mind Only School, other-powered natures are falsities, but they do not falsely exist. This is because, if they did not truly exist, they would not exist at all. Nevertheless, they are false in the sense that, due to the predispositions that exist in the mind of the perceiver, they appear to exist as entities separate from a perceiving consciousness. Realization of the fact that they truly exist prevents extreme views of non-existence, and realization of their falseness in the sense of appearing one way but existing another prevents extreme views of exaggerated existence.

Proponents of Sūtra, Proponents of Mind Only, and Autonomists all agree in their presentations of the three times and of non-affirming negatives.

> These three schools assert that a pastness and a futureness are permanent phenomena, that is, mere absences, and that present functioning things are impermanent. They, along with the Consequentialists, agree that negatives do not necessarily imply something in place of the objects that they negate.

The five sense objects—forms and so forth—do not exist as external objects because they are produced within the substantial entity of an internal consciousness through the power of predisposing latencies established by common and[1] uncommon actions in the mind-basis-

---

[1] In the the Dharamsala 1967 edition (48.15) and the Teacher Training edition (49.7) read *du thun mong dang thun mong ma yin* for *du thun mong ma yin* in accordance with the Collected Works edition

of-all.

The True Aspectarians assert that the five sense objects—forms, and so forth—are not external objects but do exist as gross objects. The False Aspectarians maintain that, if such were the case, then forms and so forth would have to be external objects; therefore, they assert that the five types of sense objects do not exist as gross objects [although they do, of course, accept part and whole].

Assertions Regarding Object-Possessors [Subjects]

The Followers of Scripture [mainly the followers of Asaṅga] assert eight consciousnesses; therefore, they assert that the mental consciousness and[1] the mind-basis-of-all is the person. The Followers of Reasoning [mainly the followers of Dharmakīrti] assert that the mental consciousness is the illustration of a person [i.e., is the person].

> This does not mean that all mental consciousnesses are the person, for there are many types of mental consciousnesses, desire, hatred, and so on. The mental consciousness

(517.3), the Peking edition (19b.6), the Go-mang 1980 edition (47.16), the Tibet Go-mang 1987 edition (16a.5), and Mimaki (93.2).

[1] In the Dharamsala 1967 edition (49.6) and the Teacher Training edition (49.16) read *'dod pas* ***yid kyi rnam par shes pa dang*** *kun* for *'dod pas kun* in accordance with the Collected Works edition (517.6), the Peking edition (20a.2) the Go-mang 1980 edition (48.8), the Tibet Go-mang 1987 edition (16b.1), and Mimaki (93.10). As with other variations noted earlier, the deletion of the reference to the mental consciousness reflects an editor's attempt to improve the text. Indeed, it is unusual to assert that both the mental consciousness and the mind-basis-of-all are held to be the person in the system of the Proponents of Mind Only Following Scripture; it is more commonly said that when the person is sought among his/her bases of designation, one finds the mind-basis-of-all, and thus the mind-basis-of-all is posited as the illustration of a person.

> that is the actual person is a subtle, neutral form of the mental consciousness which exists unceasingly throughout the whole life. It is called the mental consciousness that is the base of the name of the person. It is much like the mind-basis-of-all but is not separated off as a different entity from the other forms of the mental consciousness.

The Followers of Scripture assert that a mind-basis-of-all observes [the five senses, the five objects, and] the internal latencies.

> The actual objects of observation of a mind-basis-of-all are the five senses and the five types of objects which are apprehended by the five sense consciousnesses. The mind-basis-of-all does not actually observe the latencies, but it is *said* to observe them because all perceptions are produced by the latencies.

A mind-basis-of-all has the aspect of not discriminating its objects [it does not notice its objects and cannot induce another consciousness to notice objects], and its entity is undefiled and neutral. It is a constant main mind, associated only with the five omnipresent mental factors.

> The five omnipresent mental factors are contact, feeling, discrimination, intention, and mental activity.

Moreover, from among the two possibilities of being defiled or non-defiled, it is non-defiled and neutral.

> It is non-defiled because it is not accompanied by afflictive mental factors.

A mind-basis-of-all is not virtuous because it exists in the continuum of one whose roots of virtue are severed. It is also not non-virtuous because those of the upper realms [the Form and Formless Realms] have a mind-basis-of-all; [therefore, it is neutral].

> In the Form and Formless Realms, even the mental factors of pride and so forth are not non-virtuous but neutral.

The object of observation of an afflicted mind[1] is a mind-basis-of-all.

> However , it does not perceive the actual entity of the mind-basis-of-all as it is, for if it did, it would not perceive it as a self-sufficient person.

Its aspect is that of considering the mind-basis-of-all to be [a substantially existent or self-sufficient] I. Its entity is defiled and neutral.

> An afflicted mind has nine accompanying mental factors, the five omnipresent mental factors and four mental factors that defile it: attachment to self, obscuration about self, pride in self, and view of self. When these four defiling mental factors are cleared away, the entity of an afflicted mind still exists, but it is then pure. At Buddhahood an afflicted mind is transformed into a wisdom of equality which views all objects equally as not different entities from the consciousness perceiving them.

Their way of presenting the six operative consciousnesses agrees with the general [Buddhist presentation of these six].

Both Followers of Scripture and Followers of Reasoning] assert that prime cognitions are of two types, direct and inferential, and they also assert a presentation of four types of direct prime cognition [sense, self-cognizing, mental, and yogic prime cognitions]. Self-cognizing

---

[1] *nyon yid, kliṣṭamanas*.

direct perceptions and yogic direct perceptions are necessarily non-mistaken consciousnesses [because they are not infected by the false appearance of subject and object as different entities].

True Aspectarians assert that an eye consciousness in the continuum of the short-sighted [an ordinary being] that apprehends blue is a non-mistaken consciousness.[1]

> Etymologically, the term 'short-sighted' or 'one who looks near-by' refers to one who does not see beyond ordinary worldly appearances.

According to the False Aspectarians, all sense direct perceptions in the continuum of the short-sighted are necessarily mistaken consciousnesses. Also, they assert that mental direct perceptions in such a continuum are of two types, mistaken and non-mistaken.

> Other scholars assert that all instances of both sense direct perceptions and mental direct perceptions in the continuum of an ordinary being are mistaken because objects appear to these consciousnesses to be separate entities from the perceiving consciousness.

ASSERTIONS ON THE PATHS

This section has three parts: objects of paths, objects abandoned by the paths, and the nature of the paths.

Objects of Observation of the Paths

The sixteen aspects of the four noble truths are imper-

---

[1] The Dharamsala 1967 edition (50.8) adds 'with respect to the portion of the appearance of blue as blue' (*sngon po sngon por snang bas* [sic] *cha la*). The editor of this edition clearly wanted to make small adjustments in the text without indicating that such had been made.

manence and so forth (see pp. 203-204). The coarse selflessness of persons is a person's emptiness of being permanent, unitary, and independent. The subtle selflessness of persons is a person's emptiness of being substantially existent in the sense of being self-sufficient.

There are two subtle selflessnesses of phenomena:

1 a form and its prime cognition's emptiness of being separate substantial entities;
2 a form's emptiness of being established by way of its own character as the basis adhered to by the conceptual consciousness apprehending it.

> A form is not a separate entity from a consciousness apprehending it, and a consciousness of a form is not a separate entity from its object. Also, forms, consciousnesses, and so forth are not established by way of their own character as the referents of either conceptual consciousness or their respective terminology. The two types of emptiness are said to be intimately related.

Both subtle selflessnesses [of persons and of phenomena] are asserted to be emptinesses. However, an emptiness is not necessarily either of these, for both true cessations and nirvanas are asserted to be emptinesses.

> This is a technical point. A true cessation is an emptiness of the mind of one who has utterly extinguished an obstruction, and it must be either of the two selflessnesses. But once it can be either, in general it is neither.

Compounded phenomena are asserted to be the same substantial entity[1] as the prime cognitions that apprehend them. Uncompounded phenomena are asserted to

---

[1] *rdzas gcig, ekadravya.*

be the same entity[1] as the prime cognitions that apprehend them.

Objects Abandoned by the Paths

The objects abandoned by the paths are the afflictive obstructions[2] and the obstructions to [simultaneous cognition of all] objects of knowledge.[3]

> Less literally, these are the obstructions to liberation from cyclic existence and obstructions to omniscience.

The obstructions to liberation are, for instance, consciousnesses conceiving a coarse or subtle self of persons, together with their seeds, as well as the six root afflictive emotions and twenty secondary afflictive emotions.

> The six root afflictions are desire, anger, pride, ignorance, doubt, and afflictive view. The twenty secondary afflictions are belligerence, resentment, concealment, spite, jealousy, miserliness, deceit, dissimulation, haughtiness, harmfulness, non-shame, non-embarrassment, lethargy, excitement, non-faith, laziness, non-conscientiousness, forgetfulness, non-introspection, and distraction.

The obstructions to omniscience are, for instance, consciousnesses conceiving a self of phenomena, together with their predisposing latencies.

Bodhisattvas take the obstructions to omniscience as their main object of abandonment; they do not take the obstructions to liberation as their main object of abandonment. Lesser Vehicle Learners [Hearers and Solitary

---

1 *ngo bo gcig, ekavastu.*
2 *nyon sgrib/ nyon mongs pa'i sgrib pa, kleśāvaraṇa.*
3 *shes sgrib/ shes bya'i sgrib pa, jñeyāvaraṇa.*

Realizers on the paths of accumulation, preparation, seeing, and meditation] take the obstructions to liberation as their main object of abandonment and do not take the obstructions to omniscience as their main object of abandonment.

Nature of the Paths[1]

A presentation of the five paths—the paths of accumulation, preparation, seeing, meditation, and no more learning—is made for each of the three vehicles. The Proponents of Mind Only also assert a presentation of the ten Bodhisattva grounds for the Great Vehicle.

> The first of the ten grounds begins with the Great Vehicle path of seeing which is also the beginning of the Superior's path. Roughly speaking, the remaining nine grounds are the path of meditation.

ASSERTIONS ON THE FRUITS OF THE PATHS[2]

Those whose lineage is definite as that of the Lesser Vehicle take as their main object of meditation the thoroughly established nature in terms of the selflessness of persons.

> The three natures can be presented either in terms of the selflessness of persons or in terms of the selflessness of phenomena. The former

---

[1] All editions of the text (Collected Works, 519.4; Peking edition, 21a.3, etc.) read 'presentation of the paths' (*lam gyi rnam bzhag*); we have used 'nature of the paths' for the sake of consistency with the other chapters and thus accessibility.

[2] All editions of the text (Collected Works, 519.5; Peking edition, 21a.4, etc.) read 'actualization of the fruits' (*'bras bu mngon du byed tshul*); we have used 'assertions on the fruits of the path' which accords more with the title announced earlier.

presentation is for practitioners of the Lesser Vehicle, whereas the latter is for practitioners of the Great Vehicle. From among the three natures, in both presentations other-powered natures are impermanent phenomena produced in dependence upon causes and conditions, but the imputational nature, in terms of the selflessness of persons, is a person's substantial establishment in the sense of being self-sufficient whereas, in terms of the selflessness of phenomena, it is the establishment of objects by way of their own character as the bases adhered to by the conceptual consciousness apprehending them (or a difference of entity between subject and object). Similarly, the thoroughly established nature, in terms of the selflessness of persons, is a person's not being substantially established in the sense of being self-sufficient, whereas, in terms of the selflessness of phenomena, the thoroughly established nature is objects' not being established by way of their own character as the bases adhered to by the conceptual consciousness apprehending them (or the absence of a difference of entity between subject and object).

When familiarity with the thoroughly established nature is complete, then in dependence on the vajra-like meditative stabilization of the Lesser Vehicle path of meditation, they abandon all the obstructions to liberation and simultaneously actualize the fruit of a Lesser Vehicle Foe Destroyer.

There is not even the slightest difference between Hearers and Solitary Realizers regarding the selflessness that is their object of meditation, or regarding the afflictive emotions that are their objects of abandonment. Therefore, the presentation of the eight Approachers and Abiders applies to both. However, Solitary Realizers only live in the Desire Realm [and do not exist in the Form or Formless Realms]; therefore, the arrangement of the twenty members of the spiritual community does not apply to them.

Still, it is not the case that there are no differences at all between Hearers and Solitary Realizers. It is asserted that Hearers are inferior and Solitary Realizers are superior from the point of view that a Solitary Realizer extends the amassing of the collections of merit for one hundred aeons, whereas a Hearer does not. The fruits that arise for Solitary Realizers and Hearers through the force of these practices are also respectively superior and inferior.

The Mind Only Followers of Scripture do not assert that a Lesser Vehicle Foe Destroyer who is solely directed to peace ever enters the path of the Great Vehicle. However, they assert that a Foe Destroyer whose enlightenment becomes transformed [into that of a Bodhisattva] enters the path of the Great Vehicle. This entry is from a nirvana with remainder. There is no entry from a nirvana without remainder because they assert that there are three final vehicles.

> A remainderless nirvana is asserted to be a severance of the continuum of form and consciousness, like the extinguishing of a lamp. Thus, it would be impossible to enter the Great Vehicle at that point.

The Mind Only Followers of Reasoning assert that all Lesser Vehicle Foe Destroyers enter into the Great Vehicle because they assert that there is [only] one final vehicle.

Those who have the Great Vehicle lineage take as their main object of meditation the thoroughly established nature in terms of the selflessness of phenomena. They practice meditation on the selflessness of phenomena in conjunction with [amassing] the collections of merit over three periods of countless aeons and gradually traverse the five paths and the ten grounds. By means of the uninterrupted path at the end of their continuum [as a sentient being who still has obstructions to be abandoned], they completely abandon the two obstructions, thereby attaining Buddhahood in a Highest Pure Land.[1] They attain a Truth Body,[2] the abandonment of obstructions and realization of selflessness that is the perfection of their own welfare, and attain the two Form Bodies [Complete Enjoyment Body[3] and Emanation Body[4]], the perfection of activities for others' welfare.

According to some followers of Asaṅga's *Compendium of Manifest Knowledge*,[5] it is evident that complete enlightenment also can occur in a human life.

> They maintain that Buddhahood can be attained in a human body, not just with the special body of one in a Highest Pure Land.

Regarding the word of Buddha, Proponents of Mind Only accept the distinction of definitive[6] scriptures and scriptures requiring interpretation.[7] For they assert that the first two wheels of doctrine as described in the *Sūtra Unravelling of the Thought* are sūtras requiring interpre-

---

[1] *'og min, akaṇiṣṭa.*

[2] *chos sku, dharmakāya.*

[3] *longs sku, saṃbhogakāya.*

[4] *sprul sku, nirmāṇakāya.*

[5] *mngon pa kun btus, abhidharmasamuccaya.* For a translation of this text into French, see *La compendium de la super-doctrine (philosophie) (Abhidharmasamuccaya) d'Asaṅga*, translated by Walpola Rahula, (Paris: École Française d'Extrême-Orient, 1971).

[6] *nges don, nītārtha.*

[7] *drang don, neyārtha.*

tation and that the final wheel is comprised of definitive sūtras.

> The term 'sūtra' can refer either to a whole text or to scriptural passages. For a brief discussion of the three wheels of doctrine, see chapter three, pp. 171-173.

They posit a scripture whose explicit teaching is not suitable to be accepted literally as a sūtra requiring interpretation. They posit a scripture whose explicit teaching is suitable to be accepted literally as a definitive sūtra.

There are three types of nirvanas: with remainder, without remainder, and non-abiding[1] (see the next chapter). There are Three Bodies of a Buddha, Truth Body, Complete Enjoyment Body, and Emanation Body. A Truth Body is of two types, a Nature Body[2] and a Wisdom Truth Body.[3] Also, there are two Nature Bodies, a Nature Body of natural purity and a Nature Body of freedom from peripheral defilements.

> A Wisdom Truth Body is a Buddha's omniscient consciousness, and a Nature Body is the emptiness of a Buddha's omniscient consciousness. In the sense that a Buddha's mind has always been *essentially* free of the defilements, the emptiness of that mind is called a naturally pure Nature Body. In the sense that a Buddha's mind has become free of peripheral defilements, the emptiness of that mind is called a Nature Body as freedom from peripheral defilements.

---

[1] *ni gnas pa'i myang 'das, apratiṣṭhitanirvāṇa.*
[2] *ngo bo nyid sku, svabhāvikakāya.*
[3] *ye shes chos sku, jñānadharmakāya.*

Because they assert these points, the Proponents of Mind Only are called proponents of Great Vehicle tenets.

* * *

Stanza between sections:[1]

It is right for the discriminating to enter here with joy
To the tenets of those propounding cognition-only
Who follow the word of the Subduer, the Leader,
Since this was stated in accordance with the word of many sages.

---

[1] The poetic play of this stanza revolves around use of the term *rnam* in all four lines—either as an intensifier or as meaning 'aspect'—but it is untranslatable.

7 The Middle Way School 1: The Autonomy School

The presentation of the tenets of the Proponents of Middle Way School,[1] the Proponents of Non-Entityness,[2] is in four parts: definition, etymologies, subschools, and descriptions of the individual subschools.

DEFINITION

The definition of a Proponent of the Middle Way School is: a person propounding Buddhist tenets who asserts that there are no truly existent phenomena, not even particles.

The Middle Way School refutes true existence[3]

---

[1] *dbu ma pa, mādhyamika*. This chapter and the next have also been translated (with romanized Tibetan of the Collected Works edition) by Shotaro Iida in *Reason and Emptiness: A Study in Logic and Mysticism* (Tokyo: The Hokuseido Press, 1980), pp. 27-51.
[2] *ngo bo nyid med par smra ba, niḥsvabhāvavādin*.
[3] *bden par grub pa, satyasiddhi*.

with respect to all phenomena even down to particles. This means that through reasoning this school shows that things are not established as their own mode of subsistence, or are not their own reality. The final mode of being of a table, for instance, is not the table but its emptiness of being established as its own reality.

According to Ge-luk-b̄a expositions, in the Middle Way Autonomy School phenomena are not established by way of their own uncommon mode of existence without being posited through the force of appearing to a non-defective awareness.[1] Although objects seem to have their own unique self-established mode of being, they do not; they exist from their own side but also depend, for their existence, on appearing to a non-defective awareness. In the Middle Way Consequence School, however, the refutation of true existence includes refutation of a phenomenon's existing from its own side or existing inherently, due to which objects exist only imputedly. Since, in both sub-schools, phenomena are held to exist, the refutation of true existence does not mean that things actually do not exist; rather, they seem to be their own mode of subsistence whereas they are not and thus are falsely established.

ETYMOLOGIES

Why are they called Proponents of the Middle Way School? They are called Proponents of the Middle Way

---

[1] *blo gnod med la snang ba'i dbang gis bzhag pa ma yin par rang gi thun mongs ma yin pa'i sdod lugs kyi ngos nas ma grub pa.*

School because they assert the middle that is free from the extremes of permanence and annihilation. They are called Proponents of Non-Entityness because they propound that phenomena have no entityness,[1] that is, no true existence.

> 'Entityness' or 'inherent nature' (*ngo bo nyid/rang bzhin, svabhāva*) has three usages: (1) the conventionally existent nature of a phenomenon, such as the heat of fire; (2) the real or final nature of a phenomenon, that is, its emptiness or absence of true existence; and (3) true existence—an object's being established as its own final mode of being. All Proponents of the Middle Way School assert the existence of the first and second and refute the third.

SUBSCHOOLS

There are two types of Proponents of the Middle Way School: Proponents of the Middle Way Autonomy School[2] and Proponents of the Middle Way Consequence School.[3]

> This chapter deals with the Autonomists; the Consequentialists are the subject of chapter eight.

DESCRIPTIONS OF THE INDIVIDUAL SUBSCHOOLS

This section has two parts: descriptions of the systems of the Autonomists and of the Consequentialists.

---

1 *ngo bo nyid med pa, niḥsvabhāvatā.*
2 *dbu ma rang rgyud pa, svātantrikamādhyamika.*
3 *dbu ma thal 'gyur pa, prāsaṅgikamādhyamika.*

THE AUTONOMY SCHOOL

This section has four parts: definition, etymology, subschools, and assertions of tenets.

DEFINITION

The definition of an Autonomist is: a Proponent of Non-Entityness who asserts that phenomena exist by their own character conventionally[1] [although not ultimately].

ETYMOLOGY

Why are they called Proponents of the Middle Way Autonomy School? They are called such because they refute truly existent things through relying on a correct logical sign whose three aspects exist from their own side.

> A correct logical sign[2] or reason[3] must have three qualities: the sign must be a property of the subject; the sign must be pervaded by the predicate, i.e., the predicate must be something that is always true of the reason; and the opposite of the predicate must be pervaded by the opposite of the sign. For example, in the syllogism, 'A person does not truly exist because of being a dependent-arising,' 'person' is the subject, 'does not truly exist' is the predicate, and 'dependent-arising' is the sign or reason. The reason is a property of the subject because a person is a dependent-arising. The predicate

[1] *tha snyad du, vyavahāratas.*
[2] *rtags, liṅga.*
[3] *gtan tshigs, hetu.*

pervades the reason because all dependent-arisings do not truly exist, i.e., do not exist as their own mode of subsistence. The counter-pervasion also is true because, hypothetically speaking, a truly existent object could not be a dependent-arising. The Autonomists assert that a correct reason inherently possesses these three aspects within the context of not ultimately existing. That they do not ultimately exist means that they are not established by way of their own uncommon mode of existence without being posited through the force of appearing to a non-defective awareness.

SUBSCHOOLS

There are two divisions, the Yogic Autonomy Middle Way School[1] and the Sūtra Autonomy Middle Way School.[2]

The definition of a Proponent of the Yogic Autonomy Middle Way School is: a Proponent of the Middle Way School who asserts self-cognizing consciousness and does not assert external objects. An illustration is the master Shāntarakṣhita[3] [who is considered to be founder of this subschool].

The definition of a Proponent of the Sūtra Autonomy Middle Way School is: a Proponent of the Middle Way School who does not assert self-cognizing consciousness and who asserts that external objects exist by way of their own character. An illustration is the master

---

1 *rnal 'byor spyod pa'i dbu ma rang rgyud pa, yogācārasvātantrika-mādhyamika.*

2 *mdo sde spyod pa'i dbu ma rang rgyud pa, sautrāntikasvātantrika-mādhyamika.*

3 Shāntarakṣhita lived during the eighth century; he visited Tibet and is renowned, along with Padmasambhava, as one of the great early disseminators of Buddhism in Tibet.

Bhāvaviveka[1] [who is considered to be the founder of the Autonomy School and of this subschool].

There are also etymologies. Proponents of the Yogic Autonomy Middle Way School are so called because they assert a presentation of the basis in accordance with the Proponents of Mind Only [i.e., Yogic Practitioners]. Proponents of the Sūtra Autonomy Middle Way School are so called because, like the Proponents of Sūtra, they assert external objects that are composites of minute particles.

Moreover, Proponents of the Yogic Autonomy Middle Way School are of two types, those who accord with True Aspectarians and those who accord with False Aspectarians. Instances of the first are Shāntarakṣhita, Kamalashīla,[2] and Āryavimuktisena.[3] Instances of the second are the masters Haribhadra,[4] Jetāri,[5] and Kam-

---

[1] Bhāvaviveka lived during the sixth century. He criticized Buddhapālita's commentary on Nāgārjuna's *Treatise on the Middle (dbu ma'i bstan bcos, madhyamakaśāstra)* which was later defended by Chandrakīrti, whereby the split between the Autonomy and the Consequence Schools developed.

[2] Kamalashīla lived during the eighth century; he was a student of Shāntarakṣhita and is famed for coming to Tibet and defeating a Chinese monk in debate at Sam-yay (*bsam yas*) in the latter part of the eighth century. The outcome of the debate set the predominantly Indian-oriented tone of Tibetan Buddhism.

[3] Āryavimuktisena flourished during the first half of the sixth century; he is said to have been a student of Dignāga, Bhāvaviveka, and also Vasubandhu; see David Seyfort Ruegg, *The Literature of the Madhyamaka School of Philosophy in India* (Wiesbaden: Otto Harrassowitz, 1981), p. 87.

[4] Haribhadra flourished during the later part of the eighth century (see Ruegg, p. 101); he is famed for his commentaries on Maitreya's *Ornament for Clear Realization* (*mngon rtogs rgyan, abhisamayālaṃkāra*). Tāranātha (p. 277) explains that Haribhadra was a student of Shāntarakṣhita.

[5] Ruegg (p. 100, n. 312) relates that there are two scholars by the name of Jetāri (or also Jitāri), one who lived during the ninth century and another who lived during the eleventh century.

balapāda.[1] It is explained that Jetāri accords with the Tainted False Aspectarians, and Kambalapāda accords with the Non-Tainted False Aspectarians.

ASSERTIONS OF TENETS

This section has two parts: the system of Yogic Autonomy Middle Way School and the system of the Sūtra Autonomy Middle Way School.

TENETS OF THE YOGIC AUTONOMY MIDDLE WAY SCHOOL

This section has three parts: their assertions on the basis, paths, and fruits.

ASSERTIONS ON THE BASIS

This section has two parts: assertions regarding objects and assertions regarding object-possessors.

Assertions Regarding Objects

They maintain that any established base [i.e., object] necessarily exists by way of its own character, because they assert that, regarding any phenomenon, if the imputed object is sought, it is findable.

> The Consequence School asserts just the opposite; they maintain that when an imputed object—any phenomenon—is sought, it cannot be found and thus does not exist by way of its own character.

---

[1] Kambalapāda probably flourished during the first part of the eighth century, if Tāranātha's placing him as an approximate contemporary of Jñānagarbha is correct (see Ruegg, p. 106).

Therefore, they assert that inherently existent,[1] existing by way of its own character,[2] existing by way of its own mode of subsistence,[3] and existing in its own right[4] are mutually inclusive.

> The Autonomy School affirms these of all phenomena whereas the Consequence School refutes these of all phenomena.

When objects of knowledge are divided, they are twofold—ultimate truths and conventional truths. The definition of an ultimate truth is: an object that is realized in a non-dualistic manner by a direct prime cognition that directly realizes it.

> When an ultimate truth, an emptiness, is directly realized in meditative equipoise, it is realized in an utterly non-dualistic manner without any appearance of subject and object, conventionalities, conceptual image, difference, or true existence. It is only an ultimate truth that can be non-dualistically cognized in this way.

The definition of a conventional truth is: an object that is realized in a dualistic manner by a direct prime cognition that directly realizes it.

> Duality here refers to an appearance of subject and object, which in this system are conventionally one entity.

A pot's emptiness of true existence is an illustration of an ultimate truth. A pot is an illustration of a conventional truth.

If an extensive division of ultimate truths is made,

---

1 *rang bzhin gyis grub pa, svabhāvasiddha.*

2 *rang gi mtshan nyid kyis grub pa, svalakṣaṇasiddha.*

3 *rang gi sdod lugs kyi ngos nas grub pa.*

4 *rang ngos nas grub pa, svarūpasiddha.*

there are sixteen emptinesses. Or, in brief, there are four emptinesses.

> The four emptinesses are of compounded phenomena, uncompounded phenomena, self, and other.

There are two types of conventional truths, real conventional truths and unreal conventional truths. An example of the first is water; an example of the second is a mirage.

> A mirage exists but is commonly known to be unreal because it appears to be water but is not.

This system asserts that any consciousness is necessarily a real conventionality.

Assertions Regarding Object-Possessors [Subjects]

Both Yogic Autonomists and Sūtra Autonomists assert that [a subtle, neutral] mental consciousness is an illustration of [i.e., is] the person. Also, both subschools do not assert a mind-basis-of-all or an afflicted mind but assert six consciousnesses. There are two kinds of awarenesses, prime cognitions and non-prime awarenesses. There are two types of prime cognitions, direct prime cognitions and inferential prime cognitions.

[For the Yogic Autonomists][1] there are four types of direct perception: sense, mental, self-cognizing, and yogic. They assert that all self-cognizing and yogic direct perceptions are unmistaken consciousnesses.

> These are not mistaken either with respect to the non-difference of entity of subject and ob-

---

[1] This qualification is necessary because, as the author himself later says of the Sūtra Autonomists, '... this system asserts external objects and does not assert self-cognizing consciousness'.

> ject or with respect to the absence of true existence.

Since they do not accept external objects, they maintain that a direct perception apprehending a blue [patch] and the blue [patch] itself are one substantial entity.

ASSERTIONS ON THE PATHS

This section has three parts: objects of observation of the paths, objects abandoned by the paths, and nature of the paths.

Objects of Observation of the Paths

The Yogic Autonomists assert that a person's emptiness of being permanent, unitary, and independent[1] is a coarse selflessness of persons. They assert that a person's emptiness of being substantially existent in the sense of being self-sufficient is a subtle selflessness of persons.[2]

> The coarse selflessness of persons is also applicable to phenomena in the sense that all phenomena are empty of being objects of use of a permanent, unitary, and independent user. The subtle selflessness of persons similarly applies to phenomena in that all phenomena are empty of being objects that are used by a substantially existent or self-sufficient user. Thereby it is seen that, according to the Autonomists, the base of the emptiness of persons is not just the person but all

---

[1] *gang zag rtag gcig rang dbang can gyis stong pa, nityaikasvatantrikaśūnyapudgala.*

[2] These two assertions apply not only to this school but to all schools except the Consequence School and the five subschools of the Great Exposition School that assert an inexpressible person.

> phenomena. Also, the bases of the emptiness of phenomena are not just phenomena (excluding the person) but also the person. Thus the bases of the two emptinesses are the same; however, the object negated in, for instance, the subtle selflessness of persons is substantial existence, whereas the object negated in the subtle selflessness of phenomena is true existence. Thus, for the Autonomists the bases of the emptiness of a self of persons and the bases of the emptiness of a self of phenomena are the same, but the object negated, or that of which the bases are empty, is different. 'Base of emptiness' here means an object that is empty of a negated element and should not be misunderstood as a physical base out of which phenomena are produced. Still, it can be said that emptiness is the base of all phenomena because if phenomena were not empty of true existence, they could not be produced or destroyed.

The Yogic Autonomists assert that a form's emptiness of being an entity other than the prime cognition apprehending the form[1] is a coarse selflessness of phenomena. They assert that the emptiness of true existence of all phenomena is the subtle selflessness of phenomena.

Objects Abandoned by the Paths

The Yogic Autonomists assert that consciousnesses conceiving [the coarse and subtle versions of] a self of persons are the obstructions to liberation. They assert that consciousnesses conceiving [the coarse and subtle versions of] a self of phenomena are the obstructions to omniscience.

---

[1] *gzugs 'dzin tshad ma, *rūpagrāhakapramāṇa.*

There are two types of obstructions to omniscience. They assert that a consciousness conceiving an otherness of substantial entity of apprehended object and apprehending subject[1] is a *coarse* obstruction to omniscience and that a consciousness conceiving the true existence of phenomena, such as the mental and physical aggregates, is a *subtle* obstruction to omniscience.

Nature of the Paths

The Yogic Autonomists assert the five paths of the three vehicles, making fifteen paths, just as the other systems do. The difference is in their assertion that an uninterrupted path and a path of release of a Solitary Realizer must have the aspect of realizing an emptiness of duality [of subject and object].

> An uninterrupted path is the meditative equipoise vanquishing the obstructions of that level. It leads directly, without interruption, to the attainment of a path of release—the experience of having vanquished those obstructions.
>
> 'Emptiness of duality' here refers to subject and object's emptiness of being different entities. The aspect of a path is its mode of apprehension. A path is a consciousness which, when actualized, will lead one to high attainments.

ASSERTIONS ON THE FRUITS OF THE PATHS

Solitary Realizers take as their main object of abandonment the coarse obstructions to omniscience [the conception that subject and object are different entities]. Therefore, the presentation of the eight Approachers and Abiders is not applicable to Solitary Realizers.

---

[1] *gzung 'dzin, grāhya-grāhaka.*

> Because Solitary Realizers strive mainly to abandon the coarse obstructions to omniscience, the eight Approachers and Abiders, which deal with abandoning the obstructions to liberation, do not apply to them.

However, the eight Approachers and Abiders[1] are asserted with respect to Hearers.

Those firm in the Hearer lineage take as their main object of meditative cultivation the view realizing the selflessness of persons.

> To be 'firm in the Hearer lineage' means to enter the Hearer path and complete it without switching to the path of a Solitary Realizer or a Bodhisattva.

Finally, in dependence on the vajra-like meditative stabilization of their path of meditation, they abandon all obstructions to liberation and simultaneously[2] actualize the fruit of Hearer Foe Destroyer.

Those firm in the Solitary Realizer lineage take as their main object of meditative cultivation the view that apprehending subject and apprehended object are empty of duality. Finally, in dependence on the vajra-like meditative stabilization of their path of meditation, they entirely abandon the obstructions to liberation as well as all the coarse obstructions to omniscience and simultaneously attain the fruit of Solitary Realizer Foe Destroyer.

Lesser Vehicle nirvanas are of two types, those with

---

[1] The text (Collected Works, 525.2; Peking edition, 24b.4, etc.) literally reads 'eight half-pair persons' (*gang zag ya brgyad*) referring to the four pairs of Approachers and Abiders. For a brief discussion of the eight, see pp. 207-209.

[2] In the Peking edition (24b.5) read *dus mnyam du* for *'dus mnyam du* in accordance with the Collected Works edition (525.3), the Gomang 1980 edition (60.7), Mimaki (100.2), etc.

remainder[1] and those without remainder.[2] The first is a nirvana having the remainder of miserable [mental and physical] aggregates that were wrought by former [contaminated] actions and afflictive emotions. The second type is asserted to be a state devoid[3] of miserable mental and physical aggregates. A Hearer or Solitary Realizer Foe Destroyer will necessarily enter the Great Vehicle because they assert only one final vehicle.

Therefore, in this system, due to a difference in the objects of abandonment and in the type of realization of Hearers and Solitary Realizers, there is also a distinction of inferiority and superiority with respect to the fruits that they attain.

Those firm in the Great Vehicle lineage generate a mind of altruistic aspiration to highest enlightenment.[4] Then, during the great level of the path of accumulation [from among the division of this path into small, middling, and great levels], in dependence on the meditative stabilization of the stream of doctrine[5] they actually listen to preceptual instructions[6] from supreme Emanation Bodies. When, in dependence on their practicing the meaning of these instructions, they first produce the wisdom arisen from meditation[7] which observes emptiness, they pass on to the path of preparation.

Then at the time of heat[8] [the first of four levels in the path of preparation], the manifest conception of thor-

---

[1] *lhag bcas myang 'das, sopadhiśeṣanirvāṇa.*

[2] *lhag med myang 'das, nirupadhiśeṣanirvāṇa.*

[3] In the Peking edition (25a.2) read ***bral ba'i*** for ***'bral ba'i*** in accordance with the Collected Works edition (525.6), the Go-mang 1980 edition (61.2), Mimaki (100.10), etc.

[4] *byang chub mchog tu sems bskyed, bodhicittaparamotpāda.*

[5] *chos rgyun gyi ting nge 'dzin, srotānugatasamādhi.*

[6] *gdams ngag, avavāda.*

[7] *sgom byung gi shes rab, bhāvanāmayīprajñā.*

[8] 'Heat' (*drod, ūṣmagata*) indicates that the fire of the non-conceptual wisdom of the path of seeing will soon be generated.

oughly afflicted objects [as truly existent objects of use] diminishes.

> An example of this is the apprehension of a cup as an object of use (e.g., drinking) that truly exists. That only the *manifest* conception of this diminishes indicates that the seeds of these obstructions are not abandoned at this point; thus, these obstructions still exist latently.

At the time of attaining peak[1] [the second level of the path of preparation], the manifest conception of pure objects [such as true cessations and true paths as truly existent objects of use] diminishes. When forbearance[2] [the third level of the path of preparation] is attained, the manifest conception [of a truly existent user] with regard to a subject [i.e., consciousness] that apprehends objects as substantially existent diminishes. When highest mundane qualities[3] [the fourth and last level of the path of preparation] is attained, the manifest conception [of a truly existent user] with regard to a subject [i.e., consciousness] that apprehends objects as imputed diminishes. These four conceptions are abandoned by the path of seeing.

The four—heat, peak, forbearance, and highest mundane qualities—are respectively called the meditative stabilization of achieving perception [of emptiness],[4] the meditative stabilization of the increase of the perception

---

[1] 'Peak' (*rtse mo, mūrdhagata*) indicates that one has reached the peak, or end, of the instability (susceptibility to destruction) of roots of virtue.

[2] 'Forbearance (*bzod pa, kṣānti*) indicates a meditative serviceability with emptiness, a lack of fear of emptiness, etc.

[3] 'Highest mundane qualities' (*chos mchog/ 'jig rten pa'i chos mchog, laukikāgradharma*) indicates that this level is the supreme of levels while one is still an ordinary being, for the next level is the path of seeing, at which point one becomes a Superior (*'phags pa, āryan*).

[4] *snang ba thob pa'i ting nge 'dzin, ālokalabdhasamādhi*.

[of emptiness],[1] the meditative stabilization which understands suchness one-sidedly,[2] and the uninterrupted meditative stabilization.[3]

> The meditative stabilization which understands suchness one-sidedly is so called because for the first time yogis have attained clear conceptual perception of the emptiness of *objects* but have not yet gained such perception of the emptiness of *subjects*; thus, their concentration is one-sided with respect to emptiness. The uninterrupted concentration is so called because in the same session the yogī will proceed, without interruption, to a path of release of a path of seeing.

Right after that, the acquired obstructions to liberation[4] and the acquired obstructions to omniscience,[5] together with their seeds are removed by an uninterrupted path of the path of seeing. A path of release [of the path of seeing] and a true cessation [of the acquired obstructions] are then actualized.[6]

---

1 *snang ba mched pa'i ting nge 'dzin, ālokavṛddhisamādhi.*

2 *de kho na nyid kyi phyogs gcig la zhugs pa'i ting nge 'dzin, tattvārthaikadeśānupraveśasamādhi.*

3 *bar chad med pa'i ting nge 'dzin, ānantaryasamādhi.*

4 *nyon sgrib kun btags, parikalpitakleśāvaraṇa.*

5 *shes sgrib kun btags, parikalpitajñeyāvaraṇa.*

6 In the Dharamsala 1967 edition (63.11) read *nyon sgrib kun btags* ***dang/ shes sgrib kun btags sa bon dang bcas pa spangs nas rnam grol lam dang 'gog pa'i bden pa gnyis mngon du byed do// sgom lam skor dgus sgom spang nyon mongs bcu drug gi sa bon dang sgom spang*** *shes sgrib* for *nyon sgrib kun btags brgya dang bcu gnyis dang / mthong spang shes sgrib brgya dang brgyad kyi sa bon cig car du spong / sgom lam gyi gnas skabs su sgom spang shes sgrib* in accordance with the Peking edition (25b.3), the Collected Works edition (526.5), the Go-mang 1980 edition (62.7), Tibet Go-mang 1987 edition (20b.4), and Mimaki (100.30). Similarly, in the Teacher Training edition (64.16) read the same for *nyon sgrib kun btags dang/ sgom spang shes sgrib*. The latter is merely an omission, whereas the former shows

> Acquired obstructions to liberation refer to superimpositions of a self of persons that are not inborn but intellectually acquired. Such conviction is gained through teachings and proofs of, for instance, a substantially existent, self-sufficient person. Acquired obstructions to omniscience refer to superimpositions of a self of phenomena that derive from conviction gained through the teachings and proofs of a difference of entity of subject and object or of true existence.
>
> The path of release here is the state of having vanquished the acquired obstructions. True cessation here is the state of cessation, completely and forever, of the acquired obstructions.

It is said that, through the nine steps of the path of meditation, the seeds of the sixteen afflictive emotions and the seeds of the one hundred and eight obstructions to omniscience—which are to be abandoned by the path of meditation—are gradually abandoned. Finally, in dependence on the uninterrupted path at the end of the continuum [of existence as a sentient being] the innate afflictive emotions and the innate obstructions to omniscience are simultaneously abandoned. In the next moment highest enlightenment[1] is attained.

> Upon the attainment of Buddhahood one is no longer a 'sentient being' (*sems can, sattva*), but this does not mean that a Buddha has no mind. The term 'sentient being' specifically refers to a

---

creative editing, which again suggests that the Dharamsala 1967 edition may have been based on the Teacher Training edition and was creatively edited to make more sense.

[1] *bla na med pa'i byang chub, anuttarasambuddha.*

> being who has obstructions yet to be overcome, and thus because a Buddha does not have obstructions yet to be abandoned, a Buddha is not a 'sentient being'. The innate obstructions are the consciousnesses conceiving a self of persons and a self of phenomena that derive from the beginningless habit of viewing persons and phenomena as, for instance, truly existent. The term 'innate' or 'inborn' means that these obstructions are produced along with the mental and physical aggregates without the need of conviction gained through teachings and proofs.

This is the way the fruit is manifested by those who are firm in the Bodhisattva lineage.

They assert that a Great Vehicle nirvana and a non-abiding nirvana[1] are mutually inclusive.

> In a non-abiding nirvana, due to wisdom there is no abiding in cyclic existence, and due to compassion there is no abiding in solitary peace.

They assert that the number of Bodies of a Buddha is definitely four. Even though Āryavimuktisena and Haribhadra debated about the teachings regarding the Bodies of a Buddha [in Maitreya's *Ornament for Clear Realization*], they did not debate about the number being limited [to four].

> The Four Bodies of a Buddha are Nature Body, Wisdom Body, Complete Enjoyment Body, and Emanation Body.

With respect to the word of Buddha, a presentation of definitive sūtras and sūtras requiring interpretation is made. For, sūtras requiring interpretation are those that

---

[1] *ni gnas pa'i myang 'das, apratiṣṭhitanirvāṇa.*

teach within taking conventional truths as the main object of their explicit teaching,[1] and definitive sūtras are those that teach within taking ultimate truths as the main object of their explicit teaching.[2]

> For a scripture to be definitive, it also must be literally acceptable, without qualification. For instance, even a passage teaching that all phenomena are empty of inherent existence requires interpretation; though the main object taught is an ultimate truth, the passage cannot be accepted without the qualification 'ultimately' (*don dam par, paramārthatas*), that is, all phenomena are *ultimately* empty of inherent existence.

With respect to the wheels of doctrine as explained in the *Sūtra Unravelling the Thought*, the first wheel requires interpretation; the last two wheels are both asserted to have two types, definitive and requiring interpretation.

TENETS OF THE SŪTRA AUTONOMY MIDDLE WAY SCHOOL

ASSERTIONS ON THE BASIS

Except that this system asserts external objects and does not assert self-cognizing consciousness, their presenta-

---

[1] The editor of the Dharamsala 1967 edition (64.9) has improved the definition by adding 'those which either are not suitable to be asserted literally or' (*dang sgra ji bzhin du khas blang du mi rung bas* [sic] *mdo gang rung de*). See the indented explanation.

[2] The editor of the Dharamsala 1967 edition (64.12) again has improved the definition by adding 'suitable to be asserted literally' (*sgra ji bzhin du khas blang du rung ba'i*). For a brief discussion of this point, see the indented explanation.

tion of the basis mostly resembles that of the Yogic Autonomy Middle Way School.

ASSERTIONS ON THE PATHS

With respect to differences regarding the paths, the Sūtra Autonomy Middle Way School asserts that those firm in the lineages of Hearers and of Solitary Realizers do not realize the selflessness of phenomena. Also, they do not assert a wisdom that realizes that subject and object are empty of being different substantial entities, and they do not assert that a conceptual consciousness apprehending external objects is an obstruction to omniscience.

ASSERTIONS ON THE FRUITS OF THE PATHS

The obstructions that Hearers and Solitary Realizers abandon and the selflessness that they realize do not differ in coarseness or subtlety; hence, there is no difference in their type of realization. The Sūtra Autonomists make a presentation of the eight Approachers and Abiders for both Hearers and Solitary Realizers.

They assert that those firm in the Great Vehicle lineage abandon the two obstructions serially. For, Bhāvaviveka explains in his *Blaze of Reasoning*[1] that, at the time of achieving the eighth ground, the obstructions to liberation are exhaustively abandoned. However, unlike the Consequentialists, they do not assert that one begins to abandon the obstructions to omniscience only when the obstructions to liberation have all been removed.

---

[1] *rtog ge 'bar ba, tarkajvālā*. This is Bhāvaviveka's commentary on his *Heart of the Middle* (*dbu ma snying po, madhaymakahṛdaya*). For a partial English translation of the latter (chap. III.1-136), see Shotaro Iida, *Reason and Emptiness*. For modern editions of the Sanskrit, see Ruegg, pp. 127-128.

> The Sūtra Autonomists say that Bodhisattvas on the first ground simultaneously begin to rid themselves of the obstructions to liberation and the obstructions to omniscience but that the final removal of the two obstructions does not take place simultaneously. The completion of the abandoning of the obstructions to liberation takes place at the beginning of the eighth Bodhisattva ground, and the completion of the abandoning of the obstructions to omniscience takes place at Buddhahood.

Except for only these differences, the Sūtra Autonomy Middle Way School's presentation of the basis, paths, and fruits mostly accords with that of the Yogic Autonomy Middle Way School.[1]

* * *

Stanza between sections:[2]

> O, those whose own wish is to be wise, take up this exposition
> Expressing well, without my own fabrication, all the distinctions
> In tenets of the Proponents of Own-Power who assert that things,
> Though existent by way of their own character, do not truly exist.

---

[1] For more reading on the tenets of the Autonomy School, see Donald S. Lopez, *A Study of Svātantrika* (Ithaca: Snow Lion, 1986).

[2] The author uses the term 'own' (*rang*) in all four lines—'own character' (*rang mtshan*), 'own power' (*rang rgyud*) which has usually been translated as 'autonomy', 'own fabrication' (*rang bzo*), and 'whose own wish is to be wise' (*rang nyid mkhas 'dod*). Most likely, he is emphasizing the Autonomists' assertion that objects exist from their own side.

8 The Middle Way School 2: The Consequence School

The presentation of the tenets of the Consequentialists is in three parts: definition, etymology, and assertions of tenets.

DEFINITION

The definition of a Consequentialist is: a Proponent of Non-Entityness who does not assert that phenomena exist by way of their own character even conventionally. Illustrations are Buddhapālita, Chandrakīrti, and Shāntideva.[1]

---

[1] Buddhapālita lived around 470-540, as tentatively indicated in Ruegg, p. 58. Chandrakīrti was a seventh century scholar who came to the defense of Buddhapālita's commentary on Nāgārjuna's *Treatise on the Middle* which had been criticized by Bhāvaviveka. Shāntideva was an eighth century scholar and poet whose view is held to be that of a Consequentialist.

ETYMOLOGY

Why are they called 'Consequentialists'?[1] They are called Consequentialists [i.e., Those Who Use Consequences] because they assert that an inferring consciousness that realizes the thesis[2] [that phenomena do not inherently exist can be] generated in the continuum of other parties just by [presenting that person with an absurd] consequence [of their own position].

> The Consequentialists maintain that the mere consequence, 'It follows that a person is not a dependent-arising because of inherently existing,' can generate in another—who is properly prepared—the understanding that a person does not inherently exist (because of being a dependent-arising). The other systems hold that, after presenting a consequence, it is necessary to state *explicitly* its import in syllogistic form in order to cause an opponent to realize the intended thesis. Thus, it is not that the Consequentialists do not accept syllogistic reasoning; rather, they hold that it is not *necessary* to state a syllogism for another to generate an inferential understanding of emptiness.

ASSERTIONS OF TENETS

This section has three parts: their assertions on the basis, paths, and fruits.

ASSERTIONS ON THE BASIS

[This section has two parts: assertions regarding objects and assertions regarding object-possessors (subjects).]

---

[1] *thal 'gyur pa, prāsaṅgika.*
[2] *bsgrub bya, sādhya.*

Assertions Regarding Objects

They assert that whatever is an established base [i.e., whatever exists] necessarily does not exist by way of its own character. This is because they assert that all objects[1] are only imputed by conceptuality and that the word 'only' in the term 'only imputed by conceptuality' eliminates the existence of objects by way of their own character. Established base, object, and object of knowledge are mutually inclusive.

Objects are divided into the manifest and the hidden, and they are divided into the two truths.

The manifest and the hidden

The definition of a manifest object is: a phenomenon that can be known through the power of experience, without depending on a logical sign. Obvious object,[2] manifest object,[3] sense object,[4] and non-hidden phenomenon[5] are mutually inclusive and synonymous. Illustrations are forms, sounds, odors, tastes, and tangible objects.

The definition of a hidden object is: a phenomenon that must be known through depending on a reason or sign. Hidden object,[6] non-obvious phenomenon,[7] and

---

[1] Literally, 'whatsoever established bases' (*gzhi grub tshad*). *tshad* here does not refer to valid cognition (*tshad ma*) but to 'measure' as in 'whatsoever measure' or 'whatsoever extent'.

[2] *mngon sum, pratyakṣa*. Only the Consequentialists assert that this term primarily applies to objects; the other schools use the term primarily to refer to directly perceiving consciousnesses.

[3] *mngon gyur, abhimukhī.*

[4] *dbang po'i yul, indriyaviṣaya.*

[5] *lkog tu ma gyur pa'i chos, aparokṣadharma.*

[6] *lkog gyur, parokṣa.*

[7] *mngon sum ma yin pa'i chos.*

object of inferential comprehension[1] are mutually inclusive and synonymous. Illustrations are the impermanence of a sound and a sound's selflessness of phenomena.[2]

> These definitions are taken from the point of view of ordinary beings because there are no hidden objects for a Buddha, who realizes everything directly. Also, although an ordinary being who has a yogic direct perception that directly realizes the subtle impermanence of, for instance, a sound must depend on inference before directly cognizing it, a Superior can directly perceive the impermanence of a sound without first depending on an inference. Thus the impermanence of sound is not always a hidden object; it can be perceived directly as under the above conditions. Consequently, the synonyms given are only roughly mutually inclusive because what is an object of inference for one person could be an object of direct perception even for another ordinary being. The point here is that a hidden object is something

---

[1] *rjes dpag gi gzhal bya, anumānaprameya.*

[2] All seven editions of the text (e.g., Peking edition 27b.1) read 'a sound's selflessness of persons' (*sgra gang zag gi bdag med*) whereas it seems that they should read 'a sound's selflessness of phenomena' (*sgra chos kyi bdag med*). The reason for this is that the author himself says below that the selflessness of persons and the selflessness of phenomena apply, respectively, only to persons and to other phenomena:

> The two subtle selflessnesses [of persons and of phenomena] are differentiated from the point of view of the bases that are predicated by emptiness [persons and phenomena]. They are not differentiated from the point of view of the object of negation.

Therefore, but with some trepidation, we have taken the liberty of amending the translation.

> that an ordinary being can *newly* cognize *only* through inference. It can be understood from the illustrations that the author gives—the impermanence of a sound and a sound's selflessness of phenomena—that hidden objects are not *propositions* about phenomena inaccessible to an ordinary being's experience but are such phenomena themselves.

Therefore, in this system a manifest object and a hidden object are mutually exclusive [for ordinary beings]. Also, the three spheres of objects of comprehension [the manifest, the slightly hidden, and the very hidden] are asserted to be mutually exclusive.

> Slightly hidden objects, such as an emptiness of inherent existence, are amenable to realization by the usual type of inference. The very hidden, such as the layout of the universe, are known through such means as inference based on valid scriptures.

The two truths

The definition of something's being a conventional truth [or, more literally, a truth for a concealing consciousness] is: an object that is found by a valid cognition distinguishing a conventionality and with respect to which a valid cognition distinguishing a conventionality becomes a valid cognition distinguishing a conventionality. An illustration is a pot.

> A definition of a conventional truth sufficient to apply to anyone but a Buddha is: an object found by a valid cognition that distinguishes a conventionality (that is, any existent except an emptiness). However, a single consciousness of a Buddha distinguishes both conventionalities (everything except emptinesses) as well as the

> final nature of those phenomena (emptinesses). Thus, a Buddha is said to have a valid cognition that distinguishes conventional phenomena only from the point of view of the object, such as a pot. Similarly, a Buddha is said to have a valid cognition that distinguishes the final nature only from the point of view of the object, such as the emptiness of a pot. Thus, relative to different objects, a Buddha is said to have valid cognitions that distinguish conventional phenomena and that distinguish the final nature. However, a Buddha's valid cognition that distinguishes conventional phenomena also distinguishes the final nature of phenomena, and a Buddha's valid cognition that distinguishes the final nature also distinguishes conventional phenomena. Therefore, with respect to a Buddha, an object found by a valid cognition that distinguishes conventional phenomena is not necessarily a conventional phenomenon. Similarly, with respect to a Buddha, an object found by a valid cognition that distinguishes the final nature is not necessarily a final nature. The second part of the definition, therefore, is given for the sake of including the objects of a Buddha's cognitions within the framework of the definition.

Conventional truths are not divided into real conventionalities and unreal conventionalities. This is because there are no real conventionalities, for conventionalities are necessarily not real since conventionalities are necessarily unreal [in the sense that they appear to be inherently existent but are not inherently existent]. However, *relative to an ordinary worldly consciousness*, conventional truths are divided into the real and the unreal. For relative to a common worldly consciousness, a form is real, and relative to a common worldly consciousness, the reflection of a face in a mirror is unreal. [Still] whatever is real relative to a common worldly consciousness is not necessarily existent because truly existent forms are real relative to a common worldly consciousness [but are totally non-existent].

> Although forms exist, *truly existent* forms do not exist at all.

The definition of something's being an ultimate truth is: an object found by a valid cognition distinguishing a final nature [an emptiness] and with respect to which a valid cognition distinguishing a final nature becomes a valid cognition distinguishing a final nature. An illustration is a pot's absence of inherent existence. The divisions of ultimate truths are as given above [p. 287].

Furthermore, a pastness, a futureness, and a disintegratedness are asserted to be [functioning] things [capable of producing an effect, rather than permanent phenomena as the Proponents of Sūtra, Proponents of Mind Only, and Autonomists assert]. Also, the Consequentialists assert external objects because they assert that apprehended object and and apprehending subject are different entities.

Assertions Regarding Object-Possessors [Subjects]

Persons

The Consequentialists assert that a person is the mere I that is imputed in dependence upon its bases of imputation, which are either the five mental and physical aggregates [in the Desire and Form Realms] and or the four aggregates [in the Formless Realm].

> In the Consequentialist system, a person is the dependently imputed I, not the mental consciousness, nor the composite of aggregates,

> nor a mind-basis-of-all as the other systems say.

Persons are necessarily compositional factors that are neither form nor consciousness.

> A person is not any of his/her bases of designation and shares the qualities of all the mental and physical aggregates. Therefore, persons are included in the fourth aggregate, among non-associated compositional factors. Though a person is thus technically an instance of the fourth aggregate, a person is still not any of the aggregates that serve as that person's bases of imputation.

Awarenesses

Awarenesses are of two types, valid and non-valid. Valid cognitions are of two types, direct and inferential. Direct valid cognitions are of three types, sense, mental, and yogic direct perceptions. The Consequentialists do not accept self-cognizing direct perceptions.

All sense consciousnesses in the mental continuum of a sentient being are necessarily mistaken consciousnesses.

> Sense consciousnesses of sentient beings are necessarily mistaken in that objects *appear* to them to exist inherently even if they do not *conceive* those objects to exist inherently. This type of mistake is limited to 'sentient beings', those who have minds with obstructions yet to be removed; thus, the term 'sentient being' includes all conscious beings except Buddhas. Only *sense* consciousnesses of sentient beings are said to be mistaken because Bodhisattvas in meditative equipoise on emptiness perceive emptiness directly with their mental conscious-

> ness in a unmistaken manner. They are sentient beings because they have obstructions yet to be removed, but their mental consciousness at the time of directly cognizing emptiness is totally unmistaken. Therefore, not all consciousnesses but all *sense* consciousnesses of sentient beings are mistaken; still, except for those directly realizing emptiness, all other consciousnesses—sense and mental—of sentient beings are mistaken in that there is a conflict between how things appear and how they exist. Even when Bodhisattvas (or Hearers or Solitary Realizers) rise from meditative equipoise on emptiness, their sense and mental consciousnesses again come under the influence of previously acquired predispositions that make objects appear as if inherently existent.

Yogic direct perceptions are of two types, mistaken and unmistaken. A yogic direct perception that is in uncontaminated meditative equipoise [on emptiness] is unmistaken, and a yogic direct perception of a short-sighted person[1] that directly realizes subtle impermanence is a mistaken consciousness.

> The latter is mistaken because impermanence falsely *appears* to it to be inherently existent even though it does not *conceive* impermanence to be inherently existent. Subtle impermanence is the moment by moment disintegration of compounded phenomena and is difficult to realize. Illustrations of coarse impermanence are death, the breaking of an object, and so on, which can be realized very easily.

---

[1] Literally, 'one who looks nearby' (*tshur mthong*), i.e., someone who has not realized emptiness.

It follows that a yogic direct perception of a short-sighted person is a mistaken consciousness because it is a consciousness in the mental continuum of a common being.

> All sense and mental consciousnesses of common persons are mistaken, whereas with regard to sentient beings (a term that includes Superiors) only *sense* consciousnesses are necessarily mistaken, because a mental consciousness—in the continuum of a Superior—directly cognizing emptiness is unmistaken. Conversely, all consciousnesses of a Buddha are unmistaken. This means that a Buddha's consciousness—sense or mental—neither perceives nor conceives objects as being inherently existent whether in or out of meditative equipoise.

All subsequent cognitions are necessarily direct valid cognitions. For, the second moment of an inferring consciousness that realizes that a sound is impermanent is a conceptual direct valid cognition and the second moment of a sense direct perception apprehending a form is a non-conceptual direct valid cognition.

> In the Consequentialist system the term *pramāṇa (tshad ma)*—which is translated here as 'valid cognition' but in other contexts as 'prime cognition'—does not refer to a cognition that *newly* realizes its object in such a manner that its cognition is incontrovertible. Rather, in accordance with worldly usage of the term, *pramāṇa* refers just to a valid, right, or incontrovertible cognition that is not mistaken with respect to its prime or main object; it is not necessarily perceiving its object for the first time. Thus, for the Consequentialists, a valid cogni-

tion is an incontrovertible knower of its main object, but it is not necessarily new as the other systems maintain.

To understand what the other systems mean by 'new', consider the following. Often because of intense concentration on an object one does not notice other objects that nevertheless appear. For instance, when watching a particularly interesting object of sight, one might not notice what was said within hearing range. The ear consciousness heard the sound, but what was heard was not noticed by the mental consciousness at that time, nor could it be remembered in the future. Such a consciousness is not a *pramāṇa* because, although the object appeared to it clearly, no notice was taken of what was perceived. Thus, even though one might be in contact with an object for some time, one might not notice the object due to lack of attention. Also, a consciousness of an ordinary being cannot apprehend a single instant of an object. Whether attention is intense or not, it takes many instants before an ordinary being can notice an object.

If the object of a consciousness is not noticed, that consciousness is not a *pramāṇa*. For a consciousness to be a *pramāṇa*, there must be a noticing of the object. Thus, according to the non-Consequentialist use of the term, a 'sense direct prime/valid cognition' refers to a correct sense consciousness at that period of time when its object is initially noticed. The subsequent moments of consciousness in the same continuum of attention to that object, during which no other noticed perceptions intervene, are called subsequent cognitions. This is because in those moments an object that was formerly noticed is being cognized again through the power of the former cognition. In all systems except that of the Consequentialists, a subsequent cognition is not a *pramāṇa* because it does not *newly* realize its object. However, the Consequentialists do not gloss the *pra* (prime/valid) of *pramāṇa* as 'first' or 'new'; they gloss it as 'valid', 'right', or 'main'; and thus, for them a subsequent cognition is a *pramāṇa*, a valid cognition, or even 'prime cognition' in the sense that it is a cognition that is valid with respect to its *prime* or *main* object.

The same holds true for an inferential consciousness. Once an inference has been produced, its subsequent moments are subsequent cognitions that the Consequentialist system alone accepts as a *pratyakṣapramāṇa*, a *direct* valid cognition. Since the subsequent moments of an inferential consciousness do not rely again on a reason in order to cognize the object, the second period is no longer inferential but direct. This is because it remembers the object already inferred without renewed reliance on a logical reason. Therefore, in the Consequentialist system, unlike the other systems, a direct perception can be conceptual. A subsequent cognition of an already inferred object that does not rely again on a logical sign in its cognition is a conceptual direct perception. Even though direct, it nevertheless is conceptual because it cognizes its conceived object through the medium of a generic image. 'Direct' here means not relying on a logical sign; it does not imply that the consciousness is non-conceptual. A subsequent cognition that is the subsequent moment of a direct sense per-

> ception is a non-conceptual direct valid cognition.

Inference is of four types: inference by the power of a fact [that serves as a logical sign such as the presence of dependent-arising which is a sign of an absence of inherent existence]; inference by renown [such as coming to know that the term 'moon' is suitable to express that object]; inference through example [such as inferring what a cow without a dewlap is through knowledge of a cow with a dewlap]; and inference through correct belief [in which a scripture is realized to be incontrovertible with respect to what it teaches due to its not being implicitly or explicitly contradicted by other scriptures, inference, or direct perception].

Being mistaken with respect to an object and realizing that object are not mutually exclusive, because the Consequentialists assert that an inferential cognition realizing that a sound is impermanent is mistaken with respect to impermanent sound.

> Such an inferential cognition is mistaken in the sense that impermanent sounds *appears* to exist inherently. However, it does not *conceive* that impermanent sound inherently exists; furthermore, it correctly realizes the impermanence of a sound. Therefore, 'mistaken' here refers to the *appearance* of what does not inherently exist as inherently existent. Thus, a consciousness may correctly ascertain an object but may be mistaken in that the object *appears* to it to be inherently existent.

Dualistic consciousnesses are necessarily direct valid cognitions with respect to their own appearing object.[1]

---

[1] The text (e.g., Peking edition 28b.4) reads 'its own appearance' (*rang gi snang ba*), but we have taken this as referring to its own appearing object (*rang gi snang yul*).

This is because even a conceptual consciousness that [mis]conceives sound to be permanent is a direct valid cognition with respect to its appearing object.

> Its appearing object is merely a generic image of permanent sound; actual permanent sound does not even appear to it because permanent sound does not exist. The consciousness is valid *with respect to its appearing object* because it notices and can induce memory of this generic image, no matter how erroneous that image is.
>
> A conceptual consciousness that conceives sound to be permanent is not itself a valid cognition because it is not a correct knower. However, if one considers merely the conceptual appearance of its object, which is an idea or image of permanent sound, then it is valid with respect to this appearance because validity involves a noticing of the object and an ability to remember it. Thus, even a wrong consciousness is a valid cognition *with respect to its own appearing object*.

All consciousnesses [correct, wrong, conceptual, or non-conceptual] realize[1] their own objects of comprehension. For, a generic image of the horns of a rabbit is the object of comprehension of a conceptual consciousness apprehending the horns of a rabbit, and a generic

---

[1] In the Collected Works edition (531.5), the Peking edition (28b.5), and the Tibet Go-mang 1987 edition (23a.4) read *rtogs pas* for *rtog pas* in accordance with the Go-mang edition (69.16), the Dharamsala 1967 edition (71.9) the Teacher Training edition (72.14), and Mimaki (104.33). It should be noted that none of the old editions (either ours or Mimaki's) have the corrected reading. Without the correction, the sentence would read, 'All consciousnesses [correct, wrong, conceptual, or non-conceptual] conceptualize their own objects of comprehension.' Such an assertion would not merit mention and would not accord with a long tradition of Ge-luk-b̄a scholarship on what, with the correction, is a provocative assertion.

image of permanent sound is the object of comprehension of a conceptual consciousness apprehending permanent sound.

ASSERTIONS ON THE PATHS

Objects of Observation of the Paths

A person's emptiness of substantial existence in the sense of self-sufficiency is asserted to be a coarse selflessness of persons. Also, a person's emptiness of true existence is asserted to be the subtle emptiness of persons.

The two subtle selflessnesses [of persons and of phenomena] are differentiated from the point of view of the bases that are predicated by emptiness [persons and phenomena]; they are not differentiated from the point of view of the object of negation. This is because true existence is the object of negation, and a negative of true existence—the object of negation—in relation to a person as a base of negation is a subtle selflessness of persons and a negative of true existence—the object of negation—in relation to a mental or physical aggregate or the like as a base of negation is a subtle selflessness of phenomena. A subtle selflessness of persons and a subtle selflessness of phenomena do not differ in subtlety, and both are asserted to be the final mode of existence [of persons and other phenomena].

Objects Abandoned by the Paths

The coarse and subtle conceptions of self, together with their seeds, and the three poisons that arise through their influence, together with their seeds, are asserted to be the obstructions to liberation from cyclic existence. This is so because the Consequentialists assert that a consciousness conceiving true existence is an obstruction to liberation. The latencies of the conception of true existence, the mistaken appearances of [inherently existent] duality which arise through their influence, and the taints of apprehending the two truths as different entities are asserted to be the obstructions to omniscience.

> The *seeds* of the conception of true existence produce a *consciousness conceiving* that phenomena and persons truly exist, but the *latencies* of the conception of true existence produce an *appearance* of persons and phenomena as inherently existent. The taints of apprehending the two truths as different entities are what make it impossible for anyone but a Buddha to perceive directly both phenomena and their final nature, emptiness, at the same time.

Nature of the Paths

The Consequentialists present the five paths for each of the three vehicles. Also, relying on the *Sūtra on the Ten Grounds*,[1] they present the ten grounds for the Great Vehicle. The three vehicles do not have different types of wisdom because the Consequentialists assert that all Superiors directly cognize the selflessness of phenomena.

ASSERTIONS ON THE FRUITS OF THE PATHS

Those firm in the Lesser Vehicle lineage cultivate the view of selflessness merely through brief reasoning. In

---

[1] *mdo sde sa bcu pa, daśabhūmika*. For a Sanskrit edition, see *Daśabhūmikasūtram*, P.L.Vaidya, ed. Buddhist Sanskrit Texts No.7 (Darbhanga: Mithila Institute, 1967); for an English translation, see M. Honda, 'An Annotated Translation of the "Daśabhūmika"', in D. Sinor, ed, *Studies in Southeast and Central Asia*, Śatapitaka Series 74, (New Delhi: 1968), pp. 115-276.

dependence on this, they finally remove the conception of true existence, together with its seeds, through the vajra-like meditative stabilization of the Lesser Vehicle path of meditation and simultaneously actualize the Lesser Vehicle enlightenment.

The Proponents of the Middle Way Autonomy School and below assert that in order to attain a nirvana without remainder it is first necessary to attain a nirvana with remainder.

> This statement does not appear to cover the case of a person who is reborn in a pure land and who newly actualizes nirvana there. Since birth in a pure land is not due to contaminated actions and afflictions but is due to pure wishes, it would seem to be impossible for such a person first to actualize a nirvana with remainder, given that these 'lower' schools define a nirvana with remainder as having a remainder of aggregates that are impelled by contaminated actions and afflictions. It seems that such a person would actualize only a nirvana without remainder, and thus this would be a case of actualizing a nirvana without remainder without having first actualized a nirvana with remainder.

However, in the Consequentialist system it is asserted that prior to a nirvana with remainder it is necessary to attain a nirvana without remainder.

> The Consequentialists have a different meaning for the two terms. For them, a nirvana without remainder refers to the meditative equipoise on emptiness during which practitioners of the Lesser Vehicle finally become Foe Destroyers. At that time they have overcome the conception of inherent existence and

> thus possess a nirvana, a passing beyond sorrow, with 'sorrow' identified as the obstructions to liberation. Since at that time they are directly cognizing emptiness, they also are temporarily free of the appearance of inherent existence and thus are said not to have any 'remainder' of this false appearance. However, when they rise from equipoise, things falsely *appear* to exist inherently even though they never again will assent to this false appearance and thereby conceive things to exist inherently. Thus, Foe Destroyers first have a nirvana without remainder and then a nirvana with remainder. Gradually, Foe Destroyers enter the Great Vehicle and, after a great accumulation of merit, also purify their perception of the false appearance of inherent existence. They thereby eliminate the obstructions to omniscience and become Buddhas.

The Consequentialists assert[1] a presentation of the eight Approachers and Abiders for Hearers and Solitary Realizers, and they assert that all Approachers and Abiders are Superiors.

The way that the Great Vehicle enlightenment is actualized is this: Bodhisattvas extensively cultivate the view of selflessness through innumerable forms of reasoning and thereby remove the obstructions. Moreover, until the obstructions to liberation are exhaustively abandoned, they do not begin to abandon the obstructions to omniscience. They begin to abandon the obstructions to omniscience on the eighth Bodhisattva ground which is when Bodhisattvas who did not initially go on a Lesser Vehicle path exhaustively abandon the obstructions to liberation. Finally, through depending on the

---

[1] In the Teacher Training edition (75.3) read *khas len* for *khas mi len* in accordance with the Peking edition (29b.3), etc.

uninterrupted path at the end of the continuum [of being a sentient being with obstructions to be abandoned] they abandon, without residue, all obstructions to omniscience and simultaneously actualize the state of the Four Buddha Bodies.

The Consequentialists assert that all nirvanas and true cessations are ultimate truths.

> A nirvana is an emptiness of the mind in the continuum of one who has completely and forever abandoned all afflictions. A true cessation is an emptiness of the mind in the continuum of one who has completely and forever abandoned a portion of the afflictions.

The first and last of the three wheels of doctrine as described in the *Sūtra Unravelling the Thought* are scriptures that require interpretation because they do not contain any passages that explicitly teach [the actual] emptiness.

> This refers only to the three wheels as set forth in the *Sūtra Unravelling the Thought*. According to the Consequentialists' own way of setting forth the three wheels of doctrine, certain passages in the first and third wheels are also definitive because they teach emptiness, the final nature of phenomena, explicitly.

They assert that the middle wheel of doctrine, as described in the *Sūtra Unravelling the Thought*, is composed of definitive scriptures because the *Heart Sūtra*[1] is a definitive scripture.

The main distinguishing feature of the Consequence School is that, based on the reason that internal and external phenomena are dependently imputed, they refute that phenomena exist by way of their own charac-

---

[1] *shes rab snying po, prajñāpāramitāhṛdaya.*

ter, but within their own system and without needing to rely on [the ignorance of] others they know how to establish—without fault—bondage and liberation, cause and effect, known and knower, and so forth, conventionally, only nominally, that is, as only imputedly existent.

> Some other interpretations of the Consequence School hold that Consequentialists posit bondage and liberation, etc., only in the face of others' ignorance. The author rejects this notion and maintains that Consequentialists posit these phenomena from their own point of view and that their doing so within the context of completely refuting inherent existence is, in fact, the chief distinguishing feature of the school.[1]

Nowadays, some who are vain about having high views say that phenomena are only mistaken appearances and take them to be utterly non-existent, like the child of a barren woman; then they hold that non-attention to anything is the supreme practice. They do not have even the scent of a Consequentialist in them.

Therefore, those who seek liberation, having seen all the marvels of cyclic existence as being like a whirlwind of fire, should abandon all bad views which are fabricated to look like doctrine and should value supremely the Middle Way Consequence School's own system, the highest of all systems of tenets.[2]

---

[1] For extensive discussion of this point in the special insight section of Ḏzong-ka-ḇa's *Great Exposition of the Stages of the Path*, see Elizabeth Napper's *Dependent-Arising and Emptiness* (London: Wisdom Publications, 1989).

[2] For more reading on the tenets of the Consequence School, see Jeffrey Hopkins, *Meditation on Emptiness* (London: Wisdom Publications, 1983) and *Emptiness Yoga* (Ithaca: Snow Lion, 1987).

* * *

[Concluding stanzas:]

The depth [of the ocean] of terms and meanings, gathered on the golden earth of the systems of doctrine, is difficult to fathom.
Successive waves of various reasonings move about, causing fear in the hearts of children of low intellect.
Splitting into a thousand rivers of manifold views, it is a place of sport for birds of clear intellect.
Who can measure all the particulars of the great treasure of water of outer and inner systems of doctrine?

However, the boat obtained through birth,
Impelled by a favorable wind arisen from endeavor,
Goes to the center of the ocean of tenets
And presently finds here this precious garland of eloquence.

The youthful groups of those with clear intellect
Wishing to spread the feast of eloquent song
Before millions of the best of the wise should make use
Of this condensation of the essence of our own and others' tenets.

O, the wonder of those nowadays vainly considering themselves to be wise,
Running off from the top of their heads, without training
A long time in the great books, assuming for the sake of wealth and respect
The tiring task of the dance of composition!

Thousands of rays of eloquence from the sky of analysis

Shine forth, closing all the jasmines of faulty explanations[1]
But cause to smile the white countenance of the marvellous meanings
Of the great grove with hundreds of petals of the pure systems.

This book illuminating countless tenets upon condensing the essence
From the books of Indian and Tibetan scholars
Was not done through competitiveness or jealousy but for the sake
Of furthering the intellect of those whose lot is similar to mine.

Through this good deed rising from hard work,
Suppressing with its brilliance even the light of the moon,
May all transmigrating beings be freed from the chasm of bad views
And be restfully sustained by the pure path forever.

This brief presentation of outer and inner tenets called *A Precious Garland* was composed by the reverent Ḡön-chok-jik-may-w̄ang-b̄o during the waxing of the sixth month in the water-snake year (1773). He composed it in the face of requests by the faithful, energetic, and discriminating Ḡu-s̄hri Ngak-w̄ang-ḡel-sang[2] and the monk Ngak-w̄ang-sang-b̄o.[3] The scribe was D̄a-drin-tsay-ring.[4]

Sarvamaṅgalaṃ.

---

[1] The light of the sun is said to close jasmine.
[2] *ku shri ngag dbang skal bzang*. The term *ku shri* indicates that he was a Mongolian.
[3] *ngag dbang bzang po*.
[4] *ta mgrin tshe ring*. The Peking edition has a further colophon on the occasion of its publication; for it and the colophons of recent editions, see Mimaki, pp. 108-109.

Appendix, Glossary, Bibliography, and Index

Appendix

Collation with the *Stages of the Path*

Dzong-ka-ba's *Great Exposition of the Stages of the Path (lam rim chen mo)* offers a thorough discussion of the topics presented in Part One. The page references for the topics of Part One as found in that text (Dharamsala: Shes rig par khang, 1964) are:

How to act in the session 37a.5
How to act between sessions 41a.4
How to prepare for a session 37a.6
How to perform the actual session 40a.4
Generating ascertainment of the presentation of the path in general 58a.3
Thought on the meaningfulness of leisure and fortune 53b.4
Thought on the difficulty of finding leisure and fortune 55b.4
Refuge 86b.6
Inevitable effects of actions 103b.3
Sufferings of cyclic existence in general 136b.6
Sufferings of bad transmigrations 75b.6
Sufferings of happy transmigrations 149a.4
How to meditatively cultivate the aspiration to enlightenment 184a.5
How to achieve evenmindedness 194a.3
Recognition of all beings as mothers 195a.6
Thought of the kindness of all mothers 195b.4

Glossary

ENGLISH	SANSKRIT	TIBETAN
action	karma	las
activity	rajas	rtul
affirming negative	paryudāsapratiṣedha	ma yin dgag
afflicted mind	kliṣṭamanas	nyon yid
afflictive emotion/ affliction	kleśa	nyon mongs
afflictive obstruction	kleśāvaraṇa	nyon sgrib/ nyon mongs pa'i sgrib pa
aggregate	skandha	phung po
Analyzer	mīmāṃsaka	dpyod pa ba
anus	pāyu	rkub
appearing object	*pratibhāsaviṣaya	snang yul
apprehended object and apprehending subject	grāhya-grāhaka	gzung 'dzin
arms	pāṇi	lag pa
artificial	parikalpita	kun btags
artificial obstruction to liberation	parikalpitakleśāva-raṇa	nyon sgrib kun btags
artificial obstruction to omniscience	parikalpitajñeyāva-raṇa	shes sgrib kun btags
aspect	ākāra	rnam pa
Autonomist	svātantrika	rang rgyud pa
awareness to which an object appears without being noticed	*aniyatapratibhāsa buddhi	snang la ma nges pa'i blo
basis	sthāpana	gzhi
basis of negation		dgag gzhi
Bodhisattva	bodhisattva	byang chub sems dpa'

ENGLISH	SANSKRIT	TIBETAN
community	saṃgha	tshogs
Complete Enjoyment Body	saṃbhogakāya	longs spyod rdzogs pa'i sku
compositional factor not associated with mind or mental factors	cittacaittaviprayukta-saṃskāra	sems sems byung dang ldan par ma yin pa'i 'du byed
compounded phenomenon	saṃskṛta	'dus byas
conceived object		zhen yul
conceptuality / conceptual consciousness	vikalpa	rtog pa
Consequentialist	prāsaṅgika	thal 'gyur pa
contaminated	sāsrava	zag bcas
conventional truth	saṃvṛtisatya	kun rdzob bden ba
conventionally / in conventional terms	vyavahāratas	tha snyad du
correctly assuming consciousness	*manaḥparīkṣā	yid dpyod
cyclic existence	saṃsāra	'khor ba
darkness	tamas	mun pa
definiendum	lakṣya	mtshon bya
definitive	nītārtha	nges don
dependent nature	paratantra	gzhan dbang
Desire Realm	kāmadhātu	'dod khams
Dialecticians	rtog ge pa	tārkika
direct prime cognition / direct valid cognition	pratyakṣapramāṇa	mngon sum tshad ma
discipline	vinaya	'dul ba
doctrine	dharma	chos
doubt	vicikitsā / saṃśaya	the tshom
ear	śrota	rna
earth	pṛthvī	sa
element of [a Superior's] qualities	dharmadhātu	chos dbyings
Emanation Body	nirmāṇakāya	sprul sku
emptiness	śūnyatā	stong pa nyid
entity	vastu	ngo bo
entity / substantial entity	dravya	rdzas

ENGLISH	SANSKRIT	TIBETAN
entityness	svabhāvatā	ngo bo nyid
Enumerator	sāṃkhya	grangs can pa
established base	*vastu	gzhi grub
established by way of its own uncommon mode of existence without being posited through the force of appearing to a non-defective awareness		blo gnod med la snang ba'i dbang gis bzhag pa ma yin par rang gi thun mongs ma yin pa'i sdod lugs kyi ngos nas grub pa
exclusion-of-the-other	apoha	gzhan sel
Exemplifier	dārśtāntika	dpe ston ba
exist validly	pramāṇasiddha	tshad mas grub pa
existent	sat	yod pa
existing by way of its own mode of subsistence		rang gi sdod lugs gyi ngos nas grub pa
existing by way of its own character	svalakṣaṇasiddha	rang gi mtshan nyid kyis grub pa
existing in its own right	svarūpasiddha	rang ngos nas grub pa
existing inherently	svabhāvasiddha	rang bzhin gyis grub pa
external object	bāhyārtha	phyi don
eye	cakṣus	mig
False Aspectarian	alīkākāravādin	rnam brdzun pa
falsely established		brdzun par grub pa
falsity	mṛṣā	brdzun pa
fire	tejas	me
Foe Destroyer	arhan	dgra bcom pa
Follower of Sūtra	sautrāntika	mdo sde pa
forbearance	kṣānti	bzod pa
Forder	tīrthika	mu stegs pa
form	rūpa	gzugs
Form Body	rūpakāya	gzugs sku
Form Realm	rūpadhātu	gzugs khams
Formless Realm	ārūpyadhātu	gzugs med khams
fortune	saṃpad	'byor pa
fruit	phala	'bras bu
fundamental nature	prakṛti	rang bzhin
generally characterized phenomenon	sāmānyalakṣaṇa	spyi mtshan

ENGLISH	SANSKRIT	TIBETAN
generic image	arthasāmānya	don spyi
genitalia	upastha	'doms
god-child demon	devaputamāra	lha'i bu'i bdud
great one	mahat	chen po
ground	bhūmi	sa
Half-Eggists		sgo nga phyed tshal pa
Hearer	śrāvaka	nyan thos
heat	ūṣmagata	drod
Heavily Adorned Highest Pure Land	akaniṣṭaghanavyūha	'og min stug po bkod pa
Hedonist	cārvāka/ayata	rgyang 'phen pa
hidden phenomenon	parokṣa	lkog gyur
highest enlightenment	anuttarasambuddha	bla na med pa'i byang chub
highest mundane qualities	laukikāgradharma	chos mchog/'jig rten pa'i chos mchog
Highest Pure Land	akaniṣṭa	'og min
I-principle	ahaṃkāra	nga rgyal
illustration	lakṣya	mtshan gzhi
impermanent	anitya	mi rtag pa
imputational [nature]	parikalpita	kun btags
imputedly existent	prajñaptisat	btags yod
inferential prime cognition	anumānapramāṇa	rjes su dpag pa'i tshad ma
inherently existent	svabhāvasiddha	rang bzhin gyis grub pa
intellect	buddhi	blo
intellectual faculty	manas	yid
interpretable/requiring interpretation	neyārtha	drang don
isolate/ isolatable factor		ldog pa
Jewel/Superior Rarity	ratna	dkon mchog
Joyous Pure Land	tuṣita	dga' ldan
Kambalapāda	kambalapāda	lva ba pa
latency/predisposition	vāsanā	bag chags
leg	pāda	rkang pa
leisure	kṣaṇa	dal ba
lightness	sattva	snying stobs

ENGLISH	SANSKRIT	TIBETAN
limit of reality	bhūtakoṭi	yang dag mtha'
logical mark/sign	liṅga	rtags
Logician	naiyāyika	rigs pa can
main mind	citta	sems
Manifest Knowledge	abhidharma	chos mngon pa
manifest object	abhimukhī	mngon gyur
manifest phenomenon	abhimukhī	mngon gyur
meaning-generality	arthasāmānya	don spyi
meditative stabilization	samādhi	ting nge 'dzin
meditative stabilization achieving perception [of emptiness]	ālokalabdhasamādhi	snang ba thob pa'i ting nge 'dzin
meditative stabilization of the increase of the perception [of emptiness]	ālokavṛddhisamādhi	snang ba mched pa'i ting nge 'dzin
meditative stabilization of the stream of doctrine	srotānugatasamādhi	chos rgyun gyi ting nge 'dzin
meditative stabilization understanding suchness one-sidedly	tattvārthaikadeśānupraveśasamādhi	de kho na nyid kyi phyogs gcig la zhugs pa'i ting nge 'dzin
Meditators	snyoms 'jug pa	samāpattika
mental and physical aggregates	skandha	phung po
mental consciousness	manovijñāna	yid kyi rnam shes
mental direct perception	mānasapratyakṣa	yid kyi mngon sum
mental factor	caitta	sems byung
Middle Way Autonomist	svātantrika-mādhyamika	dbu ma rang rgyud pa
Middle Way Consequentialist	prāsaṅgika mādhyamika	dbu ma thal 'gyur pa
mind	citta	sems
mind of altruistic aspiration to highest enlightenment	bodhicittaparam-otpāda	byang chub mchog tu sems bskyed pa
mind-basis-of-all	ālayavijñāna	kun gzhi rnam shes
mistaken consciousness	bhrāntijñāna	'khrul shes
mutually inclusive	ekārtha	don gcig
Nature Body	svabhāvikakāya	ngo bo nyid sku

ENGLISH	SANSKRIT	TIBETAN
negative phenomenon	pratiṣedha	dgag pa
Never Returner	anāgamin	phyir mi 'ong
nirvana with remainder	sopadhiśeṣanirvāṇa	lhag bcas myang 'das
nirvana without remainder	nirupadhiśeṣanirvāṇa	lhag med myang 'das
nominal truth	vyavahārasatya	tha snyad bden pa
non-abiding nirvana	apratiṣṭhitanirvāṇa	mi gnas pa'i myang 'das
non-affirming negative	prasajyapratiṣedha	med dgag
non-associated compositional factor	viprayuktasaṃskāra	ldan min 'du byed
non-entityness	niḥsvabhāvatā	ngo bo nyid med pa
non-hidden phenomenon	aparokṣadharma	lkog tu ma gyur pa'i chos
non-obvious phenomenon		mngon sum ma yin pa'i chos
Non-Pluralists		sna tshogs gnyis med pa
non-prime consciousness	apramāṇabuddhi	tshad min gyi blo
non-revelatory form	avijñaptirūpa	rnam par rig byed ma yin pa'i gzugs
non-thing	abhāva	dngos med
non-wastage	avipraṇāśa	chud mi za ba
nose	ghrāṇa	sna
object	viṣaya	yul
object aspect	viṣayākāra	yul rnam
object of engagement	pravṛttiviṣaya	'jug yul
object of inferential comprehension	anumānaprameya	rjes dpag gi gzhal bya
object of knowledge	jñeya	shes bya
object possessor	viṣayin	yul can
obstruction to liberation/afflictive obstruction	kleśāvaraṇa	nyon sgrib
obstruction to omniscience/obstruction to simultaneous cognition of all phenomena	jñeyāvaraṇa	shes sgrib
obtainer	prāpti	thob pa
obvious object	pratyakṣa	mngon sum
odor	gandha	dri
Once Returner	sakṛdāgamin	lan gcig phyir 'ong

ENGLISH	SANSKRIT	TIBETAN
one who looks nearby		tshur mthong
other-powered [nature]	paratantra	gzhan dbang
Particularist	vaiśeṣika	bye brag pa
path	mārga	lam
path of accumulation	saṃbhāramārga	tshogs lam
path of meditation	bhāvanāmārga	sgom lam
path of no more learning	aśaikṣamārga	mi slob lam
path of preparation	prayogamārga	sbyor lam
path of seeing	darśanamārga	mthong lam
peak	mūrdhagata	rtse mo
person	puruṣa	skyes bu
person's emptiness of being permanent, unitary, & independent	nityaikasvatantra-śūnyapudgala	gang zag rtag gcig rang dbang can gyis stong pa
positive phenomenon	vidhi	sgrub pa
preceptual instruction	avavāda	gdams ngag
prime cognition	pramāṇa	tshad ma
prime cognition apprehending form	*rūpagrāhaka-pramāṇa	gzugs 'dzin tshad ma
prime consciousness	pramāṇabuddhi	tshad ma'i blo
principal	pradhāna	gtso bo
product	kṛta	byas pa
Proponent of a Person	pudgalavādin	gang zag smra ba
Proponent of an Equal Number of Subjects and Objects		gzung 'dzin grangs mnyam pa
Proponent of Cognition	vijñaptika / vijñaptivādin	rnam rig pa
Proponent of Mind Only	cittamātrin	sems tsam pa
Proponent of Non-Entityness	niḥsvabhāvavādin	ngo bo nyid med par smra ba
Proponent of the Middle Way School	mādhyamika	dbu ma pa
reason	hetu	gtan tshigs
reliquary	stūpa	mchod rten
Ritualist/Analyzer	mīmāṃsaka	dpyod pa ba
same entity	ekavastu	ngo bo gcig
same substantial entity	ekadravya	rdzas gcig

ENGLISH	SANSKRIT	TIBETAN
seed	bīja	sa bon
self	ātman	bdag
self-cognizing consciousness	svasaṃvedana	rang rig
self-cognizing direct perception	svasaṃvedana-pratyakṣa	rang rig mngon sum
selflessness of persons	pudgalanairātmya	gang zag gi bdag med
selflessness of phenomena	dharmanairātmya	chos kyi bdag med
sense direct perception	pratyakṣapramāṇa	mngon sum gyi tshad ma
sense object	indriyaviṣaya	dbang po'i yul
sense power	indriya	dbang po
sentient being	sattva	sems can
sets of discourses	sūtrānta	mdo sde
skin/body	sparśana	pags pa/lus
Solitary Realizer	pratyekabuddha	rang sangs rgyas
sound	śabda	sgra
sound generality	śabdasāmānya	sgra spyi
space	ākāśa	nam mkha'
special insight	vipaśyanā	lhag mthong
specifically characterized phenomenon	svalakṣaṇa	rang mtshan
speech	vāc	ngag
Spiritual Community	saṃgha	dge 'dun
Stream Enterer	śrotāpanna	rgyun zhugs
subsequent cognition	*paricchinnajñāna	bcad shes/ dpyad shes
substantial entity	dravya	rdzas
substantially established	dravyasiddha	rdzas grub
substantially existent	dravyasat	rdzas yod
suchness	tattva	de nyid/de kho na nyid
Superior	ārya	'phags pa
sūtra	sūtra	mdo
Sūtra Autonomy Middle Way School	sautrāntikasvātantrikamādhyamika	mdo sde spyod pa'i dbu ma rang rgyud pa
tangible object	spraṣṭavya	reg bya
taste	rasa	ro
tenet/established conclusion	siddhānta	grub mtha'

ENGLISH	SANSKRIT	TIBETAN
that which has the aspect of the apprehender	grāhakākāra	'dzin rnam
that which has the aspect the apprehended	grāhyākāra	gzung rnam
thesis	sādhya	bsgrub bya
thing/functioning thing	bhāva	dngos po
thoroughly established [nature]	pariniṣpanna	yongs grub
three characters	trilakṣaṇa	mtshan nyid gsum
three natures	trisvabhāva	rang bzhin gsum/ ngo bo nyid gsum
thusness	tathatā	de bzhin nyid
tongue	rasana	lce
treatise	śāstra	bstan bcos
True Aspectarian	satyākāravādin	rnam bden pa
truly established/truly existent	satyasiddha	bden par grub pa
truly existent/truly established	bden par yod pa	satyasat
truth	satya	bden pa
Truth Body	dharmakāya	chos sku
truth-for-a-concealer/ truth-for-an-obscured-awareness/ conventional truth	saṃvṛtisatya	kun rdzob bden pa
ultimate truth	paramārthasatya	don dam bden pa
ultimately	paramārthatas	don dam par
uncompounded [phenomenon]	asaṃskṛta	'dus ma byas
uninterrupted meditative stabilization	ānantaryasamādhi	bar chad med pa'i ting nge 'dzin
uninterrupted path	ānantaryamārga	bar chad med lam
vajra-like meditative stabilization	vajropamasamādhi	rdo rje lta bu'i ting nge 'dzin
valid cognition/prime cognition	pramāṇa	tshad ma
water	āp	chu
wind	vāyu/prāṇa	rlung

ENGLISH	SANSKRIT	TIBETAN
wisdom arisen from meditation	bhāvanāmayīprajñā	sgom byung gi shes rab
Wisdom Truth Body	jñānadharmakāya	ye shes chos sku
Word of Buddha	Buddhavacana	bka'
wrong consciousness	viparyayajña	log shes
Yogic Autonomy Middle Way School	yogācārasvātantrika mādhyamika	rnal 'byor spyod pa'i dbu ma rang rgyud pa
Yogic Practitioner	yogācāra	rnal 'byor spyod pa pa

Bibliography

Sūtras and tantras are listed alphabetically by English title in the first section. Indian and Tibetan treatises are listed alphabetically by author in the second section. Other works are listed alphabetically by author in the third section.

'P', standing for 'Peking edition', refers to the *Tibetan Tripiṭaka* (Tokyo-Kyoto: Tibetan Tripiṭaka Research Foundation, 1956).

1. Sūtras

Descent Into Laṅkā Sūtra
laṅkāvatārasūtra
lang kar gshegs pa'i mdo
P775, vol. 29
Sanskrit: *Saddharmalaṅkāvatārasūtram*. P.L.Vaidya, ed. Buddhist Sanskrit Texts No.3. Darbhanga: Mithila Institute, 1963; also: Bunyiu Nanjio, ed. Bibl. Otaniensis, vol. I. Kyoto: Otani University Press, 1923
English translation: D.T. Suzuki. *The Lankavatara Sutra*. London: Routledge and Kegon Paul, 1932

Perfection of Wisdom Sūtras
prajñāpāramitāsūtra
shes rab kyi pha rol tu phyin pa'i mdo
P Vols. 12-21
See: E. Conze. *The Large Sūtra on Perfect Wisdom*. Berkeley: U. Cal., 1975

Sūtra on the Ten Grounds
daśabhūmikasūtra
mdo sde sa bcu pa
P761.31, vol. 25
Sanskrit: P.L.Vaidya, ed. *Daśabhūmikasūtram*. Buddhist Sanskrit Texts No.7. Darbhanga: Mithila Institute, 1967
English translation: M. Honda. 'An Annotated Translation of the "Daśabhūmika"'. in D. Sinor, ed, *Studies in Southeast and Central Asia*, Śatapitaka Series 74. New Delhi: 1968, pp.115-276

Sūtra Unravelling the Thought
saṃdhinirmocanasūtra
dgongs pa nges par 'grel pa'i mdo
P774, Vol. 29
Edited Tibetan text and French translation: Étienne Lamotte, *Saṃdhinirmocanasūtra: l'Explication des mystères*. Louvain: Université de Louvain, 1935

2. SANSKRIT AND TIBETAN WORKS

A-ku Ḻo-drö-gya-tso (*a khu blo gros rgya mtsho*)
Commentary on the Difficult Points of (Ḏzong-ka-ḇa's) 'The Essence of the Good Explanations, Treatise Differentiating Interpretable and Definitive Meanings': A Precious Lamp
drang ba dang nges pa'i don rnam par 'byed pa'i bstan bcos legs bshad snying po'i dka' 'grel rin chen sgron me
Delhi: Kesang Thabkhes, 1982

Asaṅga (*thogs med*, fourth century)
Compendium of Manifest Knowledge
abhidharmasamuccaya
chos mngon pa kun btus
P5550, Vol. 112
French translation: Walpola Rahula. *La compendium de la superdoctrine (philosophie) (Abhidharmasamuccaya) d'Asaṅga*. Paris: École Française d'Extrême-Orient, 1971
Five Treatises on the Levels
Grounds of Yogic Practice
yogācārabhūmi
rnal 'byor spyod pa'i sa
P5536-5538, Vol. 109-10
Translation of the Chapter on Suchness, the fourth chapter of Part I of the *Grounds of Bodhisattvas* (*byang chub sems dpa' pa'i sa, bodhisattvabhūmi*) which is the fifteenth volume of the *Grounds of Yogic Practice*: Janice D. Willis. *On Knowing Reality*. Delhi: Motilal, 1979
Compendium of Ascertainments
nirṇayasaṃgraha / viniścayasaṃgrahaṇī
rnam par gtan la dbab pa bsdu ba
P5539, Vol. 110-11
Compendium of Bases
vastusaṃgraha
gzhi bsdu ba
P5540, Vol. 111

Compendium of Enumerations
paryāyasaṃgraha
rnam grang bsdu ba
P5543, Vol. 111
Compendium of Explanations
vivaraṇasaṃgraha
rnam par bshad pa bsdu ba
P5543, Vol. 111

Bhāvaviveka (*legs ldan 'byed*, c.500-570?)
Blaze of Reasoning, a Commentary on the 'Heart of the Middle Way'
madhyamakahṛdayavṛttitarkajvālā
dbu ma'i snying po'i 'grel pa rtog ge 'bar ba
P5256, Vol. 96
Partial English translation (chap. III. 1-136): S. Iida. *Reason and Emptiness*. Tokyo: Hokuseido, 1980
Heart of the Middle Way
madhyamakahṛdayakārikā
dbu ma'i snying po'i tshig le'ur byas pa
P5255, vol. 96
Partial English translation (chap. III. 1-136): S. Iida. *Reason and Emptiness*. Tokyo: Hokuseido, 1980

Ḏak-tsang Ṣhay-rap-rin-chen (*stag tshang lo ts ba shes rab rin chen*, born 1405)
Explanation of 'Freedom from Extremes through Understanding All Tenets': Ocean of Good Explanations
grub mtha' kun shes nas mtha' bral grub pa zhes bya ba'i bstan bcos rnam par bshad pa legs bshad kyi rgya mtsho
Thim-phu: Kun-bzang-stobs rgyal, 1976

Dharmakīrti (*chos kyi grags pa*, seventh century)
Seven Treatises on Valid Cognition
Analysis of Relations
sambandhaparīkṣā
'brel pa brtag pa
P5713, Vol.130
Ascertainment of Prime Cognition
pramāṇaviniścaya
tshad ma rnam par nges pa
P5710, Vol. 130
Commentary on (Dignāga's) 'Compendium on Prime Cognition'
pramāṇavārttikakārikā
tshad ma rnam 'grel gyi tshig le'ur byas pa
P5709, vol. 130
Also: Sarnath, India: Pleasure of Elegant Sayings Press, 1974

Sanskrit: Swami Dwarikadas Shastri, ed. *Pramāṇavarttika of Āchārya Dharmakīrtti*. Varanasi: Bauddha Bharati, 1968

Drop of Reasoning
nyāyabinduprakaraṇa
rigs pa'i thigs pa zhes bya ba'i rab tu byed pa
P5711, Vol.130
English translation: Th. Stcherbatsky. *Buddhist Logic*. New York: Dover Publications, 1962

Drop of Reasons
hetubindunāmaprakaraṇa
gtan tshigs kyi thigs pa zhes bya ba rab tu byed pa
P5712, Vol. 130

Principles of Debate
vādanyāya
rtsod pa'i rigs pa
P5715, Vol.130

Proof of Other Continuums
saṃtānāntarasiddhināmaprakaraṇa
rgyud gzhan grub pa zhes bya ba'i rab tu byed pa
P5716, Vol.130

Dharmamitra (*chos kyi bshes gnyen*)

Clear Words, a Commentary on (Maitreya's) 'Ornament for Clear Realization'
abhisamayālaṃkārakārikāprajñāpāramitopadeśaśāstraṭīkāprasphuṭapadā
shes rab kyi pha rol tu phyin pa'i man ngag gi bstan bcos mngon par rtogs pa'i rgyan gyi tshig le'ur byas pa'i 'grel bshad tshig rab tu gsal ba
P5194, Vol. 91

Drak-ba-s̄hay-drup (*grags pa bshad sgrub, co ne ba*, 1675-1748)

Condensed Essence of All Tenets
grub mtha' thams cad kyi snying po bsdus pa
Delhi: Mey College of Sera, 1969

D̄zong-ka-b̄a L̄o-sang-drak-b̄a (*tsong kha pa blo bzang grags pa*, 1357-1419)

The Three Principal Aspects of the Path
lam gtso rnam gsum/ tsha kho dpon po ngag dbang grags pa la gdams pa
P6087, vol. 153
English translation: Translated in this book. Also: Geshe Sopa and Jeffrey Hopkins. Including commentary from the Dalai Lama, in Tenzin Gyatso's *Kindness, Clarity, and Insight*. Ithaca, N.Y.: Snow Lion, 1984, pp. 118-56. Also: Geshe Wangyal. in

The Door of Liberation. New York: Lotsawa, 1978, pp. 126-160. Also: Robert Thurman. in *Life and Teachings of Tsong Khapa*. Dharamsala, Library of Tibetan Works and Archives, 1982, pp. 57-8

Fourth Paṇ-chen Lama, L̄o-sang-b̄el-den-d̄en-b̄ay-nyi-ma (*blo bzang dpal ldan bstan pa'i nyi ma*, 1781-1852/4)
Instructions on [D̄zong-ka-b̄a's] 'Three Principal Aspects of the Path: Essence of All the Scriptures, Quintessence of Helping Others
gsung rab kun gyi snying po lam gyi gtso bo rnam pa gsum gyi khrid yig gzhan phan snying po
n.d.
English translation: Translated in this book. Also: Geshe Wangyal. in *The Door of Liberation*. New York: Lotsawa, 1978, pp. 126-60

Ge-dün-gya-tso, Second Dalai Lama (*dge 'dun rgya mtsho*, 1476-1542)
Ship for Entering the Ocean of Tenets
grub mtha' rgya mtshor 'jug pa'i gru rdzings
Vāraṇasi: Ye shes stobs ldan, 1969

Ḡön-chok-jik-may-w̄ang-b̄o (*dkon mchog 'jigs med dbang po*, 1728-91)
Precious Garland of Tenets/ Presentation of Tenets, A Precious Garland
grub pa'i mtha'i rnam par bzhag pa rin po che'i phreng ba
The Collected Works of dkon-mchog-'jigs-med-dbaṅ-po. Vol. 6. New Delhi: Ngawang Gelek Demo, 1972. pp. 485-535, twenty-six folios. Also: xylograph in thirty-two folios from the Lessing collection of the rare book section of the University of Wisconsin Library which is item 47 in Leonard Zwilling, *Tibetan Blockprints in the Department of Rare Books and Special Collections* (Madison; the University of Wisconsin-Madison Libraries, 1984); no publication data [referred to as the 'Peking edition']. Also: Mundgod: L̄o-s̄el-l̄ing Press, 1980 [referred to as the 'Go-mang 1980 edition'], in seventy-six pages. Also: Dharamsala: Shes rig par khang, 1967 [referred to as the 'Dharamsala 1967 edition']; in seventy-eight pages. Also: Dharamsala: Teacher Training, no date [referred to as the 'Teacher Training edition']; in seventy-nine pages. Also: A block-print edition in twenty-eight folios obtained in 1987 from Go-mang College in Hla-s̄a, printed on blocks that pre-date the Cultural Revolution [referred to as the 'Tibet Go-mang 1987 edition']. Also, a critical edition: K. Mimaki. Le *Grub mtha' rnam bźag rin chen phreṅ ba* de dKon mchog 'jigs med dbaṅ po (1728-1791), *Zinbun*, number 14 (The Research Institute for Humanistic Studies, Kyoto University), pp. 55-112 [referred to as 'Mimaki edition']

English translation: Translated in this book. Also: H.V. Guenther. in *Buddhist Philosophy in Theory and Practice*. Baltimore: Penguin, 1972. Also, the chapters on the Autonomy School and the Consequence School: Shotaro Iida. in *Reason and Emptiness* (Tokyo: Hokuseido, 1980)

Gung-tang Ḡön-chok-d̄en-b̄ay-drön-may (*gung thang dkon mchog bstan pa'i sgron me*, 1762-1823

Beginnings of a Commentary on the Difficult Points of (D̄zong-ka-b̄a's) 'Differentiation of the Interpretable and the Definitive', the Quintessence of the 'The Essence of the Good Explanations'

drang nges rnam 'byed kyi dka' 'grel rtsom 'phro legs bshad snying po'i yang snying

Collected Works, volume 1, 403-723

New Delhi: Ngawang Gelek Demo, 1975

Also: Sarnath: Guru Deva, 1965

Jam-ȳang-shay-b̄a (*'jam dbyangs bzhad pa*, 1648-1721)

Great Exposition of Tenets: Explanation of 'Tenets', Sun of the Land of Samantabhadra Brilliantly Illuminating All of Our Own and Others' Tenets and the Meaning of the Profound [Emptiness], Ocean of Scripture and Reasoning Fulfilling All Hopes of All Beings

grub mtha' chen mo/ grub mtha'i rnam bshad rang gzhan grub mtha' kun dang zab don mchog tu gsal ba kun bzang zhing gi nyi ma lung rigs rgya mtsho skye dgu'i re ba kun skong

Musoorie: Dalama, 1962

English translation (beginning of the chapter on the Consequence School): Jeffrey Hopkins. in *Meditation on Emptiness*. London: Wisdom Publications, 1983

J̄ang-ḡya Rol-b̄ay-dor-jay (*lcang skya rol pa'i rdo rje*, 1717-86)

Presentation of Tenets/ Clear Exposition of the Presentations of Tenets, Beautiful Ornament for the Meru of the Subduer's Teaching

grub mtha'i rnam bzhag/ grub pa'i mtha'i rnam par bzhag pa gsal bar bshad pa thub bstan lhun po'i mdzes rgyan

Varanasi: Pleasure of Elegant Sayings Printing Press, 1970

Also: an edition published by gam bcar phan bde legs bshad gling grva tshang dang rgyud rnying slar gso tshogs pa, in the royal year 2109

Also: *Buddhist Philosophical Systems of Lcaṅ-skya Rol-pahi Rdo-rje*. Edited by Lokesh Chandra. Śata-pitaka Series (Indo-Asian Literatures), v. 233. New Delhi, 1977

Translation of Sautrāntika chapter: Anne C. Klein. in *Knowing, Naming, and Negation*. Ithaca: Snow Lion, forthcoming 1989. Commentary on this: Anne C. Klein. in *Knowledge and Liberation: A Buddhist epistemological analysis in support of trans-*

formative religious experience: Tibetan interpretations of Dignaga and Dharmakirti. Ithaca: Snow Lion, 1986

Translation of Svātantrika chapter: Donald S. Lopez jr. in *A Study of Svātantrika*. Ithaca: Snow Lion, 1986

Translation of part of Prāsaṅgika chapter: Jeffrey Hopkins. *Emptiness Yoga*. Ithaca: Snow Lion, 1983

Jay-d̄zün Chö-ḡyi-gyel-tsen, (*rje btsun chos kyi rgyal mtshan*, 1469-1546)

Presentation of Tenets

grub mtha'i rnam gzhag

Bylakuppe: Se-rwa Byes Grwa-tshaṅ, 1977

L̄ong-chen-rap-jam (*klong chen rab 'byams/ klong chen dri med 'od zer*, 1308-1363

Treasury of Tenets, Illuminating the Meaning of All Vehicles

theg pa mtha' dag gi don gsal bar byed pa grub pa'i mtha' rin po che'i mdzod

Gangtok, Dodrup Chen Rinpoche, 1969[?]

Maitreya (*byams pa*)

Great Vehicle Treatise on the Sublime Continuum/ Great Vehicle Treatise on the Later Scriptures

mahāyānottaratantraśāstra

theg pa chen po rgyud bla ma'i bstan bcos

P5525, Vol. 108

Sanskrit: E. H. Johnston (and T. Chowdhury) ed. *The Ratnagotravibhāga Mahāyānottaratantraśāstra*. Patna: Bihar Research Society, 1950

English translation: E. Obermiller. 'Sublime Science of the Great Vehicle to Salvation'. *Acta Orientalia*, 9 (1931), pp. 81-306. Also: J. Takasaki. *A Study on the Ratnagotravibhāga*. Rome: IS. M.E.O., 1966

Ornament for Clear Realization

abhisamayālaṃkāra

mngon par rtogs pa'i rgyan

P5184, Vol. 88

Sanskrit text: Th. Stcherbatsky and E. Obermiller, ed. *Abhisamayālaṃkāra-Prajñāpāramitā-Updeśa-Śāstra*. Bibliotheca Buddhica XXIII. Osnabrück: Biblio Verlag, 1970

English translation: Edward Conze. *Abhisamayālaṃkāra*. Serie Orientale Roma. Rome: Is.M.E.0., 1954

Ngak-w̄ang-b̄el-den (*ngag dbang dpal ldan*, b.1797), also known as B̄el-den-chö-jay (*dpal ldan chos rje*)

Annotations for (Jam-ȳang-shay-b̄a's) 'Great Exposition of Tenets',

Freeing the Knots of the Difficult Points, Precious Jewel of Clear Thought
grub mtha' chen mo'i mchan 'grel dka' gnad mdud grol blo gsal gces nor
Sarnath: Pleasure of Elegant Sayings Press, 1964

Paṇ-chen Sö-nam-drak-b̄a (*paṇ chen bsod nams grags pa*, 1478-1554)
Presentation of Tenets, Sublime Tree Inspiring Those of Clear Mind, Hammer Destroying the Stone Mountains of Opponents
grub mtha'i rnam bzhag blo gsal spro ba bskyed pa'i ljon pa phas rgol brag ri 'joms pa'i tho ba
Buxa, n.d.

Shāntideva (*zhi ba lha*, eight century)
Compendium of Instructions
śikṣāsamuccayakārikā
bslab pa kun las btus pa'i tshig le'ur byas pa
P5272, Vol. 102
English Translation: C. Bendall and W.H.D. Rouse. *Śikṣā Samuccaya.* Delhi: Motilal, 1971

Tu-ḡen-l̄o-sang-chö-ḡyi-nyi-ma (*thu'u bkvan blo bzang chos kyi nyi ma*, 1737-1802)
Mirror of the Good Explanations Showing the Sources and Assertions of All Systems of Tenets
grub mtha' thams cad kyi khungs dang 'dod tshul ston pa legs bshad shel gyi me long
Sarnath: Chhos Je Lama, 1963

Ū-b̄a-l̄o-s̄el (*dbus pa blo gsal*, 14th century)
Treasury of Expositions of Tenets
Grub pa'i mtha' rnam par bśad pa'i mdzod, An Introduction to the comparative siddhānta of the spiritual traditions of India, Buddhist and non-Buddhist, by Dbus-pa blo-gsal
Thimphu, 1979
Critical edition and French translation of the chapter on the Sūtra School: K. Mimaki. Le chapitre du *Blo gsal grub mtha'* sur les Sautrāntika, Présentation et édition, *Zinbun* no, 15, pp. 175-210; and Un essai de traduction, *Zinbun* no, 16, pp. 143-172
Critical edition of the chapters on the Great Exposition School, the Mind Only School, and the Middle Way School as well as a French translation of the chapter on the Middle Way School: K. Mimaki. *Blo gsal grub mtha'*. Kyoto: Université de Kyoto, 1982

Vajragarbha
Commentary on the Condensation of the Hevajra Tantra

hevajrapiṇḍārthaṭīkā
kye'i rdo rje bsdus pa'i don gyi rgya cher 'grel pa
P2310, Vol. 53
English translation of the tantra itself: D.L. Snellgrove. *Hevajra Tantra,* Parts I and II. London: Oxford University Press, 1959

Vasubandhu (*dbyig gnyen*)
Treasury of Manifest Knowledge
abhidharmakośakārikā
chos mngon pa'i mdzod kyi tshig le'ur byas pa
P5590, Vol. 115
Sanskrit text: P. Pradhan, ed. *Abhidharmakośabhāṣyam of Vasubandhu.* Patna: Jayaswal Research Institute, 1975
French translation: Louis de la Vallée Poussin. *L'Abhidharmakośa de Vasubandhu.* 6 vols. Bruxelles: Institut Belge des Hautes Études Chinoises, 1971

3. Other Works

Apte, Vaman Shivaram. *Sanskrit-English Dictionary.* Poona: Prasad Prakashan, 1957.

Bareau, André. *Les sectes bouddhiques du Petit Véhicule.* Saigon: 1955.

Bendall, C., and Rouse, W.H.D. *Śikṣā Samuccaya.* Delhi: Motilal, 1971.

Chandra, Lokesh, ed. *Materials for a History of Tibetan Literature.* Śatapiṭaka series, vol. 28-30. New Delhi: International Academy of Indian Culture, 1963.

Conze, E. *The Large Sūtra on Perfect Wisdom.* Berkeley: U. Cal., 1975.

Das, Sarat Chandra. *A Tibetan-English Dictionary.* Calcutta, 1902.

Dondup, K. *The Water-Horse and Other Years: a history of 17th and 18th Century Tibet.* Dharamsala: Library of Tibetan Works and Archives, 1984.

Edgerton, Franklin. *Buddhist Hybrid Sanskrit Grammar and Dictionary.* New Haven: Yale University Press, 1953; reprint, Delhi: Motilal, 1972.

Guenther, Herbert. *Buddhist Philosophy in Theory and Practice.* Baltimore: Pelican, 1972.

Gyatso, Tenzin, Dalai Lama XIV and Hopkins, Jeffrey. *The Kālachakra Tantra: Rite of Initiation.* Translated and introduced by Jeffrey Hopkins. London: Wisdom Publications, 1985.

Gyatso, Tenzin, Dalai Lama XIV. *Kindness, Clarity, and Insight.* Jeffrey Hopkins, trans. and ed.; Elizabeth Napper, co-editor. Ithaca, N.Y.:

Snow Lion Publications, 1984.

Honda, M. 'An Annotated Translation of the 'Daśabhūmika', in D. Sinor, ed, *Studies in Southeast and Central Asia*, Śatapitaka Series 74. New Delhi: 1968.

Hopkins, Jeffrey. *Emptiness Yoga*. Ithaca: Snow Lion, 1987.

Hopkins, Jeffrey. *Meditation on Emptiness*. London: Wisdom, 1983.

Iida, Shotaro. *Reason and Emptiness*. Tokyo: Hokuseido, 1980.

Jha, G. *The Tattvasaṃgraha of Śāntirakṣita with the commentary of Kamalaśīla*. Gaekwad's Oriental Series Vol. lxxx and lxxxiii. Baroda: Oriental Institute, 1937-9.

Johnston, E. H. (and T. Chowdhury) ed. *The Ratnagotravibhāga Mahāyānottaratantraśāstra*. Patna: Bihar Research Society, 1950.

Joshi, L.M. 'Facets of Jaina Religiousness in Comparative Light', L.D. Series 85, [Ahmedabad: L.D. Institute of Indology, May 1981], pp.53-8.

Klein, Anne C. *Knowing, Naming, and Negation*. Ithaca: Snow Lion, 1989.

Klein, Anne C. *Knowledge and Liberation: A Buddhist epistemological analysis in support of transformative religious experience: Tibetan interpretations of Dignaga and Dharmakirti*. Ithaca: Snow Lion, 1986.

Kuijp, Leonard van der. *Contributions to the Development of Tibetan Buddhist Epistemology*. Wiesbaden: Franz Steiner Verlag, 1983.

Lamotte, Étienne. *Saṃdhinirmocanasūtra: l'Explication des mystères*. Louvain: Université de Louvain, 1935.

Lati Rinbochay and Elizabeth Napper. *Mind in Tibetan Buddhism*. London: Rider and Company, 1980; Ithaca: Snow Lion, 1980.

Lopez, Donald S. *A Study of Svātantrika*. Ithaca: Snow Lion, 1986.

Mimaki, Katsumi. *Blo gsal grub mtha'*. Kyoto: Université de Kyoto, 1982.

Mimaki, Katsumi. Le chapitre du *Blo gsal grub mtha'* sur les Sautrāntika, Présentation et édition, *Zinbun* number 15 (The Research Institute for Humanistic Studies, Kyoto University), pp. 175-210.

Mimaki, Katsumi. Un essai de traduction, *Zinbun* no, 16, pp. 143-172.

Mimaki, Katsumi. Le *Grub mtha' rnam bźag rin chen phreṅ ba* de dKon mchog 'jigs med dbaṅ po (1728-1791), *Zinbun*, number 14 (The

Research Institute for Humanistic Studies, Kyoto University), pp. 55-112.

Monier-Williams, Sir Monier. *A Sanskṛit-English Dictionary*. London: Oxford, 1899; reprint, Delhi: Motilal, 1976.

Napper, Elizabeth. *Dependent-Arising and Emptiness*. London: Wisdom Publications, forthcoming 1989.

Nyima, Geshé Ngawang. *Introduction to the Doctrines of the Four Schools of Buddhist Philosophy*. Leiden, 1970.

Obermiller, E. 'Sublime Science of the Great Vehicle to Salvation'. *Acta Orientalia*, 9 (1931), pp. 81-306.

Perdue, Daniel. 'Practice and Theory of Philosophical Debate in Tibetan Buddhist Education'. Ann Arbor: U. Microfilms, 1983.

Poussin, Louis de la Vallée. *L'Abhidharmakośa de Vasubandhu*. 6 vols. Bruxelles: Institut Belge des Hautes Études Chinoises, 1971.

Poussin, Louis de La Vallée, ed. *Mūlamadhyamakakārikās de Nāgārjuna avec la Prasannapadā Commentaire de Candrakīrti*. Bibliotheca Buddhica IV. Osnabrück: Biblio Verlag, 1970.

Pradhan, P. , ed. *Abhidharmakośabhāṣyam of Vasubandhu*. Patna: Jayaswal Research Institute, 1975.

Rahula, Walpola. *La compendium de la super-doctrine (philosophie) (Abhidharmasamuccaya) d'Asaṅga*. Paris: École Française d'Extrême-Orient, 1971.

Rock, J.F. *The Amney Ma-chhen Range and Adjacent Regions*. Rome: 1956.

Ruegg, David Seyfort. *The Literature of the Madhyamaka School of Philosophy in India*. Wiesbaden: Otto Harrassowitz, 1981.

Sangpo, Khetsun. *Biographical Dictionary of Tibet and Tibetan Buddhism*. Dharamsala: Library of Tibetan Works and Archives, 1973.

Santina, Peter della. *Madhyamaka Schools in India*. Delhi: Motilal Banarsidass, 1986.

Sastri, S.S. Suryanarayana, edited and translated. *Sāṃkhyakārikā of Īśvara Kṛṣṇa*. Madras: University of Madras, 1935.

Shastri, Swami Dwarikadas, ed. *Pramāṇavarttika of Āchārya Dharmakīrtti*. Varanasi: Bauddha Bharati, 1968.

Snellgrove, D.L., and Richardson, Hugh. *Cultural History of Tibet*. New York: Praeger, 1968.

Snellgrove, David L., trans. *Hevajra Tantra, A Critical Study,* Parts I and II. London: Oxford University Press, 1959.

Snellgrove, David L. *Indo-Tibetan Buddhism: Indian Buddhists and Their Tibetan Successors.* Boston: Shambhala, 1987.

Staal, J.F. 'Negation and the Law of Contradiction in Indian Thought'. London: *Bulletin of the School of Oriental and African Studies,* Vol. XXV: Part 1, 1962.

Stcherbatsky, Th., and Obermiller, E., ed. *Abhisamayālaṃkāra-Prajñāpāramitā-Updeśa-Śāstra.* Bibliotheca Buddhica XXIII. Osnabrück: Biblio Verlag, 1970.

Stcherbatsky, Th. *Buddhist Logic.* New York: Dover Publications, 1962.

Suzuki, D.T. *The Lankavatara Sutra.* London: Routledge and Kegon Paul, 1932.

Takasaki, J. *A Study on the Ratnagotravibhāga.* Rome: IS. M.E.O., 1966.

Thurman, Robert, ed. *Life and Teachings of Tsong Khapa.* Dharamsala, Library of Tibetan Works and Archives, 1982, pp. 57-8.

Vaidya, P.L., ed. *Daśabhūmikasūtram.* Buddhist Sanskrit Texts No.7. Darbhanga: Mithila Institute, 1967.

Vostrikov, A.I. *Tibetan Historical Literature.* Soviet Indology Series No. 4. tr. H.C. Gupta. Calcutta: 1970.

Wangyal, Geshe. *Door of Liberation.* New York: Maurice Girodius, 1973; reprint, New York: Lotsawa, 1978.

Willis, Janice D. *On Knowing Reality.* Delhi: Motilal, 1979.

Wogihara, Unrai, ed. *Abhisamayālaṃkārālokā Prajñā-pāramitā-vyākhyā. The Work of Haribhadra.* Tokyo: The Toyo Bunko, 1932-5; reprint ed., Tokyo: Sankibo Buddhist Book Store, 1973.

Index

(For topical outlines of the two texts, the reader may wish to consult the guides each found on pp. 43-44 and 141-144, respectively. In the index, numbers in bold type indicate fuller explanations.)

ian, **258-259**, 285
non-wastage, 194

object-possessors, 123-127, 196-203, 238-244, 267-270, 287-288, 307-315
obstructions, 20, 48, 49, 56, 103; 126, 129, 151, 189, 204, 205, 211, 219, 264, 271, 276, 290, 296, 298, 308-309, 319; acquired, 33, 294-295; innate, 296; to liberation, 20, 129, 206, 210, 272-273, 274, 289, 291, 294-295, 298-299, 315-316, 318; to omniscience, 20, 127, 129, 206, 245, 272-273, 289-295, 298-299, 316, 318-319
obtainer, 194
omniscience, 166-167, 205-206, 217; *see also* obstructions to omniscience
Once Returner, 212-213
Ornament for Clear Realization, 134, 296
other-powered nature, 172, 249-250, **260-263**, 265-266, 274
Outsider, 150-153, 155; tenets of, 155-170

Paṇ-chen Lamas, 36-38; *see also* Fourth Paṇ-chen Lama
Paṇ-chen S̄ö-nam-drak-b̄a, 115, 256
pastness, 192, 233-235, 266, 307
path, 127-129; assertions on, 203-210, 244-248, 270-273, 288-290, 298, 315-316; *see also* path of accumulation, path of meditation, path of no more learning, path of preparation, path of seeing
path of accumulation, 31, 206, 210-211, 214, 292
path of meditation, 190-192, 206-214, 219, 246, 273-274, 291, 295, 317
path of no more learning, 190-191, 206, 210, 214, 218
path of preparation, 206, 211, 214, 218, 246, 292-294
path of seeing, 29, 190, 206-210, 214, 215, 216, 245-246, 263, 273, 293, 294; sixteen moments of, 207-209
peak, 211, 293
Perfection of Wisdom of One Hundred Thousand Stanzas, 52
person, 32-34, 149-151, 282, 302; assertions on, 123-126, 159, 161-165, 177-178, 196-197, 238-239, 267-268, 287, 307-308; valuing equally, 22; *see also* self of persons, selflessness of persons
Po-hla-s̄ö-nam-d̄op-gyay, 37
positive phenomenon, 192-193, 230-232
posture for meditation, 19-20
pramāṇa, 240, 310-313; *see also* prime cognition
Prasenajit, 91
predisposition/ latency, 48, 227, 253, 258-259, 266, 268, 272, 315-316; *see also* seed
present object, 192, 234-235, 266
Presentation of Tenets, Sublime Tree Inspiring Those of Clear

Mind, Hammer Destroying the Stone Mountains of Opponents, 115
presentations of tenets, 111-116
prime cognition, **197-199**, 226, 232-233, 239-240, 264, 265, 269-270, 271-272, 286, 287-288, 289, **310-313**
proponent of Buddhist tenets: definition, 176
Proponents of an Equal Number of Subjects and Objects, 253-258
Proponents of Cognition, 259; *see also* Mind Only School

real conventional truth, 287, 306-307
recognition of all sentient beings as mothers, 30, 83-84
refuge, 20-21, 46-48, 54, 103, 150-152, 155, 218-219, 247
reliance on a spiritual guide, 65-67, 68
repaying kindness, 30, 86-87
Rock, J.F., 131

Sāṃkhya, 158-165, 166
Saṃmitīya, 124, 177-178, 196, 204
scriptures requiring interpretation, 120, 173, 276-277, 296-297, 319
Second Dalai Lama Ge-dün-gya-tso, 115
Second Paṇ-chen Lama, Lo-sang-ye-shay, 37
seed, 191-192, 205, 253, 272, 293, 294, 295, 315-316, 317; *see also* predisposition
self, 33, 88, 94, 96, 98, 123, 152-153, 156, 158, 159, 161, 162, 167, 175, 177-178, 244, 246, 261, 262, 265, 269; *see also* person, self of persons, self of phenomena
self-cognition/ self-cognizing consciousness, 179, 197-198, 221, 239-240, 251, 258, 269-270, 283, 287, 297, 308
self of persons, 177, 205, 225, 245-246, 262, 263, 272, 289, 295, 296
self of phenomena, 204, 205, 245, 262, 272
self-sufficient, substantially existent person, 33-34, 96, 97-98, 177-178, 204, 210, 245, 262, 269, 271, 274, 288, 295; *see also* substantially established, substantially existent
selflessness, 33, 123, 147, 288-289, 298, 315; in the four seals, 178; of phenomena, 99-100, 127, 204, 244, 274-276, 289, 304, 305, 315, 316; of persons, 95-98, 123, 204, 244-245, 263-264, 271, 273-274, 288-289, 291, 315
seven branches of practice, 23, 56-59
seven quintessential instructions of cause and effect, 29-32, 81-89
Seven Treatises of Manifest Knowledge, 215
Seven Treatises on Prime